Sam Burgum's ethnography of the Occupy movement's longest enduring encampment at Finsbury Square explains not only why the movement failed but what its failure means nearly a decade after the movement's end. Occupy held out the possibility of change but it didn't change our sense of the possible. Instead, its emphases on individualism, libertarianism, and identity reaffirmed core tenets of neoliberalism and reinvigorated accompanying racisms and nationalisms. This important work is crucial reading for anyone interested in contemporary political theory, social movements, and the need for progressive change.

Professor Jodi Dean, author of Crowds and Party

Occupying London gets inside the movement that believed there is an alternative to the excesses, inequalities and moral blankness of the world we inhabit. Through meticulous fieldwork Burgum offers a balanced and reflective assessment of the protest and those involved in it. This book raises important questions about the limits of resistance, social imagination and a system that, despite our anger and dissatisfaction with it, we are apparently unable to see beyond.

Professor Rowland Atkinson, Chair in Inclusive Societies, University of Sheffield

This outstanding book draws on fieldwork with Occupy (in) London to consider the possibility of resisting neoliberalism in the post-crisis period. It centres on the curtailment of politics by neoliberal precepts that operate as 'common sense', and offers a vital contribution to our understanding of this problem and how we might move beyond it.

Professor Nicholas Gane, Department of Sociology, University of Warwick

In October 2011, tents appeared in central London as Occupy took up its place in the city, and protestors articulated a widespread and angry confusion as to why and how capitalism retained such a grip despite the financial crash and crunch of 2007/8. Through vivid description and careful attention to the voices of the protestors, Sam Burgum takes his readers to the Occupy London encampments, sharing the stories he was told and the experiences he shared. He offers us an honest, unromantic account, capturing the hope and excitement of the movement as well as its disappointments and failures. Anyone interested in the possibilities and challenges of political resistance should read this book.

Dr Cath Lambert, Associate Professor of Sociology, University of Warwick

Occupying London

Just because there has been a crisis does not necessarily mean that change will follow. And yet why, exactly, did nothing change in the face of global resistances and movements which followed the financial meltdown of 2007/8? Based on ethnographic research on the Occupy movement in London – as a case study of one post-crash attempt to bring about alternatives – this book argues that change was ultimately foreclosed by widespread 'common sense' limitations of what was considered possible after the crash.

Offering a critically constructive analysis of the Occupy movement in London and incorporating the activists' praise and indeed self-criticism of the movement, *Occupying London* discusses both the political potential suggested by the occupation of space and the slogan 'we are the 99%', as well as the problematic extension of post-crash normativity into the movement through issues of organisation, repetitions of wider norms, and an inadvertent acceptance of wider distributions of possibility. Such positives and negatives are shown to have played out in a wide range of arenas: from the occupation of space itself, through attempts to organise collective appearance and voice, as well as 'authentic' constructions of resistance and 'cynical' framings of power.

The author's intention is to provoke thought on behalf of any 'half-fascinated, half-devastated witnesses' of the financial crash and the political disappointments which followed. It is argued that such movements possess the potential to bring about progressive change, but only if they intervene into wider distributions of 'common sense' by embracing collective symbolic efficiency and avoiding binary framings of 'authentic' resistance vs. 'hidden' power.

Samuel Burgum is a Leverhulme Research Fellow at the Department of Urban Studies and Planning, University of Sheffield, UK, conducting research into squatting in the context of London's housing crisis. You can follow Sam on Twitter (@sjburgum) or read more about the project at: samuelburgum.uk.

Routledge Advances in Sociology

The Live Art of Sociology
Cath Lambert

The Sociology of Central Asian Youth
Choice, Constraint, Risk
Mohd. Aslam Bhat

Indigenous Knowledge Production
Navigating Humanity within a Western World
Marcus Woolombi Waters

Time and Temporality in Transitional and Post-Conflict Societies
Edited by Natascha Mueller-Hirth, Sandra Rios Oyola

Practicing Art/Science
Experiments in an Emerging Field
Edited by Philippe Sormani, Guelfo Carbone & Priska Gisler

The Great Transformation
History for a Techno-Human Future
Judith Bessant

Occupying London
Post-Crash Resistance and the Limits of Possibility
Sam Burgum

Populism and the Crisis of Democracy
Volume 1: Concepts and Theory
Edited by Gregor Fitzi, Jürgen Mackert and Bryan S. Turner

Populism and the Crisis of Democracy
Volume 2: Politics, Social Movements and Extremism
Edited by Gregor Fitzi, Jürgen Mackert and Bryan S. Turner

Populism and the Crisis of Democracy
Volume 3: Migration, Gender and Religion
Edited by Gregor Fitzi, Jürgen Mackert and Bryan S. Turner

For a full list of titles in this series, please visit www.routledge.com/Routledge-Advances-in-Sociology/book-series/SE0511

Occupying London

Post-Crash Resistance and the Limits of Possibility

Samuel Burgum

Routledge
Taylor & Francis Group
LONDON AND NEW YORK

First published 2018
by Routledge

2 Park Square, Milton Park, Abingdon, Oxfordshire OX14 4RN
52 Vanderbilt Avenue, New York, NY 10017

Routledge is an imprint of the Taylor & Francis Group, an informa business

First issued in paperback 2019

British Library Cataloguing in Publication Data
A catalogue record for this book is available from the British Library

Library of Congress Cataloging in Publication Data
Names: Burgum, Samuel, 1988- author.
Title: Occupying London : post-crash resistance and the limits of possibility / Samuel Burgum.
Description: Abingdon, Oxon ; New York, NY : Routledge, 2018. | Series: Routledge advances in sociology | Includes bibliographical references.
Identifiers: LCCN 2018003828| ISBN 9781138291539 (hardcover) | ISBN 9781315265254 (ebook)
Subjects: LCSH: Occupy London (Movement) | Occupy movement–England–London. | Global Financial Crisis, 2008-2009. | Income distribution–Great Britain.
Classification: LCC HC258.L6 B87 2018 | DDC 339.2–dc23
LC record available at https://lccn.loc.gov/2018003828

ISBN: 978-1-138-29153-9 (hbk)
ISBN: 978-0-367-43896-8 (pbk)

Typeset in Times New Roman
by Taylor & Francis Books

Contents

Acknowledgements viii
Prelude ix
Preface xii

Introduction: Now is the winter of our discount tents! 1

1 What is our one demand? 19

2 Whose streets? Our streets! 42

3 We are the 99% 63

4 This is what democracy looks like 87

5 They owe us 113

Conclusion: This is not a protest, it's a process 140

Interviewee demographics 152
Bibliography 155
Index 164

Acknowledgements

First, thank you to the people of Occupy (in) London who were so generous with their time and often very enthusiastic about the project, steering me in different directions and never shying from challenging my questions. Many continue to work hard on behalf of others and with great personal sacrifice. I hope they feel that my account of the movement is fair.

This research has been planned, conducted, and written in numerous institutions between 2012 and 2017, including libraries, offices, and cafes in York, Sheffield, Warwick, and Newcastle. It has therefore been supported by hundreds of anonymous baristas, cleaners, receptionists, and librarians, as well as the ever-friendly and ever-helpful administrative staff of various university departments, including Alison, Amanda, and Lynn (York) and Cheryl, Darani, Gemma, Jane, and Janet (Warwick).

I have greatly benefitted from the supervision and support of friends and colleagues in both an official and unofficial capacity, including Nick Gane, Claire Blencowe, and Dave Beer, as well as Rowland Atkinson, Gurminder Bhambra, Roger Burrows, Maria do Mar Pereira, Triona Fitton, David Hill, Hannah Jones, John Narayan, Goldie Osuri, Raphael Schlembach, John Solomos, Chris Till, and Simon Winlow. I'd also like to thank Alastair Bonnett, Cath Lambert, and Lynne Pettinger for their invaluable encouragement and for persuading me to publish.

Finally, there are many friends outside the university who have supported this work, either by offering general words of reassurance or giving me a sofa to sleep on during fieldwork, including Mike and Shiona, the 'Arlington Rovers' (Charlie, Dom, Guy, Tom, Malik, Mike, Neil, and Will), Alex and Vicky, Anthony and Caro. My parents Paul and Julia Burgum, and Val Obriain, have always been there to back me, and the unconditional support of Finn Burgum has been incredible. Without her, this work would simply never have been completed, and therefore this book is dedicated to Finn.

This research was initially funded by the Economic and Social Research Council (ESRC) on a three-year basis at the White Rose Doctoral Training Centre (York) before moving to the University of Warwick in 2013.

Prelude

Politics Within Tent

Now is the winter of our discount tents
Where people regroup from their TV sets
And start to set out the new news agenda
There are polythene estates appearing all over the place
And slogans detonate like shock waves
Inside my brain as I stand here gazing at
Neo-classical pillars
Which start to get plastered with our collective answers to this
Cardiac arresting capital city
They read:
'Your heart is a weapon the size of a fist'
'Nature is the only superpower'
'Make occupation your occupation'
And on, and on and
Fierce discussions erupt on street corners
It's like eighteenth century France all over again
The pendulum is beginning to swing
We're at the point of zero gravity between more of the same
And
A Mexican wave that won't sit back down
Now a pandemic of tented towns
Dome tent cities pop up like frogspawn
Mini tax havens for the super poor
Prime real estate for insurrection
Emergency housing for the desperate and indignant
'I'm Spartacus!'
A clinic to the trench foot of 'why fucking bother'
Hacking off the blue limbs of 'who gives a shit'
And feeding every bit of this shit that we're given
Into a giant composting system
There's a verdant pulsating energy shooting
Through the cracks of a shattering system
Seeds of change in germination
Here a ground zero indignation solidified

A population galvanised
The ninety-nine personified
We've come to talk about what's going down
Silhouetted by queues of mesmerised traffic
There are pavement fanatics
Suited sympathetics
Ecclesiastical renegades
Sandals and trainers
Ecumenical, trans-generational
Amateur, professional, dermatologically spectral
Soldered by tent pegs of love and solidarity
We meld
And become one body
'I'm Spartacus!'
There are armies of clowns and militant mothers
Tourists flash mobbing their flaky 99'ers
There are discarded bubble gum hit and run mutters
Of chewed up and spat out Evening Standards
From sickly, acidic, goblin bankers
Gripped by a shivering profit psychosis
This uniformed, suited black-block marches
Through rat race alleyways of steely glass palaces
The zombie systems tears at our walls
So we take our bubble pod tents and we spawn the
Unwanted kids of Thatcher's dirty fantasy we
Climb the rusting scaffolds of their hierarchy we
See them running upstairs with their bounty we
Come to tear the plastic from their faces we
Come to tear the botox from their faces we
Come to tear at cosmetic surgery
Subsidy to a hideous dying kleptocracy
Paid for by a people now pregnant with change
'I'm Spartacus!'
We are nail bombs of love and rag tag humanity
Antibody to an exponential cancer of money
Because *only* another world is possible
We are purging ourselves of parasites
With thriving communities of radical campsites
We want to push the banks to the brink of extinction
Armed with information, and critical discussion
And spreading
Like the advancing Sahara
Bearing tent poles and a sense of humour
'I'm Spartacus!'
We stay
When tents lend percussion to the thrashing rain
You'll have to drag us from the last blade of grass, we remain
Singing
At the doorsteps of salvation

For whom does your bell toll St Paul's,
For us, or for them?
Follow your prophets, usury is sin
Don't follow profits, usury is sin
So the meek are inheriting the earth before it dies
If Jesus was alive today he would say
'Occupy!'

Written and performed by Pete 'the Temp' Bearder,
St Pauls Cathedral, 2011. Reproduced with permission.

Preface

Finsbury Square, April 2012

Arriving at 9 a.m. sharp and without warning, I found that most of the protesters were still in their tents. But once the bodies did begin to emerge from the muddy maze of canvas, wood, and tarpaulin, I set about naïvely introducing myself as a social researcher interested in learning more about Occupy. Unsurprisingly, I was met with a mixture of weariness and scepticism towards yet another journalist/academic tourist coming to 'document' the movement,[1] but after a chatting to a few people, some agreed to sign a compulsory university consent form and to record an interview on my borrowed hand-held recorder.

I was sitting on a wall interviewing an older, seasoned activist called Nick, when we were distracted by an idling UK Independence Party (UKIP) billboard on the back of a truck which had been caught behind traffic and had stopped right in our line of vision. A few activists sprang to their feet and began shouting – 'Fuck UKIP! Fuck UKIP!' – as an occupier called Mickey jumped onto the back of the van and unplugged the coiled electric cable from the back of the cab to the screen. The screen went black and Mickey only just managed to leap off before the truck sped away. Everyone cheered.

We laughed and turned back to our conversation.

As we were talking, however, I noticed Mickey had become emboldened by the stunt and was now building a fire in a shopping trolley to our left. It wasn't long before a fire engine pulled up at the park and exasperated officers wearily climbed out. It was clear that they had been called here many times over the last six months. 'See, that's the sort of rebellious thing tied to it, y'know?' Nick explained to me. 'He likes to show off, y'know? He's had a bit of a tough life.'

It seemed Mickey had a bit of a reputation in the camp for causing trouble. I asked Nick how long he had been there for:

> Yeah, he's been here all the time. We've got homeless people come in, y'know? His bark's worse than his bite. He had a go at someone the other day and they punched him right in the mouth and knocked him out, he's only a little guy. I mean, he's like a little terrier, y'know? He gets his bone

> and he won't let go of it. It's just things like that … [pointing at the now-smouldering trolley] make us look like twats because the fire brigade gets called out.

Despite it being almost May, the wet winter and spring of 2011/12 had had a lasting effect on this previously green space in the middle of London. There seemed to be very little grass left and, where there weren't makeshift tents, there were puddles and soggy cardboard duckboards. The shadows of the Islington high-rise office blocks also made the air colder than it should be, and I decided that I had definitely chosen the wrong footwear, as mud was now seeping through the holes in my Converse. Between two trees was strung a banner which read: 'The world is in a much bigger mess than this camp. Occupy'.

The wall from which we were spectating probably once denoted the edge of the park but was now situated between the bulk of the camp and an 'info-tent' the front of which featured a picture of Rosa Parks. The patch of ground to our left was strewn with rubbish, firewood, metal bins, trollies, and now Mickey arguing with the fire officers. According to Nick,

> There are people who came to Occupy and gave up their house or whatever. But I don't think there's many though who actually given up their house and their job to come here. He [Mickey] probably never worked in his life. But he's been *dispossessed* and the only way he knows how to speak to people is like: 'I'll punch you out!' or whatever … 'Cause that's the way the system taught him how to survive, y'know? We have to tolerate him 'cause he's one of the dispossessed.

The movement in London had begun one month after the establishment of the first Occupy camp in Wall Street, New York. It was set up outside St Paul's Cathedral and the London Stock Exchange on 15 October 2011. Finsbury Square had been established later and was seen by many as the sister camp of St Paul's. But, by April 2012, Finsbury had outlived its older sibling which – following a court case contesting the public or private nature of the square outside the cathedral – had eventually been evicted on the grounds of 'public hygiene'.

This made Finsbury the longest-running Occupy site in the world (and proud of it) but the group had been sorely neglected by many of the evicted St Paul's activists who saw the mess and chaos of Finsbury as a lost cause. The St Paul's group was now withholding money which ostensibly had been donated to something called 'Occupy London', creating bitter resentment between those at Finsbury – who saw themselves as the last stand of the Occupy movement and with a rightful claim to the donation money for toilet hire and food – and those who had now become separated from the idea of material occupation and, in one activist's words, had turned into a 'cloud above the city' (Greg).

For Nick, this split between the two camps (and the many other factions of the Occupy movement in London) was part of a wider problem of collective self-definition that had plagued the movement from day one:

> We want people to come and get involved but, as I say, the way it is at the moment puts a lot of them off. We're still in a state of being defined, I think, whereas a lot of people think that Occupy has defined itself: 'this is what Occupy is, if you don't like it, fuck off …' y'know? And there's about 100 people with that idea, like: 'this is what Occupy is' and it's their little definition of Occupy. But really they're wrong because Occupy is what people come in and tell us what it's about. *The people decide what it is.* If they decide it's just a load of crap and we're a bunch of idiots running round, they're going to think: 'why the fuck should I both supporting a movement that's just a bunch of wasters?' You know what I mean?

We were briefly distracted again as two occupiers ran around laughing and blasting each other with the camp's fire extinguishers:

> I mean, you can see it happening, you can see it. Then everyone is saying: 'oh *this* is what Occupy is about …' and there's about 100 different voices saying that, but it's not them who decide, it's the public who decide! They're going to say: 'this ain't worth [it] … it's a slum, it's just a slum full of tents. That's it. *Why should we be inspired to resist a capitalist system on the basis of a load of idiots in tents?* Why should we look at the actually inherent nature of everything our lives have revolved around – going out and paying a mortgage or working or whatever – just because these people say there's a problem with it?

The info-tent to our right was supposed to 'connect' the protest with the public, but it stood abandoned with damp shelves of radical literature falling apart inside. As the besuited city workers hurried past they avoided eye contact, but cast sidelong glances at the camp and the Bistro on the Square where they used to spend working lunches (but which had been put out of business by the protest). Two young men in suits stood at a safe distance to our left and simply shook their heads at us. Nick continued:

> I mean, all this is bollocks because there's nothing happening at the moment. Because we've been kicked out of St Paul's and pushed into here, there's a sort of sense of 'oh, we're waiting for Occupy to do something.' Well, we've got to do something ourselves! We can't just sit here and lick out wounds. What are we going to actually do as some activity? I mean, at the moment, we're just making a fucking mess here, y'know? I mean, these people here [pointing at the city workers] find it difficult to find out what it is we're trying to achieve, y'know?

One month later, on 14 June 2012, Facebook informed me that Finsbury Square had been forcibly evicted in the night after a long stand-off with the police, including an incident in which one activist had climbed a tree in the middle of the park. The *Evening Standard* and the *Daily Mail* (long-term critics of the movement) hardly mentioned Occupy's politics; instead they merely reported on the mess left behind and the likely cost of the clear-up and restoration of Finsbury Square.

I stayed in contact with the activists I met that summer, returning to London in 2013 and 2014 to conduct more interviews with them, as well as with other people they put me in contact with. The research took me from anti-austerity marches at Trafalgar Square to anti-arms marches at the Excel Centre; from one-off general assemblies at St Paul's Cathedral to environmental protest camps in Cat Hill; from the Quaker Friends' House in Euston to a squatted garden centre in Camden; from university offices at Goldsmiths to anti-capitalist protests at Canary Wharf; from living rooms, to pubs, benches, cafes, and squares all over London. What follows is my interpretation of Occupy (in) London based on the activists' experiences (both positive and negative), as well as my own observations of the movement as one example of the global post-crash resurgence of protest in 2011.

Note

1 As Greg teased me later that day: 'you bullshit the public and you become a sociologist or something, [but] when you can bullshit other sociologists, that's when you become the best in your field … that's when they believe your bullshit'.

Introduction

Now is the winter of our discount tents!

Just because there has been a crisis does not necessarily mean that change will follow.

The financial crash and credit crunch of 2007/8 appeared, at first, to directly challenge both capitalist realism (an ideological assumption that the pursuit of money based upon private property is the only fair and sustainable way to run an economy (see Fisher 2009) and neoliberal normativity (the 'common sense' that we need to 'inject market principles into all aspects of society and culture' (Gane 2014: 1092). With the collapse of Lehman Brothers, it seemed that the contradictions of global finance were finally going to be revealed (see Sayer 2015), and yet, despite the catastrophic economic and social costs of this downturn, the forces which mobilised in the immediate aftermath were more *conservative* than radical. Probably the most popular discourse being peddled by the media, economic experts, and politicians circa 2008–10 was not one of a need for change, but of an international imperative to restore capitalism – to 'get business back to normal' and to 'balance the books' – while the answer to neoliberalism's failure was 'more neoliberalism', which took the form of austerity coupled with large amounts of public money being channelled into buoying the market through bailouts and quantitative easing. For the experts, there was never any question whether this was the best available approach, and the message in the UK was simply to 'keep calm and carry on' while brazenly insisting (as David Cameron did) that, rich or poor, 'we are all in this together' (Sky News 2010).

There were certainly localised murmurs of resistance right from the start, but it seemed to take a few years for the short-term effects of austerity and post-crash injustices to meet longer-term frustrations of democratic deficit, socio-economic inequality, and unjust international distribution. Against the broader rhetoric that this crisis was somehow a 'natural' phenomenon – a disaster that had come out of nowhere, which was beyond our control, but which we now simply had to deal with – protest groups began pointing out the legacies of capitalism, neoliberalism, European colonialism and American imperialism, patriarchy, racism, and ableism, which had together created severe inequalities of both wealth and voice. From December 2010 onwards, starting in Tunisia, there began a sudden resurgence of popular mobilisation and social movements which, despite arising in very different circumstances, began to develop a mutual recognition of one another as fighting for common causes of socio-economic justice and democratic voice, in cities as diverse as Tunis (Mabrouk 2011), Cairo (Rashad and Azzazi 2011), Madrid and Barcelona (Castaneda 2012), Athens (Madden and Vradis 2012), Tel Aviv (Alimi 2012), Istanbul (Ozkirimli 2014), Oaxaca (Arenas 2014), Santiago (Guzman-Concha 2012), Abuja (Adebayo 2016), Durban (Mottiar 2013), Hong Kong (Wasserstrom 2014), Taiwan (Ho 2015), Auckland (Land 2012), Toronto (Kohn 2013) and many more.

Numerous theories exist as to why 2011 was such a hotbed of activism. For some, the rise of civil disobedience that year can simply be understood as 'an idea whose time had come' (Chenoweth 2014). With the onset of the financial crisis, inevitably a moment had arrived for long-term grievances to be addressed and nothing could be done to stop this process. The claim was that pressure had been steadily building throughout the 20th century – led by movements including civil rights, post-colonial nationalism, second-wave feminism, counter-culture (anti-war and environmental), anti-Soviet nationalism, anti-neoliberal and alter-globalization – which would (at some point) simply become uncontainable by the powers that be. For the western media, for instance, the Arab Spring of late 2010/early 2011 was easily interpreted as evidence of a demand for liberal democracy which had been a long time coming, 'proving' that the rest of the 'undeveloped' world would 'inevitably' envy and desire a western governmental structure at some point (see Badiou 2012: 48–54). Change was afoot and the time had come for such ideas to be spawned around the globe.

For others, 2011 was best explained as a matter of increased consciousness and the recognition of specific common injustices spurred by the financial crisis. From this angle, the sudden upswing of activism was a direct consequence of post-crash global indignation on the part of those who had witnessed the fallout of the crash and wanted 'to restore government to citizen control, to regulate finance for the common good, and to get banks out of the business of buying legislators and influencing law' (Taylor and Gessan 2011: 4). In addition to longer-term activists, this new context saw a fresh generation taking to the streets, as they watched the liberal promises of the 1990s (accessible education, secure employment, peace, environmental justice, democracy, human rights, equal opportunities) evaporate into student debt, precariousness, war and destruction, and a democratic and economic monopolisation of influence into fewer and fewer hands. The crisis, in other words, had provided both the occasion and opportunity for an awareness and recognition of unequal and unjust social structures that had long persisted whereby, despite the meritocratic promises of neoliberal parliamentary systems and capitalism, economic security, opportunity, and distribution remained strictly a lottery of class, race, gender, geography, and (dis)ability.

Finally, a third explanation linked to this mutual identification of separate but common causes was one of technological determinism, arguing that 2011 was the direct result of new communication tools and platforms. Just as the printing press and the internet had done for previous movements, the social media of Web 2.0 was argued to be the central driving force of post-crash resistances. Not only did this technology appear to offer horizontality (which echoed aims for direct democracy), as well as portability and (relatively) covert communication, indeed it was also seen as forcing international accountability upon governments, media, and economic elites on a scale which had previously never been possible (Stekelenburg 2012). As observed by journalist Paul Mason, who was on the ground during many of the 2011 protests, one reliable similarity across the world was 'the smartphone glow on activist faces', evidence for him that this was nothing less than 'a revolution caused by the near collapse of the free market, combined with an upswing in technical innovation, a surge in desire for individual freedom and a change in human consciousness about what freedom means' (2012: 3).

However, while these three explanations all seem to capture something of a post-crash 'age of resistance' in which 'the possibility of radical change has been firmly placed on the historical agenda' (Douzinas 2013: 9), few have then gone on to ask: *why nothing actually changed in the face of such international pressure*. Since 2011, we have not seen the rise of democracy and socio-economic justice which these movements stood for, but instead their antithesis: the continued ideological justification of extreme global inequality; the plutocratic sway of the super-wealthy over politics; the democratic deficit of liberal parliamentary models of government (despite claims to the contrary); as well as a rise of anti-establishment populist nationalism and the proliferation of explicit racism, misogyny, and hate. To illustrate this point, while 2011 had seen *Time* magazine name 'the Protestor' as their prestigious 'Person of the Year', by 2016 this title had been given to Donald Trump. How do we account for such a turnaround in the space of five years? How have we moved from the hope and popular drive for equality and justice after the crash to the division and uncertainty of today? 'Of what', asks Badiou, 'are we the half-fascinated, half-devastated witnesses?' (2012: 1).

This book, based upon ethnographic data collected from the Occupy movement in London between 2012 and 2014, will offer an explanation. It is my suggestion that, despite their best intentions, post-crash movements were ultimately limited by normative ideas of what was possible, sensible, rational, and reasonable, as a response to the financial crisis of 2007/8. In the first place, the wider context of movements like Occupy (in) London made political organisation extremely difficult, with norms of individualism and libertarianism undermining collective mobilisation and symbolic efficiency. Second, these strategic problems also made it harder for movements like Occupy to make their resistance 'appear' and be 'heard' against a wider context that distributed them as 'non-sense', while, finally, unintentionally extending the norms and presuppositions of that which they were resisting against. Ultimately, it is my contention that the reason why nothing has changed is that movements like Occupy (in) London (which represented the possibility of a post-crash alternative) were simply unable to undermine the hold that 'common sense' exerted after the crisis.

This isn't to say, however, that there is nothing to learn or reflect upon, or that we can't turn the experiences of Occupy (in) London towards addressing foreclosures which persist today. Far from it. In the first place, the use of urban occupation by the movements of 2011 demonstrated that the semi-permanent occupation of urban space through protest camps and squatting possesses a radical potential. What's more, as experiments in democracy, these movements have firmly placed equality and justice back onto the public agenda, while highlighting some of the organisational problems which persist on the left, such as internal inconsistency; authority and leadership; and the problem of reconciling collective identity with horizontality and inclusivity (i.e. a structured structurelessness). And finally, as historical events, the movements of 2011 encourage us to reflect upon how we understand, configure and construct the relationship between power and resistance, and this helps us to understand the apparent paradox that – despite one of the greatest ideological crises in history and one of the most internationally connected resistance ever known – *nothing changed.*

Did nothing change?

At first glance, to say that nothing changed after 2007/8 may seem a little disingenuous. We have surely witnessed many changes in the last ten years, from previously stable economies (like Greece and Spain) going bankrupt and being forcibly steered towards austerity in order to access international loans, to the rise of right-wing populism throughout Europe (e.g. the vote for the UK to leave the European Union – EU) and the USA (e.g. the election of President Trump), as well as new refugee crises caused by global inequality and civil war in the wake of power vacuums left by the Arab Spring (e.g. Syria). Yet while these events certainly resemble change, they also indicate a lack of change at a more fundamental level. Following Žižek, we might even call these events 'pseudo-changes' or 'pseudo-events' which offer 'the semblance of a radical change … so that 'nothing would really change', so that things (i.e. the fundamental capitalist relations of production) would basically remain the same' (2008a: 231). In other words, what we have surely not seen is any fundamental change to the infrastructures and principles of global finance, nor have we seen wider cultural changes to address the role of entrenched historical structures that maintain inequality; instead we have witnessed renewed commitments and continuations from the previous world order. International markets continue to polarise extreme concentrations of wealth and poverty along traditional post-colonial/imperial lines (whether former European colonies or new American and Chinese forays into the global south for raw materials), with a continued trust in state-backed market competition to distribute fairly and set appropriate limits on the state. The civil frustration and cynicism which has resulted from this system also continues, most obviously expressed in the anti-establishment rhetoric of movements on both the left and the right.

One way in which this lack of change was covered up was through a successful framing of the crisis as a problem of the *state* (i.e. policy) and *expertise* (i.e. economists) rather than capitalism or neoliberalism itself. For instance, the suspiciously rapid post-mortems on the crisis (such as from the International Monetary Fund – IMF) blamed 'group think' and 'intellectual capture' in creating a situation in which a crash was deemed 'unlikely', while pointing the finger at incomplete economic models and a consensus culture that excluded contrarians (Turner 2017). Behind such an allocation of blame, the fundamental neoliberal belief in the capitalist market as a self-correcting ecological phenomenon that would eventually rediscover its equilibrium could continue (King 2017; see also Krippner 2011). Rather than a revolutionary shift away from such a system that perpetuated exploitation and inequality, and towards a more equitable distribution of resources and a parallel move towards democratic inclusion, since the crisis we have instead witnessed the emergence of a greater (and growing) gulf between the rich and the poor in terms of wealth and voice. Or as Sayer (2015: 1) puts it:

> the rich continue to get richer, even in the worst crisis of 80 years – they can still laugh all the way to their banks and tax havens as the little people bail out banks that have failed … generally, the less you had to do with the crisis, the bigger the sacrifices – relative to your income – you have had to make … meanwhile a political class increasingly dominated by the rich continues to support their interests and diverts the public's attention by stigmatising and punishing those on welfare benefits and low incomes, cheered on by media overwhelmingly controlled by the super-rich.

Rather than change, we have only seen the continuation of trends, with a 'growing split between the top 1% and the 99% and the dominance of politics by the 1%' (Sayer 2015: 3) who aptly demonstrated their ability 'to be the most able group at ensuring their incomes continue to rise in defiance of the economic crisis' (Dorling 2014: 4). Despite the crash, the richest 1 per cent now have as much wealth as the rest of the world combined, with the eight richest individuals now owning as much as the poorest 50 per cent (Oxfam 2017).

And yet, at the time, many activists and political theorists alike had clearly seen the crisis as a radical opportunity to bring about fundamental and historical shifts in the way in which societies and economies were organised. For instance, while admitting that 'little had apparently changed' (Gamble 2014: 16), it remains Andrew Gamble's contention that the financial crisis was a unique juncture in which 'radically different outcomes were at stake' (ibid.: 29). For Gamble, it seems, the crash clearly presented an opportunity to directly question the ideological underpinnings and premises of the economic status quo, and therefore offered a chance to undermine and upset what had previously been considered to have no alternative. He argued that 'as the crisis has unfolded, it has also begun to cause an upheaval in previously settled views of the world: in our assumptions and expectations' (ibid.: 27), upsetting the 'obviousness' of capitalist realism and neoliberal normativity. This was a chance for an alternative to pounce and capitalise upon the crisis in a system which had been dominant for so long.

On the other hand, however, others argued that despite such optimistic rhetoric which surrounded the post-crash moment and movements, the crisis actually demonstrated just how entrenched was the notion that 'there is no alternative' in political thought and imagination. As Philip Mirowski pointed out, for instance, rather than spurring transformation, it seemed instead that 'unaccountably the political right had emerged from the tumult stronger, unapologetic, and even less restrained in its rapacity and credulity than prior to the crash' (2013: 1–2). Proceeding to explain this outcome, Mirowski suggests that 'the most likely reason that the doctrine that precipitated the crisis has evaded responsibility and the renunciation indefinitely postponed is that neoliberalism as worldview has sunk its roots deep into everyday life, almost to the point of passing as the 'ideology of no ideology' (ibid.: 28). Even a crash on such a scale as this was not enough to shift the 'common sense' principles of neoliberal capitalism: that 'free market' competition, supported by compliant state and inter-state institutions, is better than any alternatives for achieving distributive justice and liberty. The fact that this neoliberal crisis had been followed by a continuation of, rather than a change in, the status quo, was an indication of just how much of an intellectual hold this doctrine had on limiting political options.

Yet neoliberalism itself had begun as a marginal school of economic thought in the early 20th century and was for a long time sidelined and marginalised in favour of Keynesian economics which attempted to use state intervention as a tool for balancing capitalism's most exploitative effects (although this humanist project was only made possible by colonial exploitation and violence elsewhere (see Bhambra 2016; Narayan 2016). It wasn't until after the horrendous experiences of big authoritarian states during the Second World War that there began to be a concerted turn away from emphasising the distributive role of the state in economic doctrine, with figures such as Hayek (1979) criticising 'totalitarianisms' of the left and right, and advocating instead state-supported market competition as a fairer method of distribution that was free from (what he saw as) the inevitably oppressive tendencies of government. Developing these ideas through international organisations (such as the Mont Pelerin Society), inconsistencies began to develop within neoliberal thought regarding how far the state could legitimately intervene in the market in order to ensure competition. But while this lack of clarity became 'neoliberalism's curse' in that 'it can live neither with, nor without, the state' (Peck 2010: 650), this loophole also gave the ideology an immense flexibility: from early justifications of Central Intelligence Agency-backed coups and the installation of free market-friendly dictators in South America in the 1970s (e.g. Pinochet in Chile (see Fischer 2009); through the rise of oligarchies in the former Soviet Union and China from the 1980s (including, for example, American and German involvement in the post-Yugoslavian civil war (see Gowan 1999); and right up to the commercialisation of military involvement in Iraq (Klein 2008).

During the recent crisis, therefore, nation states and international organisations (such as the IMF, the EU, and the World Bank) simply felt that they were acting legitimately when they decided to bail out private interests, justifying this 'socialism for the rich' (Žižek 2011: 67) on neoliberal grounds and supporting the continuation of market competition while simultaneously cutting spending on social welfare which was seen to be undermining incentives for competition. There was no alternative. Neoliberalism, to use Mirowski's phrase above, now passed as an 'ideology of no ideology', meaning that it was no longer recognised as one political option among others, but instead was considered to be the rational, reasonable, common-sense political model for managing capitalism. Subsequently, 'any naïve leftist explanation that the current financial and economic crisis necessarily opens up a space for the radical left [was] … without doubt dangerously short-sighted' (Žižek 2009a: 17), because such a position simply failed to recognise the extent to which neoliberalism has become unrivalled in its ability to capture and police the political imagination and possibility of alternatives.

This ideological limit is what theorists before the crash were already referring to as 'post-politics' or 'the foreclosure of the possibility of politics and the tacit embrace of global capitalism' (Dean 2006: 115). The obvious problem this presents for advocates of radical change is that such a foreclosure automatically undermines the potential to even imagine the possibility of an alternative, and is therefore 'radically reactionary' because it automatically 'forestalls the articulation of divergent, conflicting and alternative trajectories of future … possibility and assemblages' (Swyngedouw 2009: 610). Under such conditions, an alternative future simply cannot be fathomed. It has 'no name' (ibid. 2010: 18) and the very viability of a change in direction is denied. Neoliberalism therefore survived its crisis, because it had become the means of distributing reason, common sense, and normality, with any alternatives (both imagined and yet to be imagined) pre-positioned as unreasonable, abnormal 'non-sense'. What we might call 'neoliberal normativity' therefore defines a political rationality that came to operate as a 'normative order of reason' which could 'legitimately govern as well as structure life and activity as a whole' via discourses that 'constitute a particular field and subjects within it … norm and deviation are the means by which subjects and objects in any field are made, arranged, represented, judged and conducted … discourses, when they become dominant, always circulate a truth and become a kind of common sense' (Brown 2015: 117).

Under neoliberal normativity, there is very little consideration for motivations, drives, or aspirations outside of instrumental economic ones (Brown 2015: 44), with the facilitation of competition through state and legal support (ibid.: 36) legitimising inequality in policy, jurisprudence, and the popular imaginary (turning people into 'winners or losers' – 'shirkers or strivers' – rather than democratic citizens who deserve better) (ibid.: 64). And yet, in the post-crash moment, those who spoke from a position that advocated this approach were simply heard and seen from a position of rationality, expertise, truth, knowledge, and authority, while those who advocated for an alternative were already pre-positioned – and often internalised the position – of speaking and appearing from a position of irrationality, falsity, ignorance, naivety, powerlessness, and 'non-sense'. Such a dynamic was itself a direct consequence of neoliberal normativity, creating (what Rancière 2001, 2010 calls) a distribution of the sensible that shaped, designated and policed sensible or non-sensible – legitimate or illegitimate, meaningful or non-meaningful, rational or irrational, political or apolitical – voice and appearance.

So, how might we understand the possibilities and limitations of post-crash resistance within this situation of foreclosure? This will be the overarching theme of the book, but I do not wish to develop this discussion in a way that unfairly dismisses the Occupy movement (nor, by clumsy extension, the other movements of 2011). Those who quickly dismiss post-crash movements as naïve, pointless, disorganised, facetious, apolitical events, I argue, simply play into those wider norms that also seek to dismiss the possibility of alternatives. From a position of public theorising and assessing such movements, academics must be careful to be constructive as well as critical, recognising that their critique can add to the wider normative efforts to foreclose and limit political imaginations.

For example, while I might agree with Mirowski that 'the neoliberal worldview has become embedded in contemporary culture', I would also encourage a more nuanced reflection on the consequences of this for post-crash movements, than his (rather condescending and dismissive) diagnosis that:

> when well-meaning activists sought to call attention to the slow-motion train-wreck of the world economic system, they came to their encampments with no solid conception of what they might need to know to make their indictments stick; nor did they have any clear perspective on what their opponents knew or believed about markets and politics, not to mention what the markets themselves knew about their attempts at resistance.
>
> (2013: 328–29)

As I will unpack throughout this book, while there is certainly truth to Mirowski's observations that the Occupy movement tended to confuse 'openness with democracy', that it over-emphasised individual self-expression which denied the movement a collective identity, and that it had a problematically libertarian preoccupation with formal organisation (ibid.: 328); I nevertheless argue that this critique needs to be made in a manner that doesn't simply end up dismissing the post-crash movements as 'non-sense'. Instead, I hope that my account, rather than extending efforts to limit and police the alternative possibilities post-crash movements represented, supports the empowerment of alternatives and helps to overcome such foreclosures by backing activists' 'capacity to intervene in our setting, making it and us different from what we were before … not of continuity with … capitalism but of rupture, of a hole or break' (Dean 2012: 216).

While I will therefore endeavour to build a constructive critique that doesn't end up further diminishing or foreclosing possibilities, there also remains a responsibility to be critical of post-crash movements, and 'ensure that our desire to see real politics return does not prompt us to misidentify political dissatisfaction with the current order as the dawning of a new political age' (Winlow 2012: 20). Most importantly, in order to explain why 'so rarely in history have so many people voiced their discontent with the political designs of the elite … yet rarely has mass protest resulted in so little political gain' (Swyngedouw 2011: 8), we need to understand the operations of power during the crisis in foreclosing and ultimately preventing change. How was it, for example, that those prominent pundits of neoliberalism – whether politicians, economists, or journalists – were able to speak from a position of authority even as this worldview was collapsing around them? And how was it that, while encouraging us to stick with pre-crash models of society, economy, and government, such individuals and institutions were able to respond so coolly 'to calls for a radical overhaul of their management by calling them unviable and unrealistic' (Worth 2013: 49)? These are the questions I will explore below, but first there follows an introduction to our case study.

Occupy (in) London

The Arab Spring and European Summer of 2011 were followed by the American Fall. Attributed by many to the Canadian magazine *Adbusters* – itself a product of the North American element of the alter-globalization movement of the late 1990s (see Klein 2001) – the common story is that 'it was an exchange between [editors] White and Lasn … in early June 2011 that produced the idea to camp out, the actual name of the movement: Occupy Wall Street, and the start date: September 17th' (Kaneck 2012: 12). Lasn registered the domain name 'occupywallstreet.org' on 9 June 2011, before sending an email to subscribers stating that 'America needs its own Tahrir', and publishing the now-infamous poster of the ballerina pirouetting on the Wall Street bull with the caption: 'What is our one demand? Occupy Wall Street. 9.17.11'. But we might want to push this origin story a bit wider. As the reference to Cairo's Tahrir Square itself demonstrates, Occupy Wall Street surely came about as a result of something more than a conversation between two magazine editors, and was directly inspired by and connected to events taking place in North Africa, the Middle East, and Southern Europe. In particular, the very tactic of occupying urban space, while it possessed a long history, was an idea which, in this context, was directly adopted from those movements.

It could also be easily argued that the Occupy movement was itself a result of pre-existing activist networks who actually responded to the call to protest and occupied Zuccotti Park (near Wall Street, New York). Thus, the Occupy movement could be seen as a direct descendant of connections that were formed in the alter-globalization movement, as well as in the 2003 international march against war in Iraq (widely recognised as the largest international march in history) and various environmental, climate, anti-poverty, and economic protests since (such as regular rallies at G8 and G20 meetings). What's more, Occupy itself was immediately preceded by post-crash resistances in the USA that directly fed into it, such as attempts by Anonymous to occupy Washington, DC in June 2011, or the online Tumblr campaign of 'we are the 99%' (when people shared 'selfies' in which they held placards detailing their debt or lack of employment/educational opportunities, ending with the common tagline 'I/we are the 99%').

But whatever its origin, what was truly exceptional about Occupy was the way in which it soon 'erupted around the world in a synchronised fashion' using 'similar symbols and narratives' even while 'the actual protests were sustained by quite different local networks in different cities' (Uitermark and Nicholls 2012: 1). According to one count, there were at least 1,518 different Occupy camps established in 70 different countries around the world (Occupy Directory 2015), yet each protest adopted a slightly different take on the overall sentiments of the movement which – carried through from the Arab Spring and the European Summer – might be described as based on democracy and socio-economic justice. In different contexts this took on diverse meanings, with 'resistance' assuming a different significance for Occupy Wall Street (as the symbolic centre of capitalism, international finance, and the crisis); in contrast with Occupy Central in Hong Kong (which was fighting for the right to democratic sovereignty from the Chinese government); with Occupy Nigeria (which was sparked by the removal of fuel subsidies in the context of poverty and post-colonial exploitation; while the country exports more oil than any other African nation, it still relies on imports of refined fuel); and with Ocupa Sampa in São Paulo (which took on the increasing militarisation of university campuses and the criminalisation of student activism).

In London, the movement began one month after Occupy Wall Street on 15 October 2011. Inspired by the New York activists, Occupy LSX targeted the London Stock Exchange and had originally intended to set up a protest camp in Paternoster Square (the location of the Exchange). However, when the activists arrived, they found themselves forced back by police and 'kettled' onto the steps of the adjacent St Paul's Cathedral, where they remained until their eviction in February 2012. While this original protest outside the cathedral remained the focus of much media and public attention – usually incorrectly identified using the universal moniker of Occupy London (hence why I use Occupy (in) London to describe the city-wide movement) – a number of other camps and squats were also established throughout the city, including the Bank of Ideas (a squat in a former bank which held events and talks); Occupation Finsbury Square (initially a relief camp for the over-crowded St Paul's site); Occupy Leyton Marsh (a community-led occupation which attempted to protest against construction work for the 2012 Olympic Games); and Occupy Nomads (who, when I met them, had set up camp at Mile End). In addition, a number of working groups were also established to focus on specific issues, such as Democracy Action (DAWG); Energy, Equity and Environment (EEE); Economies (EWG); the New Putney Debates; Press/Social Media; the Occupied Times Newspaper; and the (controversial) Occupation Records. Some of these groups opted to meet away from the campsites and squats, with one particularly popular site being the Quakers' Friends House in Euston (where many of my interviews took place).

With so many different groups, there were many alternative objectives expressed by the movement in London, and these were occasionally even self-contradictory. This makes it especially difficult to pin down exactly what Occupy (in) London wanted to achieve, and this, as will be argued in Chapter 4, also created a major strategic problem of organisation. But one way in which we might try to get an initial idea of what motivated the occupations in London is through the 'About' section of the occupylondon.org.uk website:

> Ordinary people and communities around the world are being devastated by a crisis we did not cause. Our political elites have chosen to protect corporations, financial institutions and the rich at the expense of the majority.
>
> Occupy London is part of a global movement that began in 2011 – the year of protest.
>
> Inspired by Occupy Wall Street and the Arab Spring, and answering to the call out made by the Spanish *Plataforma ¡Democracia Real YA!* in May 2011 for a Global Day of Action on October 15th 2011, Occupy London began outside the London Stock Exchange in solidarity with protests in Spain, Rome, New York, Portugal, Chile, Berlin, Brussels, Zagreb, and many more. By mid-afternoon on October 15th 2011, the 2000–3000 Occupy London protestors moved onto the grounds of St Paul's and stayed there (around 170 tents) until they were forcibly evicted on 28th Feb 2011.
>
> Occupy London brought together concerned citizens to fight for a new political and economic system that puts people, democracy and the environment before profit.
>
> OL values equality, diversity and horizontality.
>
> Decisions are made democratically in ASSEMBLIES that are open for everyone to attend and actions are implemented by WORKING GROUPS.

To begin with, this public statement gives us a clear sense of post-crash injustice and indignation, pointing to the undemocratic and devastating consequences of the current system, but (importantly) stopping short of naming what that system *is* (i.e. neoliberalism, capitalism, colonialism, imperialism, parliamentarianism, patriarchy, and so on). The connections are then made with other movements around the world, offering a mutual recognition and solidarity with other struggles for democracy and socio-economic justice, as well as with their roots in the initial call to action by the Spanish Indignados. Finally, we get an idea of the broad principles that the movement stands for – putting people, democracy and the environment before profit, as well as valuing equality, diversity, and horizontality.

These principles also guided the movement's organisational mechanisms and the 'assemblies' mentioned in the passage refer to Occupy's processes of decision-making. The General Assembly (GA), in principle, was designed to allow anyone within or outside of the movement to contribute and speak. Consensus had to be reached for a motion to be passed, and individuals and groups could 'block' motions if they did not agree. The GA also adopted an array of collective hand signals that prevented interruption but allowed interjection – such as waving hands to show agreement, or raising one hand to ask the randomly selected chair permission to speak – with the aim of facilitating democratic debate. It soon became apparent, however, that despite these measures to create a horizontal and inclusive decision-making process, hierarchies, divisions, exclusions, fractures, and cliques were beginning to appear within the movement. Starting from within the GA, these then became further exasperated by the eviction of the St Paul's group, whose decision *not* to reoccupy opened up a fundamental divide within the movement over the importance of the Occupy movement actually occupying physical space.

Perhaps the greatest divide was personified by two groups: on the one hand, the former St Paul's contingent (who had appropriated the universal name Occupy London), and on the other, the remaining occupiers of Finsbury Square. The former St Paul's group had the upper hand, consolidating its adoption of Occupy London through bank account access, press releases, invite-only organising committees, as well as ownership of registered domain names, Facebook pages and Twitter accounts. The group began to distance itself from Finsbury Square, seeing this camp as a lost cause that was plagued by violence, alcoholism, drug (ab)use, homelessness, disorganisation, and dirt (all of which were problems that, if anything, were only made worse by the division and the withholding of money that had been donated to something called 'Occupy London'). As the post-camp St Paul's contingent had managed to monopolise the symbolic and material resources of the movement, as well as attempting to cut off Finsbury Square, this left the remaining occupiers in the camp with little choice but to try to somehow maintain the site by themselves. They also began bitterly denying any ties to Occupy London which caused severe symbolic confusion for the public. Splits like this, as I will argue in Chapter 4, had serious implications for the movement's organisation and identity, allowing un-checked structures and hierarchies to persist within the (ostensibly) structureless and horizontal democratic space, as well as undermining the efficiency of their collective symbolic appearance.

Outline

Given that there were many other Occupy movements outside of the USA, there has been very little sustained research into groups beyond Wall Street. My selection of Occupy (in) London as a case study was therefore intended as more than one of convenience, in that I wanted to add to the wider literature on Occupy a study into one of the major nodes of the international movement, as well as into a post-crash protest at the heart of international finance, capitalism, and colonialism. Beginning in April 2012 in Finsbury Square, I conducted participant observation at the camps, squats, and one-off protest events, while keeping up with the movement's literature, online activity, and mailing lists. I also organised a total of 42 interviews with 36 activists over three years, who were mostly recruited via snowball sampling, and with repeat interviews taking place in separate years (see Appendix 1). My aim was to experience the movement's culture and to learn how its members viewed their own resistance as well as the 'powers' they were up against; why they saw occupation as an important tool; and about the challenges and struggles they were facing. In addition, my approach was also guided by an attempt to avoid three broad epistemological stances which seemed to typify much of the research into the Occupy movement: (1) abstract empiricism; (2) romanticism; and (3) cynicism.

By abstract empiricism, I mean a tendency within the social sciences and social movement studies to see data collection as an end in itself, with the aim of simply documenting social phenomena in order to further scientific knowledge or advance methodology. For C. Wright Mills, while it was also true that researchers should not rely solely on grand theory (1981: 46–7), the penchant for abstract empiricism had created a problematic 'tendency to confuse whatever is to be studied with the set of methods suggested for its study' (ibid.: 59). Rather than emphasising the demands and politics of movements like Occupy, or seeing research as an opportunity to support social change, instead abstract empiricism gives the impression that these new movements were simply an exciting opportunity to retest previous scientific models. Many researchers appeared to respond to post-crash resistance only by diligently reapplying concepts and frameworks, producing papers which emphasised their own data collection, rather than the political, radical, and normative aims of the movement itself. Overlooking how 'any statement of fact is of political moral significance' (Wright Mills 1981: 178), the goal of such work was to produce grounded theories (see Glaser and Strauss 2017) which might accurately describe objective laws and patterns that create the phenomenon of social movements.

Occupy began and the race was on to develop 'a novel data-collection methodology' (Thorsen *et al.* 2013), such as proposing 'the use of cognitive linguistics as a tool in narrative analysis' (Catalano and Creswell 2013); or by introducing 'a methodological framework we have designed to gather empirical data on the affective, every day encounters, or micropolitical life, of the protest camp' (Feigenbaum *et al.* 2013); or how about a content analysis of movement material to examine similarities and differences in cultural orientations (Kern and Nam 2013); or perhaps a novel application of 'three Information Studies paradigms' (Skinner 2011); or a chance to combine 'Melucci's theory of collective identity with insights from the field of organisational communication' (Kavada 2015: 872); or to develop 'new social movement' theory towards understanding Occupy as 'a new new social movement' (Langman 2013).[1] While such approaches certainly have some merits in developing methods and schemes through which we can better understand social movements, this is nevertheless where they tend to stop – as if this was the task as an end in itself – rather than using this as a starting point to develop strategy or promote the politics of the movement in question. While I would certainly agree, therefore, that 'analysing Occupy is important for understanding both the political importance of social movements and the theoretical limits of social movement approaches' (Pickerill and Krinsky 2013: 280), abstract empiricism tends to overemphasise the latter task at the expense of the (arguably more important) former responsibility of emphasising the importance of social movements.

The scramble to understand the role of social media is indicative of this, offering insights 'into the media culture of the Occupy movement … based on mixed qualitative and quantitative methods' (Costanza-Chock 2012); seeking to describe 'the ways in which individuals can use a particular social media platform, the microblog Twitter, to learn about the Occupy Wall Street movement' (Gleason 2013); or examine 'the temporal evolution of digital communication activity … using a high-volume sample' (Conover *et al.* 2013). There is a place for such empirical work – and it would be wrong (as well as simply inaccurate) to suggest that researchers aren't sympathetic to the movements they study (with many being initially drawn to the research through political empathy) – but such empiricism simply *must* be situated within wider political theory and context, as well as promoting the voices of activists themselves. Rather than asking soulless ontological questions about 'why and how people do things they do, especially why they do things together' in order to 'understand why [people] cooperate in general' and get 'to the heart of human motivation' (Goodwin and Jasper 2015: 4), we need to ask why movements are not more successful, why change appears so elusive despite resistance, and what are the key problems of strategy and political possibility.

However, this would require taking an approach that emphasises the democratic voice and appearance of activists, while also taking a critical and constructive position to their experiences and arguments. Researchers should not define their role as perfecting a methodological toolkit that can unlock some objective 'truth' behind social movements, and must avoid an 'uncritical repetition of a reductionist account' which bears 'no resemblance to the social theories and processes of movement theorising we encounter within movement' (Cox and Flesher-Fominaya 2013: 8). Instead, as Prentoulis and Thommassen have argued, academics could 'treat the protestors as political theorists rather than as objects of social reality … the aim is to let the protestors speak for themselves, and to treat their language as the language in which our analysis is cast' (2013: 169). While admitting that 'this is at once necessary and impossible' (ibid.) because research inevitably involves a level of translation and interpretation by the investigator, this nevertheless should be a guiding principle, even if we admit that 'the research will not get the authentic and unmediated truth about the protestors, as if such a thing existed in the first place' (ibid.: 171). This approach is politically significant and, by not adopting it, academics risk denying the democratic voice and appearance of protestors, undermining and dismissing their politics (which is already being foreclosed), and silencing them 'just at the point when they are trying to make their voices heard' (ibid.: 169).

Our aim should be to emphasise the politics and goals of the social movements we study; however, this should not allow us to fall for the second popular approach which was taken by researchers of the Occupy movement: *romanticism*. At the expense of a more critical or constructive reading, this included over-the-top praise for the movement by, for instance, comparing Occupy to famous moments of leftist history, describing the camps as 'much like the Paris Commune, a truly autonomous democratic community' that was 'reclaiming public space and transforming it into a 'public sphere' (Benski *et al.* 2013: 550). As I will argue below, such a fetishisation of Occupy as (somehow) removed and autonomous from wider society – creating a 'physical and political space for reasserting the power of the people' (Lubin 2012: p184) – was problematic insofar as it overlooked structures of inequality and complicities with post-crash normativity. Thus, I argue that it is overly celebratory to argue that 'the overall Occupy movement was an example of communicative action in the weak public sphere and it serves as a place of developing citizenship, which contributed to the theory of deliberative democracy in many meaningful ways' (Min 2015: 73) as, while Occupy certainly had democratic potential, it was far from able to simply achieve this in practice.

To be fair, much of the romantic gushing over the movement was focused, unsurprisingly, around the exciting period in which the camps were still on the ground, and before a more patient and critical reflection could take place. Speaking at Zuccotti Park, for instance, Naomi Klein suggested that we might 'treat this beautiful movement as if it is the most important thing in the world … because it is … it really is' (2011), while others made similar grandiose claims that 'this changes everything' and that 'historians may look back at September 2011 as the time when the 99% awoke, named our crisis, and faced the reality that none of our leaders are going to solve it… this is the moment when we realised we would have to act for ourselves' (Van Gelder 2011: 3). There was a clear feeling at the time that this was something important, something consequential, and something that would affect a lasting change. This was nothing short of a revolution, and any politicians or elites who dismissed or criticised Occupy would do so at their own peril, because 'like the spokesmen for Arab dictators … [they] couldn't be more wrong and, as time will tell, may eventually be forced to accept the inevitability of their own obsolescence' (Rushkoff 2011).

Because so much of the romantic research on Occupy finished once the camps had been evicted, such accounts could only tell us so much about the movement in the optimistic heat of the event when theorists and activists were more likely to be upbeat, enthusiastic, exuberant, and (above all) defensive in the face of critique. Subsequently, I argue that the temporal distance of my data from the height of the London movement (even by a few years) helped to alleviate this, allowing the activists I met to be more self-critical and reflexive than they might have been at the time. During the post-crash period of crisis and uncertainty, when events appeared to be happening simply 'too fast' to allow for sustained reflection, this approach also permitted me to 'slow down' my analysis (Gane 2006). Indeed, as Žižek has argued in defence of social theory, there is 'a fundamentally anti-theoretical edge' to the injunction that there is simply 'no time to reflect on all of it, we have to act now … *now* is our chance, we need to do *something quickly*, not slowly reflecting and *doing nothing*' (2008b: xv; emphasis in the original). On the contrary, Žižek invites us to respond to such rallies against thought and reflection, and to 'gather the courage to answer: 'yes precisely that! … there are situations where the only truly 'practical' thing to do is to resist the temptation to engage immediately, and to 'wait and see' by means of a patient critical analysis' (ibid.). This book is unusual in continuing the study of the movement into 2014 – two years after the camps in London had been totally evicted – but this has made possible a patient critical analysis.

Finally, the third broad approach of cynicism encompasses attempts (such as Mirowski's, see above) to dismiss the movement as a loose group of facetious, naïve, middle-class, apolitical youngsters who didn't really know what they were doing.[2] This attitude reflects a wider political context of *cynicism* (see Chapter 6 in this volume, also Burgum 2015) and is also indicative of a profound *melancholia* on behalf of the left, or 'a certain narcissism with regard to one's past political attachments and identity that frames all contemporary investments in political mobilisation … a mournful, conservative, backward-looking attachment to feelings, analyses, or relations that have become fetishised and frozen in the heart of the critic' (Brown 2001: 169–70). For example, while theorists like Roberts (2012) make important points about the lack of cohesive organisation in the Occupy movement, his criticism is nevertheless based upon a rose-tinted contrast with the past, such as 'in the late 1970s' when 'the labour movement would have been the most obvious mechanism for resisting neoliberal policies' (ibid.: 756). Such comparisons, written while tents were still on the ground, seem to come from a position that *expected* the movement to fail, suggesting a melancholia among such commentators who are 'attached more to a particular political analysis or ideal – *even to the failure of that ideal* – than to seizing possibilities for radical change in the present' (Brown 1999: 191; emphasis added), revealing a 'paradox of an intention to mourn that precedes or anticipates the loss of the object' (Žižek 2008c: 146). The melancholic and cynical left, as I will demonstrate in Chapters 5 and 6, tends to opt for an underdog mentality, seeming more comfortable with *not* winning power or authority, and instead remaining authentic and powerless; righteous and marginal. Rather than supporting new movements for progressive change, this approach is sympathetic to their politics, but presupposes that they will fail (which undermines their support, reaffirms their distribution as 'non-sense', and turns into a self-fulfilling prophecy).

It has been my aim to take a position that fits between these three approaches of abstract empiricism, romanticism, and cynicism. While using empirical data to learn from Occupy (in) London, ground my thinking, and emphasise activist voices, I also aim to be both critical and constructive about the movement, choosing to take the position that there is much to learn from Occupy about the foreclosure of political possibilities and how we might overcome them. What's more, while Occupy (in) London certainly had limitations which need to be outlined and addressed, they were more often than not criticisms which were expressed by the activists themselves. Following Brown, I intend my research to make 'visible why particular positions or visions of the future occur to us, and especially to reveal when and where those positions work *in the same "political rationality" as that which they purport to criticise*' (2001: 109–10; emphasis added). The Occupy movement in London, as a case study of post-crash resistance and the possibility for change, needs to be understood within the context of the financial crisis and the perplexing (or perhaps not) lack of change which took place during that period. Therefore, I will make a series of arguments which seek to clarify how Occupy (in) London was ultimately unable to undermine capitalist realism and neoliberal normativity, elaborating on the foreclosures of possibility faced by the movement, before drawing together some naïve, easier said than done suggestions in the Conclusion as to how movements like Occupy might strategically approach, frame, and organise protest in the future. We will begin, however, with a theoretical discussion of power and resistance, in order to firmly root the argument which follows.

Readers who are not interested in social theory and political philosophy may wish to skip Chapter 1. While this section seeks to justify and ground the approach that I take in later chapters, having a prior knowledge of where such arguments and concepts come from is not a requirement for following (or enjoying) the rest of the volume.

Notes

1 As was debated by academics at the Manchester Activism Conference in 2013, does Occupy even 'count' as a social movement? Does it fit into our academic definitions?
2 As I overheard an Israeli academic refer to Occupy Tel Aviv at the International Sociological Association conference in 2014, it was just the 'Jewish Woodstock'.

1 What is our one demand?

By way of a literature review, this chapter will establish a baseline and theoretical background for the discussions which follow, building a position on the complexities of contemporary power and resistance by focusing on a number of key theorists who do not always fit comfortably alongside one another. However, while they may approach the problem from different angles – using different traditions and presuppositions – I intend to play them off against one another in order to establish themes and concepts which will be developed throughout the book: authority, collective organisation, and aesthetics. Moreover, while Foucault, Butler, Brown, Žižek, Badiou, Dean, and Rancière may differ in their philosophical pedigrees, they nevertheless share a common and overlapping interest in understanding the counterintuitive mechanisms of power and resistance in the context of (post-)modern capitalism. It is this common focus which has led me to mix their contributions despite the infighting that exists between their followers; for instance, we might highlight the rifts between post-structuralists and Marxists, which in the case of these specific theorists have usually taken the form of mistaken accusations of Foucault himself being a neoliberal (e.g. Zamora 2014) and post-structuralists (among many others) unfairly dismissing Žižek as a charlatan or a facetious clown (Chomsky 2016; see also Burgum 2014).

We will begin with Foucault, outlining his observations of the way in which power began to operate differently under modernity, changing into something decentralised, non-concentrated, and rarely wholly 'possessed' by a group or sovereign individual. If power ever did seem to be centralised (e.g. in the nation state), he argues, this is in fact an outcome of wider distributions and relations of power, rather than the starting point from which all coercion emanates. For Foucault, modern power plays out via societal norms which can be simultaneously a matter of knowledge and a mode of coercion (a 'norm' being both 'a statistical derivation and a standard to which people are subjected' (Elden 2017: 28). Understandings of the 'normal' are shared and asserted in common, making this a capillary power which is affirmed by historical discourses and hierarchies of expertise. Thus, power is not something that simply oppresses from above and maintains that oppression through hiding its truth or perpetuating false consciousness; instead, it is something that becomes internalised and perpetuated by the individuals and populations subjected to it. Rather than theorising power as radiating from a central position, therefore, Foucault implores us to 'cut off the head of the king' in political thought and analysis (1998: 88–9) in order to break with understandings of power as something acting upon us and towards seeing it as something which can be exercised and extended by those subjected to it. This has important implications for the way in which we frame resistance. Rather than seeing protest as something which needs to be autonomous and 'outside of power' in order to be authentic – or that takes aim at an all-powerful central point which is, by definition, untouchable – I will argue that movements like Occupy need to assert their own authority in order to make their voices heard and appearances seen.

We will then move onto problematising contemporary resistance further by thinking about what such opposition requires in practice (something which, as Brown (2015) points out, Foucault never outlines explicitly). Using Žižek's ideas about the counterintuitive operations of identity and culture in postmodern capitalism – which, following Jameson (1992), he also refers to as 'cultural capitalism' or 'late capitalism' – I will outline what he has called a 'decline in symbolic efficiency' in contemporary society. This decline, encouraged by the flexibility and injunction to enjoy under consumer capitalism, as well as the notion of 'freedom' being individualised under (neo)liberalism, has had the effect of *undermining the authority and desire for collective organisation*. For Žižek, this problem is often overlooked in left-wing theory, praxis, and strategy, which has tended to champion values such as individual liberty, pluralism, and libertarianism at the expense of collective organisation and symbolic efficiency, and Occupy (in) London (as I will demonstrate) often attempted to dismiss and avoid any attempt at collective discipline for fear that it would prove oppressive and exclusive. Yet, as pointed out by many within the movement itself, this approach problematically extended wider norms of individualism and fluidity while undermining the movement's appearance and resistance. I will therefore use Dean (2012) and Badiou (2012) in particular to extend these ideas and make an argument for the importance of collective organisation and symbolic efficiency within the context of postmodern capitalism.

Finally, Rancière will push us further by asserting that this interplay between power and resistance is ultimately expressed materially and aesthetically, and this takes on especial importance when we are dealing with Occupy-type urban movements. On the one hand, appearing to agree with Foucault, Rancière perceives resistance as policed and limited by a normative (common-sense) distribution of what should (or should not) be heard or seen as legitimate. However, on the other hand, his turn towards aesthetics also makes Žižek's plea for symbolic efficiency and Badiou's argument for disciplined organisation even more crucial. Because it is the tendency of (what he calls) 'the police order' to materially and structurally dismiss and deny the appearance of resistance, this dismissal and denial becomes easier if that which is being labelled as 'disorganised non-sense' actually resembles this label. Rancière builds on this idea by providing a persuasive outline for what a resistive politics should involve, provocatively aligning this with 'democracy' and thinking what it means to make 'non-sense' appear against its designation as such.

In sum, Foucault first gives us an unrivalled account of power and resistance under modernity as two sides of the same normative distribution. Brown, Žižek, Dean, and Badiou then allow us to probe further the consequences of Foucault's insight further in order to think about the counter-intuitive nature of this relationship under postmodern capitalism, as well as what this means for collective organisation. Finally, Rancière then enables us to consider the aesthetic and material practice of democratic resistance under such conditions of normative and decentralised power, pushing us to think about resisting with authority those policing forces that seek to dismiss and deny the appearance of alternatives, as well as not getting too carried away and insisting that we recognise where foreclosures are taking place too. This chapter will take a path between these thinkers, overlooking many contradictions between their thinking in order to allow their interaction to create a framework that incorporates slightly different elements of post-crash power and resistance. This approach therefore implies a synergy between Foucault's *structures of normative power*, Žižek's *ideological symbolic order*, and Rancière's *distribution of the sensible*, treating these concepts as interchangeable in a move that readers from these camps might find distasteful (at best) or illogical (at worst). However, I maintain that all three capture something about the nature of power after the financial crash, helping us to ask the right questions about how and why political alternatives were foreclosed, as well as to identify the strengths and limitations of movements like Occupy (in) London.

Foucault, power and resistance

Having been inspired by the student protests and civil resistance against the Habib Bourguiba dictatorship in March 1968, as well as changes which had occurred in France after the protests of May 1968 (which took place while he was in Tunisia), Foucault returned to Paris in 1969 and adjusted his research focus 'from the political stakes of knowledge to the workings of power' (Elden 2017: 1). His aim was to deconstruct and decentralise the way in which we had become accustomed to understanding power by genealogically tracing and unsettling its development through modern history. It was Foucault's contention that, contrary to popular opinion and political theory which tended to understand power solely as *sovereign* – i.e. a top-down, centralised, and negative force that acted through decrees and threats of punishment – modernity had seen the development of types of power which acted through a normative 'art of distribution' and that could either discipline via 'the distribution of individuals in space' (1991: 141) or control populations through distributions of knowledge and security. In other words, these new forms of power were acting through common sense, what is considered to be 'normal'. This can operate either at the individual or collective level, because 'the norm is something that can be applied to both a body one wishes to discipline and a population one wishes to regularise' (ibid. 2003: 253).

In contrast to the sovereign power of a monarch, Foucault was therefore identifying 'new methods of power whose operation is not ensured by right but by technique, not by law but by normalisation, not by punishment but by control, methods that are employed on all levels and in forms that *go beyond the state and its apparatus*' (1991: 89; emphasis added). As he then went on to demonstrate throughout his work in the 1970s – such as *Discipline and Punish, The History of Sexuality*, vol. 1, as well as the recently published *College de France* lectures – this was a power that operated in ways that could not be reduced to trans-historical economic class war (as in Marx and Engels 2002) nor simply to a sovereign authority supported by charisma, tradition, bureaucracy, and a 'monopoly on the legitimate means of violence' (as in Weber (2003). Instead, modern power was operating as an art of distribution, through norms that were being developed and perpetuated via historical discourses and the institutions which embodied them.

First, at the individual level, Foucault argues that this new power disciplines subjects through a 'specification of place' (1991: 141). He saw such disciplinary power being adopted by those institutions which were necessary for the development of modern capitalism – law, medicine, science, knowledge, reason – before becoming dispersed beyond those institutions and into wider society as organising norms. By coercing subjects through both surveillance (a general gaze which is internalised by those subjected to it) and normalising sanctions, this power created a 'perpetual penalty that traverses all points and controls every instant in the disciplinary institutions … [it] compares, differentiates, hierarchizes, homogenizes, excludes … in a word, it normalises' (Elden 2017: 150). In any given context, then, an individual could now be thought of as 'normal' or 'abnormal' – included or excluded, in place or out of place – and coerced accordingly. Such a disciplinary distribution is then supported by the creation of hierarchy and value:

> Organising 'cells', 'places' and 'ranks', the disciplines create complex spaces that are at once architectural, functional and hierarchical … it is *spaces* that provide fixed positions and *permit circulation*: they carve out individual segments and establish operational links; they *mark places and indicate values*; they guarantee the obedience of individuals, but also a better economy of time and gesture … they are mixed spaces: real because they govern the disposition of buildings, rooms, furniture, but also ideal, because they are projected over this arrangement of characterisation, assessment, hierarchies.
>
> (Foucault 1991: 148; emphasis added)

The emphasis on space here – as well as the idea that design and architecture can 'govern the dispositions' of spaces – will be picked up in the section on Rancière below (as well as in the next chapter). But, for now, suffice to point out that this type of disciplinary power was seen by Foucault as following the example of the botanical sciences which were being developed under modernity, fixing and categorising positions, marking places and indicating values, developing hierarchies and operational links. In other words, the individual is being controlled here, because they are on the receiving end of wider understandings of a 'normative order' in which they 'carve out their place'. This is an order, therefore, that is *internalised* by those subjected to it, and that 'exists, is reproduced, only insofar as subjects recognise themselves in it and, via repeated performative gestures, again and again assume their places in it' (Žižek 2008a: 312).

Second, at the collective level, Foucault argues that this new normative power not only disciplines, but regularises and controls populations, on the grounds that it is necessary to protect life (even if this means killing or letting people die in the name of that protection). Thus, norms of security are maintained through institutions that survey, prescribe, assess, judge, decide, and divide between the normal and abnormal, internal and external (think about the algorithms now deployed at borders in order to 'sort out' potential threats to life within the nation; see Amoore 2013). Where collective control ends and individual discipline starts is unclear, but Foucault is explicit that one type of power does not simply replace another, but compliments it (2003: 240), creating an art of distribution which is internalised by those individuals and populations subjected to it. Modern normative power is therefore positive (i.e. constitutive) in character, and is repeated through everyday actions, identities, voices and appearances, as well as every appeal to something as being normal, truthful or sensible. The point is that power is not simply a nefarious, negative, oppressive force from above, because it can discipline, coerce, regularise and control through distributions being held in common. More than censoring, excluding, or repressing, Foucault's 'shift is away from a power that binds, dazzles and subjugates' (Venn 2007: 113) and towards a power that operates through the very 'processes of subject formation that constitute (or enable the self-constitution of) autonomous subjects' (Blencowe 2010: 123). Or in Foucault's words:

> Power would be a fragile thing if its only function were to repress, if it worked only through the mode of censorship, exclusion, blockage and repression … if on the contrary power is strong, this is because, as we are beginning to realise, it produces affects at the level of desire – and also at the level of knowledge. Far from preventing knowledge, power produces it.
>
> (1980: 59)

Normative power is not a matter of violence or ignorance (as in sovereign power), but is an art of distribution that operates via 'a grid of intelligibility of the social order' (Foucault 1998: 93). It disciplines, regularises and controls, coercing through shared norms, meanings, attitudes, values, desires, knowledges, truths, designations, and possibilities in everyday life, internalised through notions of 'common sense'.

But if power is so widespread and integrated into everyday actions, knowledge, and meaning, then what about resistance? Foucault concludes that, if power is a normative art of distribution, then there can be 'no outside' (1991: 301) to its influence, elaborating in a well-worn passage from *The History of Sexuality*, vol. 1, that 'where there is power there is resistance, and yet, or rather consequently, this resistance is never in a position of exteriority to power' (1998: 95). This is in sharp contrast to common understandings of power and resistance as an oppositional binary, with power seen as only acting negatively to prevent resistance. While many participants in Occupy (in) London, for instance, were very critical about the way in which the movement framed their resistance, there was certainly a general tendency to treat power in this way: as emanating from a single, central, top-down position (be that the state, international organisations, 'the 1%', or global conspiracy networks; see Chapter 6). The consequence of this was that resistance was seen to be something that needed to find an autonomous space from which to operate, somewhere authentic which was immune from the influence of power's corrupting influence, so that the movement could 'take the power back' from 'the powers that be'. Positioning themselves as aligned with 'the 99%' – who they saw as the powerless, rising up to fight for democratic freedom and socio-economic justice – power became defined as something *they did not possess*, something out of reach and untouchable. Power became something that was acting upon and against the movement, that 'we' (the weak and marginal) were now attempting to take from 'them' (the powerful).

And yet the obvious problem with Foucault's mingling of power and resistance is that this appears to leave little opportunity or possibility for resistance. If power is 'manifested and sometimes extended by the position of those who are dominated' (Foucault 1991: 141), then what chance is there to overcome and change this domination? Many theorists, including Žižek, have criticized Foucault on precisely this point. While at first agreeing that 'power and resistance are effectively caught in a deadly mutual embrace … resistance to power are generated by the very matrix they seem to oppose' (Žižek 2008a: 298), Žižek nevertheless dismisses Foucault for 'remaining uncomfortably trapped within this cycle' and ignoring 'the dialectical path which would allow him to break out of the vicious cycle of power and resistance as an effect which can outgrow its cause and overturn it' (Armstrong 2008: 20).

I would argue, however, that this is a misreading of Foucault's position, which has most likely come about because of his failure to give an explicit and elaborated view on what effective resistance might look like under this new form of power (as his friend and colleague Giles Deleuze suggested, this lack of an outline may be down to Foucault's main inquiry being one of *problematising* power through historical research, rather than elaborating on the consequences for present resistance, which he was more inclined to offer in interviews and lectures (see Elden 2017: 6). Elaborating in a later interview, and no doubt in answer to such criticism, Foucault explained that 'to say one can never be "outside" power does not mean that one is trapped and condemned to defeat no matter what' (1980: 142) and that he was 'simply saying: as soon as there is power relation, there is a possibility of resistance … we are never trapped by power, we can always modify its grip in determinate conditions and according to a precise strategy' (ibid. 1989: 153). In other words, Foucault's response to decentralised power is decentralised resistance:

> Points of resistance are present everywhere in the power network. Hence there is no single locus of great Refusal, no soul of revolt, source of all rebellions, or pure law of the revolutionary. Instead there is a plurality of resistances … it is doubtless the strategic codification of these points of resistance that makes a revolution possible.
>
> (1998: 96)

Judith Butler can help us to understand this position further. On the one hand, she argues, normative power can be 'oppressive when it requires the speaking subject, in order to speak, participate in the very terms of that opposition – that is, take for granted the speaking subject's own impossibility of unintelligibility' (2006: 157). Because power operates through normative positions and distributions of what counts as meaningful speech, voice, and identity, this means that opportunities for discipline, control, and foreclosure are multiplied, as we rely on this distribution to make ourselves visible, audible, and identifiable. Thus, problems begin to arise when 'we think we have found a point of opposition to domination [but] then realise that we have unwittingly enforced the power of domination through our participation in its opposition' (ibid. 2000: 28). And yet, on the other hand, we might also consider methods of resistance that begin from *within* this distribution – 'reverse discourses' (Foucault 1998: 101) or instances of *détournement* (see Vaneigem 1983: 144; Bonnett 1989: 135) – which twist and turn norms and hierarchies in order to force through an oppositional voice or appearance. Or, as Butler puts it, 'language has a dual possibility; it can be used to assert a true and inclusive universality of powers, or it can institute hierarchy in which only some persons are eligible to speak and others, by virtue of their exclusion from the universal point of view, cannot speak without simultaneously deauthorising that speech' (2006: 164). Subsequently, she concludes that resistance does not require a space outside of power in order to operate effectively, as 'if subversion is possible it will be subversion from within the terms of the law, through the possibilities that emerge when the law turns against itself and spawns unexpected permutations of itself' (Butler 2006: 17).

The argument, then, is to somehow find a way of developing resistance from a position that begins *within* those wider normative distributions that produce shared common sense. This can only be possible, however, if we assume that 'it is clearly possible to speak with authority without being authorised to speak' (Butler 1997: 157), and 'authority' is a tricky concept for any movement on the left to negotiate, bringing with it as it does the uncomfortable baggage of 20th-century history and claims from the right/centre that movements for equality and justice always end up with some sort of authoritarianism. Indeed, as Blencowe has pointed out, authority is unavoidably an anti-egalitarian concept and 'necessarily a matter of hierarchy and inequality' (2013: 12) which is a greater problem for the left (in pursuit of equality and democracy) than it is for the right (who celebrate leadership and clarity). But if we carefully define authority as providing 'guidance, judgement or witness from the position of 'knowing better' (ibid.), then perhaps the possibility also arises for voices and appearances 'from below' to assert a democratic authority in matters of equality and justice. For Blencowe, authority could also be seen as inherently collaborative and constitutive, insofar as it 'depends upon collective acceptance of some criteria of knowing' (ibid.) or what Rancière might recognise as 'the distribution of the sensible' (see 'Symbolic inefficiency and collective organisation'). Upon accepting 'some collective criteria of knowing', authority as 'knowing better' can help to establish collectivity, because 'insofar as we are a community, we are bound by a common objectivity … authoritative relationships, voices and statements concretise around such 'ideas of objectivity'… this binding is authority' (Blencowe 2013: 17). In this roundabout way, we can keep Foucault's all-encompassing model of power, while still recognising and allowing for resistance to be mobilised from below with authority.

Foucault's insights into the complexities of modern power allow us to understand the subtle coercive and normative policing that is taking place. As I will show in this book, seeing power as a normative art of distribution gives us new understanding of challenges and possibilities faced by contemporary movements like Occupy (in) London, such as the authoritative possibilities of occupying public space (Chapter 3); the structures that persist within movements despite attempts to establish *structurelessness* (Chapter 4); the pointlessness of attempting to establish an authentic resistance which is 'autonomous' from wider power (Chapter 5); and the problem with binary models of power that pre-position opposition as marginal and powerless (Chapter 6). So long as we see power as decentralised and capillary, then we can begin to develop ways of acting from within its distributions, and 'make allowance for the complex and unstable process whereby discourse can be both an instrument and an effect of power, but also a hindrance, a stumbling block, a point of resistance and starting point for an opposing strategy' (Foucault 1998: 101).

Symbolic inefficiency and collective organisation

While Foucault offers us an important ontological starting point, he nevertheless fails to outline exactly what this means for organisation, and he never really develops what he means by a 'precise strategy' or 'strategic codification' which 'makes revolution possible' (see quote above). What's more, as had been argued by Wendy Brown, while Foucault's distancing from Marx allowed him 'to bring forth undertheorized aspects of the emergence of political economy and permits a novel staging of the relationship between liberalism, the state, the economy, and the modern subject … this refusal also had its costs … [as] Foucault averted his glance from capital itself as a historical and social force' (2015: 74–5). Although Foucault certainly didn't ignore the contributions made by Marxism, his focus was on modern discourse which had developed in tandem with capitalism – science, medicine, social sciences, religion, the state, politics, economics – across a range of institutional contexts (which in turn had a normative effect beyond their specific settings). The clinic and the psychiatrist, for example, made claims about truth and knowledge which perpetuated wider norms about health and heterosexuality, maintaining the reproduction of the workforce; while the penal system and law were able to protect private property, with the panopticon (Bentham's model for a utilitarian institution) being the example par excellence of wider changes in normative surveillance, distribution, and the internalisation of coercion and control (Foucault 1991; Elden 2017: 152). Foucault's concentration on these discourses and institutions was extremely valuable and gives us a richer insight into both the development of capitalism and modern power, yet his aim to decentralise power (and undermine both the Marxist insistence on the centrality of economics and the Hobbesian model of the sovereign state) nevertheless left capitalism as a normative force somewhat overlooked.

As Brown argues, this oversight meant that Foucault tended to underemphasise the adverse effects of both capitalism and neoliberalism on collective organisation and democracy:

> Foucault does not draw his account of neoliberal reason into a reflection on its intersection with or effect on democratic political life and citizenship. The remaking, corrosion, and transformation of these domains is ignored in his analysis, and resistance, if it appears at all, happens in other forums and venues. Again, put sharply, Foucault's coordinates of analysis do not permit him to ask: What effects does neoliberal rationality have on democracy, including on democratic principles, institutions, values, expressions, coalitions, and forces?
>
> (2015: 74)

Given his insistence that we decentralise power, Brown points out that Foucault's account of neoliberalism in *The Birth of Biopolitics* lectures was strangely state-centric, offering an analysis in which 'governing emanates from the state and always works on the populations and the subject … there is no *political* body, no demos acting in concert (even episodically) or expressing aspirational sovereignty; there are few social forces from below and no shared power of rule or shared struggles for freedom' (Brown 2015: 73; emphasis in the original). Thus, there is little consideration of the normative effects of neoliberalism and capitalism, let alone how collective democratic authority might be organised in such a context.

What's more, because Foucault's history of neoliberalism is set in the 1970s/1980s, we also need to be aware that his account misses a number of more recent developments, including the rise of finance, financial crises and austerity politics, shifts to responsibilised and managed subjects guided by norms of individual interest and freedom, as well as devolved authority, massification and isolation (Brown 2015). Subsequently, Brown argues that 'insofar as Foucault's investigation and analysis of neoliberalism is driven by a concern with the birth of biopolitics, by shifts from sovereignty to governmentality, and by reformations of liberalism, these coordinates are insufficient for capturing what neoliberalism has done to social life, culture, subjectivity, and above all, politics' (ibid.: 73). She therefore argues that the answer to this problem is to create a 'triangular space' between Foucault, Marx, and democracy that allows us to think about political action in terms of challenging normative power (Foucault), as well as the 'hyper-exploitative or colonising effects of capital' (Marx) and 'assaults on democracy' (adding that '*really* effective political action … tries to have all these going at once' (see Burgum *et al.* 2017; emphasis in the original). I argue that Žižek, Dean, and Badiou can help us to develop the Marxist corner of this triangle in today's context, while also allowing us to discern the limits of Foucault's response to the decentralising of power with a 'plurality of resistance'.

For Žižek, contemporary capitalist societies can be defined by a 'crisis of meaning', arguing that if we agree that 'our identity is performatively grounded in symbolic identifications' and that 'the symbolic order is counted on to provide the horizon that allows us to locate every experience in a meaningful totality' (2008a: 33), then postmodernity's incredulity regarding metanarratives (Lyotard 1984) problematically promotes inefficiency in this symbolic locating. The consequence of the crisis in meaning is that when we think we are acting with individual liberty and flexibility, adopting a plurality of resistive positions in order to avoid the disciplining of collective identities and organisations, we are in fact *extending the norms of postmodern capitalism*. As Žižek argues, this limits the effectiveness of social resistance and the possibility of change:

> Postmodernity as the 'end of grand narratives' is one of the names for this predicament in which the multitude of local fictions thrives … which is why the politics advocated by many a leftist today, that of countering the devastating world-dissolving effects of capitalism modernity by inventing new fictions, imagining 'new worlds'… is inadequate, or at least, profoundly ambiguous: it all depends how these fictions relate to the underlying Real of capitalism – do they just *supplant* it with the

> imaginary multitude, as the postmodern 'local narratives' do, or do they *disturb* its functioning?'
>
> (2009b: 33; emphasis in the original)

Žižek's point is that the multiplicity and plurality of resistance movements (which Foucault appears to advocate) does not disturb the normal functioning of capitalism; instead it extends symbolic inefficiency as a norm. This is perhaps clearest in the consumer-dominated global north-west, but is also steadily being extended through the neo-imperialist globalisation of a 'cultural capitalism' that weds an insatiable drive for enjoyment and symbolic inefficiency to virtues of individual liberty, allowing the subject to feel that they are a meaningful and autonomous individual with each symbolic purchase and consumer experience. Žižek uses the example of Starbucks to illustrate this point, whereby the ethical action is built into the demand to enjoy a coffee and the freedom not to be tied down to a political commitment to eradicating poverty:

> When confronted with the starving child, we are told: 'for the price of a couple of cappuccinos, you can save her life!'... the true message is: 'for the price of a couple of cappuccinos, you can continue in your ignorant pleasurable life, not only not feeling any guilt, but even feeling good for having participated in the struggle against suffering.
>
> (2010: 117)

Rather than attacking the objective violence of the normal running of global capitalism, ethical and political action is reduced down to an individualised action that undermines collective organisation. Considering oneself to be free, rational, and sceptical, unable to be conned or cajoled into collective narratives and ideological commitments, the subject of postmodern capitalism opts for this cause or that cause without ever having to offer fidelity to a political ideal.

The problem is that not only does this 'freedom' actually further 'the fragmentation, cynicism, pan-scepticism, and symbolic inefficiency on which the system thrives' (Winlow *et al.* 2015: 7), but it also forecloses collective possibilities for organisation as 'our ability to identify crucial issues that bond us together as a collective ensures the dispersal of radical political sensibilities before they have the chance to cohere into a comprehensibly ideological alternative to our present way of life' (ibid.: 22). The result of the cultural injunction to keep on enjoying and avoid symbolic efficiency under postmodern capitalism creates a situation that 'does not offer subjects a symbolic identity; it offers them imaginary identities – ways to imagine themselves enjoying … these identities shift and change, taking on different meanings and attributes in different contexts' (Dean 2006: 99). Interestingly, Žižek even pre-empts the recent rise of popular fascism in the West, arguing that symbolic inefficiency 'produces the atmosphere of confusion and undecidability –

all ideas are equal, none is better than another – into which the fascist decision for order intervenes' (ibid.: 50). When there is no collective organisation upon which can be asserted the appearance of democratic authority, it is the authoritarianism of the right which intervenes and offers symbolic certainty, explaining why white working-class men in the global north – who have experienced a steep decline in their symbolic and economic certainty under neoliberalism – are so often the demographic that fills the ranks of Trump, UKIP or Le Pen.

It is Žižek's contention that it is therefore necessary to secure symbolically efficient collectivities that can find their 'ideas of objectivity' (Blencowe 2013) in left-wing ideals of justice, equality, and democracy, or face a continuing uptake of fascism. So long as the left advocates that 'the overall demands (complaining) of a particular group is reduced to just this demand, with its particular content' (Žižek 2008a: 243) then it will problematically extend norms of 'liberal neutrality and so-called postmodern relativism' which 'overlap in a scepticism about convictions' (Dean 2006: 50) and leave the door open for the right. By encouraging individualism, symbolic inefficiency reduces the possibility of collective identifications and solidarity, as 'political intensities become shorn of the capacity to raise claims to the universal, persisting simply as intensities, as indications of subject feeling' (ibid. 2009: 39) caught up in a postmodern distribution of 'plural, hybrid and mobile imaginary identities' (ibid.: 55). Writing on Occupy in particular, Dean therefore asserts that it was a mistake for the movement 'to emphasise individuality' as this 'reinserts the movement within the dominant culture, as if occupation were a choice like any other' (2011: 91). In contrast, therefore, Žižek, Dean, and Badiou (among others) argue strongly for the importance of re-establishing a collective politics that can allow resistance to avoid some of the more 'detrimental effects' that hinder 'the movement's ability to take a strong stand against capitalism' by overcoming an 'emphasis on plurality and inclusivity' currently 'prevalent in movement rhetoric' that 'merges seamlessly into capitalism' (Dean 2012: 222).

In *The Rebirth of History*, Badiou offers a persuasive insight into the issues of movement organisation, which he argues is 'the problem of politics par excellence' (2012: 42). For Badiou, early oppositional organisation initially tends to take the form of an 'immediate riot', which nearly always follows a violent episode of state coercion (e.g. Paris 2005, London 2011, Baltimore 2015). Such immediate riots might be considered either 'blindly progressive or blindly reactionary', but 'what they all have in common is that they stir up masses of people on the theme that things as they are must be regarded as unacceptable' (2012: 21). If we take London 2011, for example, we would point to the killing by police of unarmed black teenager Mark Duggan as the catalyst for the riots, but we would also recognise that Duggan's death sparked outrage over longer-term grievances of institutionalised racism and socio-economic inequality in London along ethnic lines. The riots that followed saw widespread protesting, looting, and vandalism, which lasted for a few days in which the police appeared to have completely lost authority and control, yet they ended just as soon as they had begun. Thus, while this might be the initial form of organisation, Badiou argues that immediate riots have a number of characteristics that prevent them from making a political intervention, such as spreading by *imitation* (rather than qualitative extension) and with a lack of a rooted political Idea. The immediate riot, in other words, is 'a rage with no purpose other than the satisfaction of being able to crystallise and find hateful objects to destroy or consume' (Badiou 2012: 25).

The immediate riot can only progress, Badiou argues, 'when it constructs – most often in the city centre – a new site, where it endures and is extended', adding that 'stagnating in its own social space is not a powerful subjective trajectory' (ibid.: 23). This observation seems fair, but given that Badiou is advocating an egalitarian movement, it is also problematic that he doesn't recognise that this transfer to the city centre is heavily limited, and easier for some groups than others. More often than not, the language of 'the riot' that Badiou is using carries class and race connotations, used by more dominant discourses in order to exclude and dismiss grievances. Simply advocating a 'move to the city centre', therefore, not only implies that those involved in the immediate riot would have the resources at their disposal to sustain an occupation there, but also overlooks how such spaces are distributed and policed by wider norms of what counts as a sensible (or non-sensible) appearance in the urban centre. While white middle-class activists may be considered non-threatening if they descend on the city centre, working-class BAME (Black, Asian, and Minority Ethnic) protestors are surely more likely to be viewed as an illegitimate appearance, who can be clamped down upon and swiftly 'moved along'. Badiou's lack of discussion of this issue therefore suggests that he is repeating Habermas' (1987) mistake of assuming an 'ideal speech-situation' where each is supposed to be able to interact and express their discontent equally, regardless of context. Indeed, the only characteristic that Badiou does consider is a suggestion that the shift from an immediate riot is more often than not spearheaded by the youth, because of 'their capacity for assembly, mobility and linguistic and tactical intervention, like their inadequacies in discipline, strategic tenacity and moderation when required, are constants of mass action' (2012: 23).

Despite this oversight, however, Badiou's move from an immediate riot via consolidation in the city centre – which indicates for him a change into a *historical riot* – starts to give us a sense of why collective organisation is so important for going 'beyond the bound (of selfishness, competition and finitude) … set by individualism' (2010: 234). The historical riot is halfway between an immediate riot and an ideal political organisation, because it can 'indicate the possibility of a new situation in the history of politics, without for now being in a position to realise that possibility' (2012: 27). On the one hand, the historical riot indicates a transformation in the right direction, because it achieves (a) 'the construction of an enduring central site'; (b) 'a transition from extension by imitation to qualitative extension'; and (c) 'a transition from the nihilistic din of riotous attacks to the intervention of a single slogan that envelopes all disparate voices' (ibid.: 24–5). Yet, on the other hand, the historical riot also remains pre-political, because 'in the first instance … it cannot *draw strength from the sharing of an idea* … [it] remains essentially negative … it does not deploy a slogan in the affirmative element of the idea' (ibid.: 40; emphasis in the original). For Badiou, Occupy, the Indignados and the Arab Spring all fall into this category. Writing in the context of the 2011 riots, and clearly having in mind these post-crash movements as the object of his critique, he argues that the problem with these examples of resistance was that 'being indignant has never sufficed … a negative emotion cannot replace the affirmative Idea and its organisation' (ibid.: 97). Instead, he argues, these movements needed to progress to the final stage of a political event, which is defined by *localisation, intensification*, and *contraction*.

By localisation, Badiou means the establishment of a central site (like the historical riot) but with 'firm rules of conquest' (2012: 65) adding that 'a non-localised Idea is impotent; a site without an Idea is merely an immediate riot, a nihilistic spurt' (ibid.: 92). By intensification, Badiou means that this localising also denotes the concentration of 'subjective energy' which requires a certain commitment and fidelity to the Idea, in that 'people know they are needed night and day; enthusiasm and passion are everywhere' (ibid.: 58). And finally, by contraction, Badiou means that the movement becomes focused through its commitment, turning it into an *exclusionary* ideal which is 'guarded by strict rules of membership of the organisation … a formal demarcation is created between those who are of it and those who are not' (ibid.: 64–5). Ultimately, then, the move from a historical riot to a political event means creating discipline in the movement's organisation. As Badiou argues, 'by formalising the constitutive features of the event, organisation makes it possible for its *authority* to be preserved' (ibid.: 66) allowing 'the possibility of an efficacious fragmentation of the Idea into *actions, proclamations and inventions* attesting to a *fidelity to the event* … an attempt to preserve the characteristics of the event' (ibid.: 69–70; emphasis in the original) and 'extending it to ensuring questions of strategy and tactics' (ibid.: 99).[1]

As was demonstrated by the post-crash movements, and in contrast to Foucault's pluralism, it is the contention of Žižek, Dean, and Badiou that 'mass spontaneism is not enough … some organisational form is needed at some point to carry local protests beyond the local to generate more lasting, system-wide effects' (Badiou 2012: 290). It was both an outside criticism and a self-critique of the Occupy movement in London that it was unable to form a cohesive and clear collective identity, with critics and sceptics berating the movement for 'not really standing for anything' and 'having no clear message'. Internal conflicts also reflected this problem, with contradictory calls to maintain the plurality, multiplicity, and openness of the movement's politics, or coalesce around a set of formal principles and collective organisation (even to the point of potentially forming a political party). Those who advocated the former position argued strongly against any type of collective organisation that might discipline the movement in anyway, withholding 'any clear ideological identification, preferring instead to reassert the movement's broad scope and universalism ... there were to be no exclusions, be they ideological or otherwise, in the 99 per cent movement' (Winlow *et al.* 2015: 159). In contrast to the plutocratic parliamentary system, their aim was to create an autonomous space that would allow a more horizontal, structureless, and openly inclusive type of organisation. Yet, as I will demonstrate in Chapter 4, Occupy (in) London was not only unable to achieve this in practice, but was also, paradoxically, unable to address any persisting structures *because of their desire to overcome them.* By viewing identity and action as autonomous and outside the reach of wider power structures, not only were they unable to tackle hierarchies and exclusions head on, but also they were unable to speak with any kind of collective symbolic authority and efficiency.

Rancière, democracy, and aesthetics

Rancière allows us to do two things. First, we can use his ideas to tie together Foucault's power as a 'normative art of distribution' with the concerns outlined in the previous section for collective appearance and symbolic efficiency. What's more, we can do this within one framework and language, using one set of concepts – 'the distribution of the sensible'; 'the police order'; and 'democratic politics'. Second, Rancière also allows us to emphasise the role of *aesthetics* in resistance as the basis of democratic authority. If power is all-encompassing and resistance necessarily positioned within and in relation to normative structures, then the aim of 'resistance' – or 'politics' and 'democracy' which Rancière argues are all the same thing – is to anticipate a world in which dismissed grievances could themselves *count as grievances.* Overall, Rancière gives us a method through which to understand both the foreclosing consequences of normative power in distributing and policing aesthetics, as well as the importance of aesthetics in creating authority 'from below' and making the 'non-sense' of dismissed grievances (e.g. post-crash protests) appear. In other words, I will deploy Rancière in order to consider the power structures of Foucault and the collective politics of Žižek *et al.*, before applying this to the specific case study of occupying public urban space in Chapter 3.

Rancière's project began with a fundamental break from his teacher Louis Althusser, following the latter's involvement with the French Communist Party (PCF) who dismissed the student-worker uprisings of May '68. These infamous events – which constituted the 'largest mass movement in French history, the biggest strike in the history of the French workers' movement, and the only 'general' insurrection that over-developed world has known since World War II' (Ross 2002: 4) – took place spontaneously and *without* the leadership of the PCF. In fact, one of the main aims of the protestors was precisely 'to contend the domain of the expert [and] to disrupt the naturalised sphere of competences (especially the sphere of specialised politics)' (ibid.: 6) which the PCF represented. This attitude against formal parties and organisations was then cemented even further when the PCF dismissed the uprising as 'a petit bourgeois movement' (Rancière 2011: xiv) making the hypocrisy of their politics clear, in that 'the masses make history, certainly, but not the masses in general, only the ones that we instruct and organise … [history can] only be known or 'made' through the mediation of intellectuals' (ibid.: 11). By adopting the position that only they had the authority to designate legitimate resistance, Althusser and the PCF had refused to recognise or support the protest, and instead added their voices to wider state and police dismissal of the protests as 'non-sense'.

Withdrawing his contribution to *Reading Capital*, Rancière argued that Althusser's hypocrisy was deepened further by the publication of *Lenin and Philosophy* three years later, in 1971. This text included Althusser's widely read essay on 'ideological state apparatus', in which he argues that power should be thought of as existing materially within institutions, such as 'the school (but also other state institutions like the church or other apparatus like the army)' because these organisations embody 'know-how but in forms that ensure subjections to the ruling ideology of the mastery of its "practice"' (ibid.: 128). In other words, Althusser takes a Foucauldian line, arguing that power can be understood as operating through hierarchies of knowledge and distributions of authority which designate what does or does not 'count' as legitimate, reasonable, or rational. While Rancière does not disagree, his point is that this was precisely the critique raised against Althusser and the PCF by the protestors of May '68, arguing that Althusser had only "discovered' in the course of his research something that the actions of the masses had already amply demonstrated, but which he advances as a very daring hypothesis' (2011: 32). This break with Althusser indicates the beginning of Rancière's lifelong project to locate democratic sources of authority 'from below' which do not need to rely on the 'top-down' recognition from vanguard authorities.

For Rancière, power can be understood as operating through *le partage du sensible* which has been commonly translated into English as 'the distribution of the sensible' (although, as Oliver Davis has pointed out, this translation doesn't quite capture the nuance of the phrase in French, as *partage* actually derives 'from the verb *partager*, meaning both share out and divide up' and therefore it 'evokes simultaneously the sharing-out and dividing-up of the sensory' (2010: 91).[2] We therefore have something akin to Foucault's normative order and Žižek's symbolic order, as designating, distributing, and partitioning what may (or may not) be considered meaningful or legitimate knowledge, voice, appearance, or identity. Rancière refers to this order as an all-encompassing arena for both coercive power *and* resistance, defining the distribution of the sensible as 'a specific regime for identifying and reflecting … a mode of articulation between ways of doing and making, their corresponding forms of visibility, and possible ways of thinking about their relationships' (2004: 10). This is therefore a fundamentally aesthetic structure of visibility and articulation which designates some appearances and voice as legitimate, and others as illegitimate, acting as a normative set of coordinates, contours, and frameworks which are continually being reasserted whenever there is an appeal to something as 'sensible' or 'non-sensible'.

The distribution of the sensible, in other words, acts as 'a general law that defines the forms of part-taking by first defining the *modes of perception* in which they are inscribed … [it] presupposes a partition between what is visible and what is not, of what can be seen from the inaudible' (Rancière 2001: 20; emphasis added). On the one hand, then, the distribution of the sensible can operate as a disciplinary and coercive power – a police order – which can designate and therefore foreclose what may or may not appear or be heard within a given context or space. Rancière defines this 'police order' as something which:

> consists, before all else, in recalling the obviousness of what there is, or rather of what there is not, and its slogan is: 'Move along! There's nothing to see here!' The police is that which says that here, on this street, there's nothing to see and so nothing to do but move along. It asserts that the space for circulating is nothing but the space of circulation.
>
> (2010: 37)

By 'recalling the obvious', Rancière is suggesting that the policing of aesthetics takes place in accordance with a wider 'common sense' of what should or should not be seen, done, heard, or named within a given space. Thus, the police order is clearly a normative power, able to 'move along' illegitimate appearances or designate them as 'nothing to see here' (i.e. 'non-sense'). Like Althusser and the PCF's dismissal of May '68, this is a form of power that can also operate through authority, or objective ideas and hierarchies which distribute the sensible (and non-sensible) within a given context and space. As with the designation of 'rioters' discussed in the previous section, the power of the police order lies in disciplining and denying recognition to some, while affording this recognition to others, because 'if there is someone you do not wish to identify as a political being, you begin by not seeing them as the bearers of politicalness, by not understanding what they say, by not hearing that it is an utterance coming out of their mouths' (Rancière 2001: 23).

For this reason, the distribution of the sensible can be mobilised as a useful concept for not only understanding the consequences of the PCF's dismissal of the events of May '68, but also for understanding Occupy (in) London as a movement which (through occupying space) attempted to create an aesthetic appearance in the context of post-crash neoliberal hegemony. I argue that we can use Rancière's ideas to think about the ways in which the Occupy-type movements were foreclosed by such a policing of the sensible, but that in order to do this effectively, we need to take quite a broad reading of the word 'sensible'. Playing on the ambiguity of the word in English, we can bring out the subtleties and implications of Rancière's theory by treating 'sensible' as both an aesthetic value judgement and the related 'common sense' distinction between the rational (sensible) and the irrational (non-sensible). In other words, I intend to use the distribution of the sensible to mean, at the same time, a material policing of what may or may not appear in space, as well as the related recognition that such a distribution must rely on a presupposed distinction of what is 'reasonable' and 'rational' in the first place. The distribution of the sensible is both a partition of who may (or may not) appear to the senses, as well as who may (or may not) be sensible – that is 'legitimately' – be heard or seen.

The other side of the distribution of the sensible, therefore, goes beyond the coercive and restrictive police order, to think about ways in which democratic authority might be asserted 'from below'. Provocatively arguing that there is no difference between questions of 'democracy' (rule by the people) and 'politics' (using Aristotle's definition of humans as political animals because they possess 'voice'), Rancière argues that both involve the 'part-taking' of those who are being distributed without voice and appearance, making an intervention into the police order:

> Politics … consists in transforming the space of 'moving along', of circulation *into a space for the appearance of the subject*: the people, the workers, the citizens. It consists in *re-figuring* the space, that is what is to be done, to be seen and to be named in it. It is the instituting of a *dispute over the distribution of the sensible.*
>
> (Rancière 2010: 37; emphasis added)

Rancièrean politics is more than simply the mechanisms of government or citizenship, it is a collective radical dispute over the very co-ordinates and presuppositions of what is considered 'sensible', re-figuring (i.e. Foucault's 'reverse discourse' or the Situationist *détournement*) what is designated as sensible or non-sensible appearance. In his own words, 'if there is something 'proper' to politics, it … is not a relationship between subjects, but between two contradictory terms that *define* a subject' (2010: 28–9; emphasis in the original) and therefore 'political struggle is not a conflict between well-defined interest groups; it is *an opposition of logics that count the parties and parts of the community in different ways*' (2001: 19; emphasis added).

In practice, then, Rancière argues that politics requires 'first and foremost an intervention upon the visible and the sayable' (2001: 21) which makes 'what was unseen visible, in getting what was only audible as noise to be heard as speech' (ibid.: 23). Subsequently, the goal of resistance (i.e. the democratic actions of the part-of-no-part) becomes less about fighting the 'powers that be', than something which:

> must demonstrate the world in which this argument *counts* as an argument and must demonstrate it as such for those who do not have the frame of reference enabling them to see it as one … political

> argumentation is at one and the same time the demonstration of a possible world in which the argument could count as an argument.
> (2010: 39; emphasis added)

In the context of normative power, politics becomes a matter of asserting a world in which the 'non-sense' argument (e.g. that there could be an alternative to neoliberalism, capitalism, liberal democracy, post-colonialism, nationalism, etc.) would no longer be non-sensible. This also means that the mode of resistance is ultimately one of aesthetics: making 'non-sense' appear and be heard against that which would dismiss it and move it along. And, as such, 'the principal function of politics is the configuration of its proper space … it is to disclose the world of its subjects and its operations … the essence of politics is the manifestation of dissensus, *as the presence of two worlds in one*' (Rancière 2001: thesis 8; emphasis in the original).

Bassett (2014) has argued that this demonstrates clear resonances between Rancière's theory and the Occupy movement. First, in line with a political approach which 'is not just a conflict of interests and opinions between counted groups within the police order; it is the *staging* of a deeper clash between police logic and egalitarian logic' (2014: 887; emphasis in the original), Bassett argues that Occupy 'did not seek recognition as a new interest or identity group within the existing political structure, nor did it aim to seize control of existing state structures, but challenged the legitimacy of the structure as a whole' (ibid.: 892). Rather than staying within existing distributions and foreclosures, Bassett argues that Occupy managed to establish new subjectivities by emerging in gaps in the police order, and was right to avoid formal participation in the state or existing political parties, as this would not have met Rancière's criteria 'for a genuinely emancipatory, collective action, which is by its nature something far more fleeting, egalitarian and subjectifying' (ibid.: 889). On the one hand, we might agree that under the parliamentary options at the time (the coalition of the Conservatives and Liberal Democrats or Ed Miliband's Labour Party), it surely would not have made sense for Occupy (in) London to participate. However, on the other hand, this libertarian interpretation of Rancière suggests a kind of distrust of *all* formal organisations, which (I will argue) was one of the reasons Occupy were unable to assert authority, symbolic efficiency, or long-term visibility. Some sort of disciplinary organisation, as Badiou and Dean argue, is surely necessary to make this politics *more* than simply a 'fleeting' intervention.

As I will demonstrate in Chapter 4, we should also be sceptical about the extent to which Occupy was able to go beyond pre-existing structures of identity and subjectivity. In the second instance, Bassett finds agreement between Rancière and Occupy in that they both put a commitment towards radical equality into practice and avoided making collective demands which might impose an overall framework on the movement, instead opting to enact horizontal equality and remaining openly inclusive. However, in the same vein as above, Bassett's interpretation seems to undermine the importance of collective organisation and identity, championing instead an openly inclusive organisation. It's true that Rancière himself does insist on equality as a presupposition rather than as a future aim, but he also alludes to this requiring a certain amount of formal organisational discipline in order for it to happen, referring to 'that which separates and excludes … that which allows participation' (2001: 20).

Finally, Bassett points out the concordance between Rancière's insistence on aesthetics and the emphasis placed upon occupying space by post-crash movements, pointing out that 'these spaces were never entirely out of police space, but the occupations materialised people power through a subversion of the 'normal distribution' of police spaces (between circulation, commerce and public functions)' (2014: 893). We can certainly agree with this to some extent, although we perhaps need to be less assertive over whether Occupy was actually successful in materialising this subversion. Instead, I argue that we should use more careful language, perhaps by arguing that the occupation of space harbours the potential of intervention and subversion, even if this is sometimes foreclosed in practice. Having said that, I argue that Bassett is right to point out that these spaces were never outside of power, despite activist insistence that autonomous space was desirable and achievable. Thus, the crossover between Rancière's aesthetics and the occupation of space should be taken more as a model of political possibility to use occupation in order to overcome foreclosures and make 'two worlds appear in one'.

Rancière does not see democratic authority as emerging from autonomous spaces. Instead, it's the appearance of two worlds in one which makes an intervention into the normative distribution of the sensible possible. This is because, for Rancière, echoing Foucault and Butler, 'the egalitarian struggle is necessarily entangled with the police order' and it 'must therefore use its language, though in subversive ways, and even recognise there can be differences between 'good' and 'bad' police orders in terms of giving democratic struggle 'more or less room' (Bassett 2016: 283). Thus, Rancière provokes us to redefine how was understand 'politics' and 'democracy', seeing these as more than their common limited designations to parliamentary and electoral system would allow, and instead presupposing a world in which his radical definitions might count as legitimate. For him, 'politics means the irruption of the so-far invisible, unheard, "part of no part" into the space of the police through stagings of dissensus and thus "re-partitioning the sensible" in a material and symbolic sense' (Bassett 2016: 287).

Conclusion

So, we now have both our framework and our fundamental problems to explore:

1 Power and resistance are locked in a mutual structural embrace. Power is not simply a nefarious, centralised, sovereign operator which acts upon us

'from above' and beyond our control, and such a model can only lead to righteous marginalisation and ideas of authenticity which are not useful for framing collective resistance. Instead, we need to 'cut the head off the king' and understand power as operating through internalised norms which are shared in common through a symbolic order that can discipline, control, and coerce those subjected to it. Resistance is not futile, but must begin from a self-understanding of complicity (rather than overlooking persisting structures by attempting to find an authentic 'autonomous' space outside of power). We can call this normative symbolic order 'the distribution of the sensible' which can act either in the mode of disciplining and controlling (i.e. *the police order*) or in the mode of democratic politics. In the latter, the 'part of no part' must force through the appearance of (what is being distributed as) 'non-sense', pre-empting an alternative future distribution in which their voice and appearance (grievances) would count as legitimate.

2 The problem of politics is the problem of *organisation*. This needs to be based upon shared ideas of objectivity, which form the basis of a democratic movement's collective authority. Such authority, however, is undermined under conditions of neoliberalism and postmodern capitalism, which maintain anti-organisational, non-committal norms of libertarianism and individualism. This therefore needs to be countered with an insistence on symbolic efficiency, formal discipline, and collective commitment to the appearance and voice of a political ideal. However, because the organisation of authority is unavoidably hierarchical and exclusive, the problem of the left today becomes how to speak with collective democratic authority *while maintaining the democratic ideals of inclusivity and horizontality*, of equal voice and appearance within its organisation.

3 The problem of organisation is the problem of *aesthetics*. Against the distribution of the sensible propagated by the police order – which would dismiss resistance by 'moving it along' as 'nothing to see here' – democratic politics must make 'non-sense' appear. This means forcing through voices and appearances which are deemed irrational, unreasonable, and abnormal from the perspective of wider 'common sense' and norms. Subsequently, the occupation of spaces of power has the potential to twist and *détourne* the normal distribution, creating an intervention which could refigure what is considered to be possible. While the power of the police order is about denying the legitimacy and authenticity of voice or appearance; politics is about making those illegitimate aesthetics appear and creating the appearance of 'two worlds in one' (i.e. the current order and a future alternative in which such grievances might count).

In Chapter 3, we will develop the problem of aesthetics. It is my contention that the post-crash Occupy-type movements – which were initially inspired by the Arab Spring and came to the fore in 2010–11 across a wide range of contexts – offer the possibility for making 'non-sense' appear. We will begin with an outline of the movement at St Paul's Cathedral, before moving on to the challenges and difficulties of occupying space (including problems of exclusion and hierarchies). While it will be argued that contemporary resistance *must* involve (what one of my interviewees dubbed) 'the spatial imperative' – granting movements publicity, semi-permanence, and contextual narratives – I will also use Lefebvre and Debord in order to outline the potential problems of extending wider consumerist norms while doing so. Notwithstanding some caveats, it will be argued that occupying space allows for both Badiou's localisation, intensification, and contraction, as well as the need to make 'non-sense' appear.

Chapter 4 will then move onto problems of organisation. Starting with the issue of (what one of my interviewees called) 'inclusivity for the sake of it', it offers a critique of Occupy (in) London alongside Jo Freeman's uncanny description of 'the tyranny of structurelessness' in creating unaccountable and undemocratic hierarchies despite people's best intentions. By attempting to establish an autonomous space outside of power and aiming to prefigure a more democratic society, it will be shown how the movement ultimately left structures unaddressed. The open inclusivity and horizontality of the movement will then be criticised further as creating a situation of symbolic inefficiency, playing into wider distributions of the Occupy movement as 'non-sense', while extending wider libertarian and individualist norms. It will be concluded that movements require a disciplined collective organisation which, counter to many arguments on the new left, must involve negotiating exclusions.

In the final two chapters, we will address how the movement framed and developed a self-understanding of power and resistance, which pre-positioned them as powerless and marginal. Chapter 5 will first discuss the 'pursuit of authenticity' within the movement. This will initially be shown as problematic in creating a complex and subtle hierarchy of those activists who considered themselves 'more authentic than others' (as well as those who considered themselves 'more authentic' than those who thought they were 'more authentic'). Using the idea of boycotting and *buy*cotting, it will then be argued that such an approach to resistance actually plays into wider distributions of the movement as consisting of 'hypocrites' who can easily be 'dismissed', before demonstrating how myths of co-optations actually extended wider consumer norms. This chapter will conclude that activists should avoid wasting energy in pursuing authenticity and recognise that political responsibility (rather than the moral high ground) is more important for making grievances seen and heard.

Finally, Chapter 6 will focus on 'conspiracy theories' within the movement, taking a broad definition of conspiracy that is less concerned with whether the theory is 'true' than with the way it frames 'power' as unreachable and therefore resistance as powerless. To begin with, we will discuss the siege mentality adopted towards undercover police, demonstrating the way which this theory spread distrust, fracturing, and a loss of collective organisation in the movement. Going up a level, we will then discuss 'the 1%' and the way in which this idea reinforced activist voice and appearance as marginal and powerless in relation to governmental and economic institutions and networks. Finally, at the most extreme, it will be argued that conspiracies around nefarious organisations (e.g. the Illuminati, the Bilderberg group, the Rothschild family, etc.) are not so problematic because they might not be true, but because they render power untouchable and unchangeable. We will conclude that activists need to avoid adopting a 'cunning of impotence' and instead recognise the way in which power operates normatively in order to organise an effective and authoritative resistance.

Notes

1 This process of formalisation, Badiou is clear, must be different from the political system which preceded it. The political event 'presupposes the formation of an organised and disciplined body … necessarily different from any political party' (Bassett 2016: 283) and, in order to assert 'a new previously unknown possibility … the organisation of this new political possibility is presented in an explicitly authoritarian form' (Badiou 2012: 61).

2 Owing to this awkward translation, I have used two English versions of Rancière's *Ten Theses on Politics* in order to really get to grips with the distribution of the sensible. The first was published in the journal *Theory and Event* (2001) while the second is from the Continuum collection *Dissensus* (2010).

2 Whose streets? Our streets!

Finsbury Square, July 2013

Returning to Finsbury Square just over a year since my first visit – and just under a year after the occupiers had been forcibly evicted by Islington Council – I found that there was no longer any trace of the camp. Occupy took its name and character from the tactic of establishing public and semi-permanent urban protest camps, but now the space had been landscaped over and new green turf laid to replace the cardboard pavements and mud. As I sat on a bench at the far end of the park, I tried to picture where the kitchen, dining tent, and that spaceship-like structure had been. The unwashed activists who had sat and talked to me the previous summer had now been replaced by slick city workers on their lunch breaks, lounging in the sunshine, eating paninis, and sipping iced coffee.

Where once had stood the info-tent, the library of radical books, and a banner which read 'Capitalism Isn't Working: Another World Is Possible'; there was now a brand-new memorial to the casualties of the Moorgate underground train disaster on 28 February 1975, reasserting an 'official' urban history of the space. The fenced-off monument declared that this was *not* a place for the appearance of resistance, but for remembering the collective sacrifices made for an efficient city transport system, and the ability to commute from the suburbs.

I did a lap of the buildings around the square, peering inside the foyers and making a list of the companies which were based there. Concerned security guards frowned and stood up from behind their desks when they saw a white guy with dreadlocks and a notepad appear at the door (no doubt they flashed back to the events of the previous summer).

To the north, the Alphabeta Building offers facilities that promise to reject 'traditional notions of the controlled office and instead, offers an adaptable space designed for the enjoyment of a creative and empowered workforce … restoring and reformatting a series of historic buildings with a sophisticated urban aesthetic, an active and vibrant communal area has been created'.[1] Also on this side stands the Royal London House luxury hotel, £250 per night.

Moving around to the east, the American consultancy and accountancy firm Grant Thornton LLP which claims to have 'an instinct for growth' and argues that 'together we are building a vibrant economy' by 'building trust and integrity in markets', 'unlocking sustainable growth in dynamic organisations' and 'creating environments where businesses and people flourish'.[2] Next door, Invesco UK LTD (now Invesco Perpetual) is one of the largest investment management firms in the UK, claiming a 114 per cent return in the five years after the financial crash and responsible for £91.59bn worth of assets (*The Telegraph* 2013). In 2009, Invesco's Chief Economist, Dr John Greenwood, was one of the signatories to a letter published in *The Telegraph* (2009) that blamed the crash on 'government failure', adding that 'the prevailing view amongst the commentariat (reflected in the recent deliberations of the G20) that the financial crash of 2008 was caused by market failure is both wrong and dangerous … government failure had a leading role in creating the conditions that led to the crash'. Also situated on this side of the square, the University of Liverpool in London is undergoing construction work, adorned with Overbury Construction site boards carrying the slogan 'passion for perfection'.

On the south side can be found Herbert Smith LLP (property management) and Bloomberg LP (a global organisation delivering international business news, data, and analysis, conveying real-time financial information to 320,000 subscribers). On the ground floor is Bloomberg Space which is 'not a conventional corporate art collection, but rather a dynamic space, where artists and audience can explore new ideas and relationships in an innovative way … open to employees, clients, and the community at large'.[3] In the corner, Wasabi Sushi as well as the obligatory Starbucks are 'open as usual' behind scaffolding and inviting passers-by to 'get together over coffee'.

Finally, to the west, 1 Finsbury Square with Wood MacKenzie LTC (analytics) and Simply Business (insurance). Next door, an empty glass executive office space of the recently constructed 10 Finsbury Square is flanked by an All Bar One restaurant, a Pret A Manger outlet and an itsu 'health and happiness' café. Also on this side, a ramp leads underneath the square to a 24-hour NCP car park, £16,00 for two hours.

At the park entrance, a sign reads: 'Welcome to Finsbury Square. Opening Hours 8 am to Dusk Daily' and includes instructive diagrams of a picnic bench and a figure with a ball. This is an area designated for leisure and enjoyment – an escape from the rat race – not a place for protests over socio-economic inequality, neoliberal capitalism, or post-crash plutocratic governance. While the businesses, firms, chains, and corporations which surround the square offer 'adaptable', 'dynamic', and 'vibrant communal areas' for interaction and getting together, it was clear that the square itself was not the proper place for the unsightly appearance and disruptive noise of public discussion and debate.

Introduction: occupy in space

This chapter focuses on the politics of space. Using Rancière's terminology, we will use the idea of the 'distribution of the sensible' in order to consider the possibilities and foreclosures that the semi-permanent occupation of public urban space might afford movements like Occupy (in) London. If Rancière's police order is able to assert power through a normative partition of some grievances as 'legitimate', 'rational', 'reasonable', and 'sensible' – while denying this recognition to others – then this is ultimately an aesthetic distribution which must map out onto material space. Thus, I argue that occupation holds a certain potential to challenge normative distributions (such as the neoliberal normativity and capitalist realism which played out after the crash) by making what is policed as 'non-sense' appear. In a context in which the dominant narrative was to get business back to normal, that there could be no alternative except a return to 'common sense' by addressing neoliberalism with more neoliberalism (austerity, bailouts, quantitative easing); occupation harboured the possibility of *making 'non-sense' appear against its designation as such.*

We will begin with a discussion of the aesthetic possibilities offered by the occupation of space, focusing in particular on Occupy LSX (London Stock Exchange) outside St Paul's, which is a setting that appeared to have three useful characteristics: (1) being public; (2) allowing a semi-permanence; and (3) taking place in a meaningful symbolic context that activists could then twist, *détourne*, and refigure. It will be argued that by virtue of these traits the occupation of space has the radical potential to intervene in the police order and to challenge the given co-ordinates of the situation. However, following the experience of Occupy (in) London, we will also highlight the challenges faced by activists in maintaining urban occupations, in particular focusing on problems of exclusions and hierarchies that were brought about by occupying space in the middle of a city (particularly around what became known as 'the homeless question'). While insisting that there is a spatial imperative to intervene in wider distributions, therefore, it will also be argued that there is a risk of occupations becoming sites of 'unproductive enjoyment' which extend wider consumerist norms of the creative city.

In order to push this idea further, I will follow the wider literature that has sought to understand Occupy using Situationism, noting how 'the daily practices of occupation associated with [Occupy] reveal a remarkable congruence with the central features of Lefebvre's formulation' (Schein 2012: 336). However, while I agree that Lefebvre is useful for drawing out the subtle power distributions of urban infrastructure, architecture, and design, I will argue against his formulation of the festival (*la fête*) as 'unproductive enjoyment' possessing radical potential in challenging the instrumental norms of the city. Not only is this idea complicit with neoliberal ideas of marketing urban deviance and the 'creative city', but it also relies on a presupposition that resistance must find a pure and authentic space 'outside' of power. Against such ideas, I argue that the concept of *détournement* carries a much more radical potential and is much closer to Rancière's injunction to refigure distributions of the sensible.

St Paul, the patron saint of tent-makers

On 15 October 2011, a large group of activists met at Paternoster Square – home of the London Stock Exchange – with the express intention of establishing a protest camp (as they had done at Zuccotti Park near Wall Street, New York). Paternoster Square is the centre of the financial district – the 'square mile' of the City of London – and a major global centre for capitalism, neoliberalism, and colonialism. The aesthetic of the area matches this history, following much of central London as being completely framed by the 'arrogant verticality of skyscrapers' whose very purpose is to 'display … to convey an impression of authority to each spectator … the spatial expression of potentially violent power' (Lefebvre 1991: 28). Situated at the top of Ludgate Hill, Paternoster Square is well hidden behind St Paul's Cathedral, marked off by a stone gateway (which was relocated here from Fleet Street in 2004, where it once acted as a toll gate to mark the outer reach of the City of London's jurisdiction (City of London 2017). By the time that Occupy LSX arrived, these gates had been reinforced by rows and rows of steel fencing, blockading the entrance to the Stock Exchange. In the context of the financial crisis, this represented *materially* a neoliberal policing of the space, asserting that the market was the realm of 'private property' where 'politics' should not enter and should not be seen or heard. The police had denied political appearance within the square through an aesthetic and normative re-establishment of the Stock Exchange and the financial system as the limit of politics (i.e. not a space for democratic intervention after the crisis).

Subsequently, Occupy LSX was pushed back from the Stock Exchange and 'kettled' onto the steps of St Paul's Cathedral next door. After a quick general assembly, the decision was made to set up a protest camp outside the cathedral and in front of the gates of Paternoster Square. Some, however, saw this as a founding foreclosure of the movement right from the start:

> Even Occupy starting off, that was originally an attempt to occupy Paternoster Square where the … the London Stock Exchange … and it was only the fact that people got kettled onto St Paul's that they ended up there! It's the same with this place [Finsbury Square], people were in a building down there and they got kettled onto here, so they stayed here. So really, it's the police who started this! *It's the police who started this movement and that's why we're at the whims of the system.* All these people say: 'oh yeah, we're having a great rebellion' and all this … well, it's actually *them* who forced us into this place, they've forced us in here.'
>
> (Nick)

For Nick, the fact that Occupy LSX had been prevented from occupying the Exchange, and had compromised by setting up outside St Paul's Cathedral, indicated that the movement had failed right from the beginning by allowing itself to be policed by the 'whims of the system'. For others, however, this accidental occupation of St Paul's was seen differently, and they described the turn of events as a 'godsend' (2014, int. 3), 'unbeatable' (2014, int. 10) 'magical' and 'brilliant' (Brian). Despite the fact that the police had corralled the activists here, a number of my interviewees argued that this had created unforeseen possibilities and permutations for the movement, expanding the potential of their resistance in at least three different ways: (1) increasing publicity; (2) facilitating semi-permanence and longevity; and (3) offering useful contextual narratives.

In the first instance, it was pointed out how the steps of St Paul's Cathedral were simply more public than the secluded Paternoster Square (which was surrounded by buildings, bars, and chain restaurants). For Shaun, for example, the occupation outside the cathedral may have been unintentional, but 'it was very central, with people going past all the time … a massive flow through'. He argued that this gave the occupiers a necessary platform for 'distributing flyers, making a scene, getting people to contribute stuff … you want to be central and open'. This argument was also echoed by Lucy:

> I think first and foremost, the fact that it was smack bang in the City of London and it's such a prominent place where there's such high footfall outside St Paul's. In terms of relationships with our surroundings – I'm really against this idea that somehow St Paul was a 'saviour' in really keeping the movement alive, that somehow organised religion was working with us, I immediately discount that – but in terms of space … if you look at Occupy London in terms of inclusivity and diversity, then it's *almost a PR exercise based on a social movement*. It was in a good space to attract people to walk through.

Clearly overlapping with Badiou's (2012) argument for localisation, intensification, and contraction, Lucy also emphasises the prominence of the cathedral steps giving the movement the ability to appear, be heard, and relate to the public by showcasing inclusivity and diversity. In particular, the 'high footfall' of this space is key. Redesigned in the 1990s, the road which curves around the cathedral was meant to facilitate the efficient and fast flow of traffic, tourists, and workers through the centre of London, but it also provided the protestors with a regularly circulating audience. The public nature of the space therefore allowed Occupy to make its appearance seen and its voice heard, fulfilling practical needs like handing out leaflets, receiving public donations, or interacting with the public.

As one activist, Ollie, put it to me, 'I'm interested in actions that take part on the street and cause onlookers to interact with those of us that are here … because [of the public occupation] people will be saying 'what's going on? Why are you doing that?' And that's what I'm interested in, that conversation'. Others also emphasised the fact that the open and public character of the space outside St Paul's helped to underline the democratic aims of their protest, something which was particularly highlighted by the camp's juxtaposition with Paternoster Square next door. The construction of the police barricade clearly demonstrated the democratic deficit of neoliberalism, that 'only a specific type of public is welcome and their activities are restricted to those of work and consumption' making 'the camp itself … an intervention, a critique of the undemocratic design and control of the urban space that surrounded it' (Koksal 2012: 447).

The context was therefore crucial to the appearance and voice of the occupation, and the public character of the space was not merely an instrumental benefit for interaction and exercise of democracy; it also contributed to a further benefit of urban occupation in facilitating semi-permanent longevity. As a space designated as 'public' by law (compared to the 'private property' of Paternoster Square), the protestors were sitting in a legal grey area and were able to remain in that space for a prolonged period of time. For Jenny, 'St Paul's was perfect!' for precisely this reason:

> I mean, as I'm sure you know, we didn't original intend to occupy St Paul's, we originally intended to occupy outside the stock exchange. We didn't realise there was already an injunction on it. So, the St Paul's option turned out to be absolutely perfect because, in every way, it juxtaposed the state and the church. The most iconic building in London, thousands of tourists all the time, then the church foolishly got themselves embroiled in the argument and ended up with resignations and all the rest of it.

Occupy LSX had avoided the injunction on Paternoster Square to remove any protestors or 'blocks in the highway', and instead was able to exploit a grey area in the legal designation of the steps of St Paul's, allowing its appearance and voice to be sustained for a longer period of time than might have been afforded by other spaces or tactics. As one interviewee explained, the tactic of occupying space made the movement's intervention more than 'just a march in the street, a march in the street is more like a party, a gathering of people' (2012, int. 9). The legal grey area outside the cathedral therefore meant that Occupy had established a public platform, a material base with no rent or costs – from which the activists could make themselves seen and heard, from which they could be found by those looking to get involved – and which had a *longevity* to it.

Yet when compared to the concrete, steel and glass institutions which surrounded them, Greg pointed out that there was also political virtue in this longevity having a semi-permanence. Gesturing towards the tents and structures in Finsbury Square, he explained that:

> All that can actually go. And yeah, the grass would be fucked for a few months, but then it can all be disappeared. Whereas these things [pointing to the Islington office blocks] they could be here for 500 years if people just abandoned them. They would take years and years and years

> to grow over. And that … there's so little potential. But you see that [the camp] and you go: 'oh, lots of potential for doing things'.

So, longevity, yes, but also a semi-permanence which facilitated a creative, flexible, and dynamic protest. By avoiding the oppressive nature of other dominant institutions and designs in the city, the tactic of occupation was seen as providing a location for open, fluid, and non-hierarchical interaction. When compared with the anti-democratic inflexibility of the steel and glass, the tents and canvas were seen as a providing a counter-aesthetic to their surrounding context.

Such contextual narratives were seen as the final benefit of occupying space. The accidental occupation outside the cathedral furnished Occupy (in) London's 'non-sensible' appearance and voice, by operating as a 'monumental space … a metaphorical and quasi-metaphysical underpinning of society' which offers 'each member of a society an image of that membership, an image of his or her social visage … it thus constitutes a collective mirror more faithful than and personal one' (Lefebvre 1991: 220). The majority of people observing the Occupy movement through mainstream or social media would probably never have heard of Paternoster Square (which itself indicates the distance and undemocratic isolation of the stock exchange); but St Paul's Cathedral – as a national monument – was able to act as a clear reference point which ensured public, journalist, and politician attention.

The wider distribution of the occupation was more fundamental to the definition of the movement than any attempt at an organic self-definition from within, and some activists pointed towards the 'messianic' (Shaun) character of this backdrop, enabling Occupy to tap into moral narratives of religious imagery. In addition to the legal distribution of the space (which had provided a grey area for the movement to stay put), the religious distribution of the space provided a *moral* grey area which allowed Occupy LSX to claim a certain *authority* to be there. This space was specifically partitioned for making moral (in this case, Christian) arguments for charity, equality, and social justice. Or as Dan put it to me:

> If we ended up in Paternoster Square, we would have probably just been there for the weekend. But because we were in St Paul's churchyard, there were buses passing by and people become more curious. People were saying we were desecrating St Paul's Cathedral, but we pointed out that *St Paul was actually the patron saint of tent-makers* and he wouldn't have been put off by it. Where do you think St Paul the tent-maker would be, in the cathedral or in the tents?

This is indicative of a whole series of religious symbolism and imagery which the protestors outside St Paul's adopted, twisted, and refigured as their own. Some of the placards outside the cathedral, for instance, questioned 'What would Jesus do?' and 'for anyone who's read the New Testament', Greg argued, 'they're going to look at that and go: 'that's odd, because Jesus was throwing the moneylenders *out* of the temple, but this particular temple is being propped up by the moneylenders!' The question of whether the protestors had a moral right to be there proved so controversial that they managed to stay put for five months, by which time there had been a number of high-profile resignations from the cathedral *on both sides of the debate*: with Canon Chancellor Giles Fraser quitting in support of the movement, and Cathedral Dean Graeme Knowles quitting in protest at the movement (stating that his position had simply become 'untenable' in the face of the occupation).

In addition to the publicity and semi-permanent longevity, such *détournement* and twisting of spatial norms allowed Occupy LSX to claim a certain authority and legitimacy for its appearance and voice, which might have been more difficult to make public, and to be legally and morally maintained in Paternoster Square. What is considered to be 'obvious' and 'sensible' within a given space – its conventions and restrictions, the designing and planning of large swathes of the city for the needs of capital – can therefore be directly challenged by the occupation of space. Indeed, the very *language* of 'occupation' suggests that the movement's appearance disrupted the 'proper use' of such space (Pickerill and Krinsky 2012) which, as Angela Davis argued, is in direct contrast to the military use of such language: 'we transform the meaning of 'occupation'... we turn 'occupation' into something that is beautiful, something that brings community together ... something that calls for happiness and hope' (2011: 133). That the St Paul's camp was eventually evicted on the grounds of 'public hygiene' demonstrates that all the police order could do in the end was to reclaim its distribution of the space by removing the 'dirt' – the 'matter out of place' (see Douglas 1966: 35) – and scrub the space clean of the rogue cells which had threatened the city's health.

The challenges of occupying space

However, while the occupation of space provided the movement with publicity, semi-permanent longevity, and a symbolic context which allowed them to tap into wider discourses and create a certain moral authority, there were nevertheless numerous attempts to 'police' the movement ('move them along') as well as to designate them as 'non-sense' ('nothing to see here'). Many of the occupiers I met, for example, had either first-hand experience or tales of different ways in which the police force was attempting to deny the legitimacy of their appearance, including issuing Anti-Social Behaviour Orders (or ASBOs) and injunctions on the green outside the Houses of Parliament 'where you're only allowed to protest for 24 hours and then you've got to go' (Harry). Others also pointed out more subtle efforts to police their protest. One particularly notorious incident was an investigation by the *Daily Mail* (2011) which used thermal imaging equipment to 'prove' that 90 per cent of the tents outside the cathedral were empty at night, leading the investigators to extrapolate from 'the damning images' that 'the vast majority of the demonstrators who gather around the cathedral to denounce capitalism during the day go home or to a hotel to stay warm at night'. This leap from the failure to pick up heat signatures to supposed hypocrisy and inauthenticity, can perhaps be translated into Rancière's language as a *literal* attempt to designate Occupy as 'nothing to see here' (see also Cissel 2012). Some even blamed the media and political sensationalism for distorting the movement's appearance, portraying Occupy as a niche group rather than the openly public and democratic organisation they were attempting to establish, 'because if you get *The Guardian,* the *Daily Mail,* or the *Evening Standard* sending a journalist down to St Paul's or something and they want to run a story about it … they're going to get a photograph of the person they think is the most strangest-looking person' (2014, int. 4). This concern with being cast as an exclusive cult also blurred with criticisms of the way in which politicians were framing the movement, with Boris Johnson (who was the Mayor of London at the time) being quoted as describing the occupiers as 'hemp-smoking, fornicating hippies' (2012, int. 5) and the movement needing to be 'pounded' in his reference to Occupy as 'like snowflakes, you must not let them settle' (Dan).

These examples demonstrate the police order in action. By dismissing the movement as 'anti-social' or limiting its aesthetic to certain clichés, such narratives played into wider normative policing of London's space and what should (or should not) legitimately appear there. Thus, post-crash power did not need to operate through physical violence, but instead through a distribution of the sensible that limited its appearance and put the onus on movements like Occupy to try and manage the image of their occupation. Yet, as the winter turned wetter and colder – as tents and tempers became tired and frayed; as sleep deprivation, the lack of food and hygiene, and the constant proximity to others was compacted by the effect of the cold paving slabs and the cathedral bells; and as local patrons of the pubs and cathedral alike shouted abuse and sometimes even turned violent – the persistent media scrutiny became more and more difficult to cope with.

What's more, making provision for people already living on London's streets, sometimes with mental illnesses or problems with addictions, added extra strain on the movement. Sally, who had a background in social care and supporting addicts, told me about the role she automatically assumed at the St Paul's camp in providing welfare to those who needed it. For her, the context of post-crash austerity and cuts to social support made welfare the biggest challenge that the movement faced:

> Welfare at Occupy meant, by default, becoming a street outreach worker, because we were on the street and a lot of homeless people and so on come in, and our job was to support them and refer them to agencies. And you know, sometimes there was some really dangerous situations to address. *It wasn't always a perfect little community of thriving activists looking after each other.* The cops, for example, quite happily if given the

> opportunity, would come in and bust somebody if they thought there was a pot deal going on or something like that. Then that would create a lot of tension, sometimes violence, you know, it was hard. And there was lots of moments like that. It's got to be said that just living in those circumstances, where you are constantly at risk of people being arrested or kicked out or something going on (it wasn't the safest of spaces) was in itself going to lead to disillusionment and burnout.

Taking a thoughtful sip of her tea, Sally proceeded to draw links between these experiences and the constant battle to present a positive aesthetic of the movement in front of media and public scrutiny, willing the protestors on to do *something* that would prove everyone's cynicism correct, which would permit them to then dismiss the movement and move on. For Sally, because St Paul's was so prominent a protest, it became *the* site where this aesthetic management was most at stake:

> I mean, one of the things that used to drive me absolutely mad was the constant cameras. It's like, just go away! I mean, I'm naturally a little bit paranoid by nature and I got to the point where I just … because I didn't know who they were, I didn't want to know who they were, I had a job to do. So I was really frustrated that I couldn't move ten yards without somebody else sticking a camera in my face. I mean, it was literally 'dodge the camera'. Often time they would just show up out of the blue, you didn't know who they were, you didn't know if they were going to be friendly in the press or not … Being at St Paul's was really important for giving publicity to the movement, but it had its limitations and, in some ways, it was human frailty or vanity or whatever … which was the limitation. *Some people were just there because they wanted to be on telly*, not many I imagine, but it was really exciting.

What was dubbed the 'homeless question' at Occupy Wall Street (Taylor and Gessan 2011, see also Smith *et al.* 2012; Schein 2012), became a sticking point whereby the politics of the movement appeared to clash with a desire to control appearances and avoid being dismissed as 'non-sense'. It was also one of the main points of contention that accelerated the fracturing of the movement in London, with some seeing the provision for those in need as distracting from their protest activity by directing scarce resources away from direct action, and others seeing the movement as rooted in such questions of social justice and provision for those suffering under the very system they were protesting against. For the former, the homeless question was one gladly answered by the eviction of St Paul's, but this also spatialised the division as some of the homeless who had been staying outside the cathedral moved to Finsbury Square (which simply did not have the resources to support more people).

So, while many activists spoke about the chaos and disorganisation at Finsbury Square with a certain sympathy, they also saw it as being emblematic of the problems within the movement that prevented Occupy from resisting effectively. For Harry, the remaining campers at Finsbury were 'the fringes of society' and therefore 'prone to the afflictions of being on the fringes of society … I was quite saddened by what I saw … it was mass alcoholism, drug-taking … it stank of piss, it really did … and I felt a bit sad about that'. Lucy also echoed these statements, suggesting that, at Finsbury Square, 'the identities and the people were an issue, especially in the later days, because *it became less about the movement and more about containing and trying to help homelessness and people with mental health problems* … it lost its way in that sense'. Others also talked about Finsbury Square in terms of strategy and made direct comparisons with St Paul's:

> I knew some people that made the first move to Finsbury Square when it was occupied and I was never quite sure why this happened … but I think Finsbury Square especially was not a very tactical use of space because it was in a little area of parkland surrounded by office buildings … whereas St Paul's was in a kind of … there's about three different major public walkthroughs and causeways in that areas, so it was a channel of the public and this was really important, I think.

In contrast, staunch defenders of Finsbury Square and self-nominated champions of the principle of occupying space as the core definition of the Occupy movement, talked about Occupy LSX in bitter terms. When I first met Greg at Finsbury Square, he was clearly right in the middle of fighting for exactly this point:

> For me, Occupy is about *occupying a space physically*, and like I said, people come along, and if you can help the community that's good, and if you can't then maybe you should jog on and go and start one somewhere else.

What Greg had found particularly distasteful was a new slogan being promoted by the former St Paul's contingent – 'You Don't Need A Tent to Occupy' – arguing that, if they weren't occupying space, then what made them any different from any other past failure? His anger was palpable and worsened as he told me about the St Paul's group adopting the name 'Occupy London' (the universal signifier) and speaking on behalf of the movement as a whole, while claiming any donation money as theirs.

As these splits demonstrated, while the occupation of urban space was certainly a popular tactic and one of the clearest common motifs of the post-crash movements, there were major challenges and difficulties faced in their organisation and maintenance. While recognising the potential of occupying, therefore, we also need to remain critical and recognise its limitations. Or, in other words:

> [while] mass occupations [have] certainly become an important element in the broader politics of 'anti-systemic' uprisings across the world, and those involved in such movements have often stressed the importance of occupation as such because of its symbolic value and role in providing a 'counter-space' for democratic experiments and the creation of new forms of community … *there are dangers in fetishizing physical occupation and ignoring its negative aspects* – it's exclusivity, the unequal struggle with forces of law and order, and the fragility of movements when their spaces are repossessed by those forces … Occupation might thus be seen as an important tool in any array of political practices, but more appropriate in some contexts than others.
>
> (Bassett 2016: 289; emphasis added)

At the same time as recognising the potential of occupation to intervene with authority in the distribution of the sensible, we must also identify the challenges and limitations of maintaining such an appearance against the police order, as well as the difficulties of sustaining an urban occupation in practice. We must also understand how the context of the occupation and its wider distribution is absolutely crucial, even if we insist that occupation possesses a radical potential to refigure that context.

The spatial imperative

The first time I arranged to meet James was at a café in Bethnal Green in 2013. After getting us both a coffee, and assuring him that I wasn't undercover police, we sat down in the corner to conduct the interview. He seemed particularly interested in discussing the importance of space and occupation for activism and resistance, labelling this the 'spatial imperative':

> I think to come back to this point of sticking your flag in the ground and saying: 'this is ours!' in a world where they are privatising everything in a heartbeat. The act of occupying space … there's a *spatial imperative* to all activism now I believe. Because *without space, you can't organise, you can't come together, you can't socialise, you can't have a free exchange of ideas.*

Once again, occupying space permits an authority, a democratic intervention ('this is ours'), as providing a material base on which organisation, socialisation, and exchange can focus. James' descriptions were evocative and full of imagery, linguistic twists, and metaphor:

> Ten per cent of the world is on land it 'shouldn't be on'; ten per cent of the world are squatters. So it's as old as humanity, it will continue, it will become more vital, and *people will continue to stand up by sitting down* [even if] it's also become increasingly difficult for us to occupy space.

After the eviction of Occupy LSX, Paternoster Square had been reclassified as a 'city walkway', enabling the police and City of London Corporation security to close off the square (as well as the six adjoining lanes and alleyways) if they deemed an 'imminent threat' or 'unforeseen events' to be likely (Gander 2014). Yet as James made clear, 'Occupy has never really cared if it's illegal; its cared whether its *right* … and that's a really important principle, not to work within the restrictions of 'you can't stand here, you can't stand here'. Using language reminiscent of Rancière, he elaborated further:

> Every space has its conventions. And if public space is taken away (and it is being taken away, large swathes of the city are being taken over as private enterprise zones) well, you can't leaflet, and you can't busk, and you can't beg, and you can't loiter (because that brings down sales), and you can't congregate … I mean human rights, left, right and centre … so the occupation of space, the defiant occupation of space – saying: 'this is ours, the city's ours because we are citizens' – is the most valuable thing that Occupy can bring (and it will continue to bring that in many different forms). We will continue to assemble in crisis; just as they are all over the world.

City space has its normative conventions, and in cities like London, the common sense which rules (neoliberalism, capitalism, colonialism, etc.) is zoning space in favour of private enterprise rather than the general public. For James, the 'defiant occupation of space' is therefore 'the main value of Occupy', and precisely what was lost after the camps had been evicted and large sections of the movement decided not to reoccupy. For him, 'when there's no space to occupy, things fragment and unravel a bit unfortunately … because there's no nucleus. I often describe it as kind of like a speck of dust: the site is a like a speck of dust around which the raindrop gathers, and then if you have enough raindrops, of course, you have a downfall.'

The second time we met was a year later at an impromptu General Assembly which was held (symbolically) on the steps of St Paul's. Many of the occupiers I had met during the course of three years of fieldwork were there, including Dan (who recorded the obligatory Livestream and had sheepishly set up a green pop-up tent at the bottom of the steps) and Greg (who was sitting at the back with a cynical air about him). James was attempting to invite the public to come and join in, but the turnout was poor and the atmosphere lacklustre. To make things worse, during the speeches and discussions a wedding party emerged from the cathedral and headed down the steps, placing us in a very awkward position. James and I headed to a café just across the road and we quickly returned to discussing the potential and limitations of occupation as a method of resistance. Reflecting on the assembly we had just attended, I asked him whether he thought St Paul's had been a good space for the protest. 'Absolutely', he said:

> It benefitted from the spectacular setting … what a stage! I mean, you can see the difference. When I was at Finsbury Square, people didn't tend to come (and that was actually closer to the head of many of the corporations and businesses we were protesting about). So, the setting is very important. Space is very important. This is a space designed for social interaction and photographs, it's hundreds of years of architectural knowledge has gone into making this a place where you can come and look at things. So, in many ways, it's perfect. And also, the contrast: juxtaposing such opulence with people in tents; the idea of the tent and the cathedral, David and Goliath, the money-lenders and the believers outside the temple. So, it's just dramatic and media-framing … the image is quite important.

Once again, the importance of public context and the symbolic setting for the staging of the movement's appearance and voice is key, and at the mention of 'media-framing' I recalled some of the other conversations I had been having regarding aesthetics and managing the movement's appearance. James agreed and discussed this problem in his own words:

> Yeah, I mean it's more photogenic to photograph people like yourself or me, who have dreads, than it would be to photograph [someone 'normal'] who does a lot in Occupy. So, the media is responsible for perpetuating these stereotypes and from the beginning was good at asserting … *maybe a cultural or politically engineered attempt to marginalise the movement*, with the visual representations and the lies basically.

La fête and the creative city

While the policing of space may become clearest at moments when movements like Occupy appear, the distribution of the sensible is by no means restricted to such events, and can be understood as operating through everyday designs, architecture, and planning in the city. Adopting a very similar position to Rancière in outlining how power in the city is fundamentally material and aesthetic, operating through a normative distribution, it was contended by Lefebvre, for instance, that 'the city writes and assigns, that is, it signifies, orders, stipulates' (1996: 102), arguing that we can easily formulate 'all the problems of society into questions of space and all that comes from history and consciousness in spatial terms' (ibid.: 99). For example, we might point towards the use of so-called defensive architectures like 'homeless spikes' (studs which are implanted into the floor to prevent rough-sleeping) which, despite often being 'added onto the street environment at a later stage' are increasingly being included in urban plans, making it 'apparent that questions of 'who do we want in this space, who do we not want' are being considered very early in the design stage' (Quinn 2014). Such political artefacts (see Winner 1980), which resemble the infamous 'bum-proof' benches described by Davis (1990), demonstrate a clear partitioning of the sensible within the city, using design and planning to subtly coerce and designate who may or may not appear in a given space and context.

The wider problem is that planners and architects tend to adopt 'a mechanised, calculated, controlled, measured way of operating' (Elden 2004: 114), which overlooks alternative and democratic uses of urban space. This technocratic approach, Lefebvre argued, can limit the vision of some architects, as they only achieve a 'concept of habitat by excluding the notion of inhabit, that is, the plasticity of space, its modelling and the appropriation by groups and individuals of the conditions of their existence' (1996: 79). In other words, because 'the experience of the architecture is [often] the experience of the architect' (Hill 1998: 5), the planning and design of urban space tends to operate from a presupposition of the 'sensible' that does not recognise democratic uses of urban space from below. In the neoliberal city especially, this means the needs of the market take precedence over the needs of the citizens. Everything must become efficient and productive. Streets must facilitate the slick flow of workers and transport, as well as the necessary superfast communication links. Squares and parks need to provide facilities for tourists, as well as a calendar of entertainment and popular urban events (all with high levels of security). Houses and homes, for those who can afford to compete for them, must also be secured from risks (see Atkinson 2017). Subsequently, post-crash London could accurately be described as 'a city in thrall to capital' (Atkinson and Burrows 2014), a position cemented in both its physical design and designation of space.

In contrast to this technocratic, capital-dominated approach to the city, it is contended by Lefebvre (as well as the Situationists) that resistance to such a distribution can be organised by asserting 'the eminent use of the city, that is, of its streets and squares, edifices and monuments' (1996: 66) that redefines urban space as *la fête* or a 'true space of pleasure' (ibid.: 150). Yet in the context of postmodern capitalism and the dual consumer injunctions of symbolic inefficiency and enjoyment, we need to question whether the call for 'unproductive enjoyment' (1991: 359–60) is really a radical gesture. As detailed in Richard Florida's manifesto for post-industrial economic growth – *The Rise of the Creative Class* – enjoyment has become *the* formula for economic success in the neoliberal city. Florida's vision is that those cities who offer unproductive enjoyment – such as post-industrial cultural quarters, urban festivals, streets markets, independent shops and entertainment, with 'edgy' neighbourhoods, graffiti, flash mobs, and pop-up excitement – will be the cities that attract lucrative talent and create for themselves a competitive advantage over others, by establishing spaces 'where everyday innovation occurs through spontaneous interaction, a place literally seething with the interplay of cultures and ideas, a place where outsiders quickly become insiders' (2002: 227).[4] The blueprint for the creative city is therefore to *encourage* the deviancy and unproductivity of Lefebvre's *la fête*, while working 'quietly with the grain of extant "neoliberal" development agendas, framed around inter-urban competition, gentrification, middle-class consumption and place making' (Peck 2005: 740–1).

As has been pointed out by others, the creative city indicates a problematic convergence between the competitiveness of the city and the apparent autonomy of its citizens, and 'whilst not wanting to allow the complete co-optation of creative thought and action by the neoliberal agenda … there is arguably no space entirely free from the kinds of creative imperatives celebrated by the capitalist entrepreneurs like Richard Florida' (Lambert 2013: 5–6). The main problem with Lefebvre's formulation, therefore, is that in attempting to locate a space 'outside' (or at least 'in between') market relations of capitalism that dominate cities like London, his argument for resistance as 'unproductive enjoyment' misses the way in which seemingly independent activities of enjoyment actually *extend* normative distributions of the city. As Bonnett (1989) has pointed out, whether or not such autonomous space is necessary (and whether or not it actually exists) is actually one of the main points of difference between Lefebvre and the Situationists. The latter, such as Debord, tended to argue instead that resistance (or 'situations') had to be understood as taking place *within* and *in relation to* wider aesthetic distributions (or 'the spectacle') 'because such alienating images have now spread throughout the entirety of social representation' and therefore 'merely to oppose them through a series of 'alternative' or 'oppositional' clichés and roles is to become part of the spectacle' (Bonnett 1989: 135). For Debord, the problem for urban resistance is that 'even the most eccentric or oppositional stance towards the conventional landscape cannot break out of the spectacular chain of meaning' (Bonnett 1989: 139) and therefore no 'authentic' space 'outside' of the police order can actually be found. As with Foucault, this seems to leave resistance with nowhere to turn, but the answer offered by Situationism is to frame resistance as a *détournement* which 'involves taking elements from a social stereotype and, through their mutation and reversal, turning them against it so it is disrupted and exposed as a product of alienation' (Bonnett 1989: 135). If a movement is unavoidably distributed by its context and is therefore putting forward an appearance and voice which is being immediately designated and dismissed as 'non-sense' by the police order, then elements of its wider context – such as the juxtaposition of the tents with steel, glass, and closed-off square, or the religious imagery of St Paul's – can be refigured, marking a move 'away from technocratic solutions' and 'towards social problems' through 'the re-use, and political resignification, of the existing environment' (ibid. 2006: 35).

On the one hand, then, while Lefebvre does recognise the prevalence of market norms in urban culture – noting, for instance, how cities have become 'a high-quality consumption product for foreigners, tourists, people from the outskirts and suburbanites … a place of consumption and a consumption of place' (1996: 73) – he nevertheless overestimated the potential of unproductive enjoyment to intervene in the context of postmodern (creative) cities. And, on the other hand, while the Situationists also emphasised festivity and play as 'the concrete construction of momentary ambiences of life and its transformation into a superior passional quality' (Debord 1957), the important difference is that the latter see this as stemming from a position of structural *complicity*, and as an 'opportunity for unofficial and popular elements to playfully *invert* social and cultural conventions' (Sadler 1999: 34; emphasis added).

And yet there were many who insisted that the political potential of Occupy lay in creating autonomous spaces from which to anticipate and experiment with a future alternative, by locating a space 'outside' of the city's productive enjoyment from which to launch resistance. A long-term supporter of the movement, David Graeber argued that what was particularly exceptional and radical about the protest camps was their engagement in a form of autonomous and prefigurative politics. Writing specifically about Occupy Wall Street, he suggested that the way in which the protestors made everyday decisions in general assemblies and their approach to organising mundane tasks were in themselves indicators of political possibility, and should be understood as an 'experiment with creating institutions of a new society … all operating on anarchist principles of mutual aid and self-organisation' (Roberts 2012: 757). Simply by being *in* the park – and being 'outside' of the system – the idea was that in itself this was enough to enact and prefigure an alternative society, with everyday actions 'laying the framework for a new world' (ibid.). Or, in other words:

> the Occupy movements [were] not based on creating either a programme or a political party that will put forward a plan for others to follow. Their purpose [was] not to determine 'the' path that a particular country should take but to create the space for a conversation in which all can participate and in which all can determine together what the future should look like. At the same time, these movements [attempted] to prefigure that future society in their present social relationships.
>
> (Sitrin 2012: 74)

This was also a popular approach to understanding Occupy (in) London. For Howard and Pratt-Boyden (2013), for instance, Occupy LSX may have been 'throughout its lifetime persistently dogged by one line of widely repeated and, for many, damning criticism: that it lacked direction, that it failed to make any concrete demands, and that, ultimately, it was consequently pointless' (ibid.: 732), but the authors argue that the problem with this criticism was that it failed to recognise how Occupy was *prefigurative*. By being 'the change they wanted to see in the world' and creating a microcosm of an alternative society, 'social actors within such movements are supposed to directly 'embody … the change the movement seeks' in all elements of social life, including movement organisation as well as identity and lifestyle … thus acting as a kind of 'working utopia' … a living model, or vision of the proposed society' (ibid.: 733–4). While admitting, therefore, that 'Occupy

London had many problems and that, for all its valiant efforts, its striving for pre-figuration was often unsuccessful, which necessarily raises questions about whether pre-figuration is a viable political strategy' (ibid.: 738); Howard and Pratt-Boyden nevertheless insist that criticism of Occupy being 'rudderless' ignores the possibilities of prefiguration, because 'protest, as with any social formation, is an ongoing journey as opposed to a pre-defined destination … pre-figurative politics are thus processual' (ibid.: 740).

This idea was equally widespread within the movement itself, with the organisation of the occupation seen as facilitating the movement's ability to establish a space from which to prefigure a future inclusive and horizontal society. More than simply a 'reclaiming of that right … the right to public space; the right to free assembly; the right to actually have a say in decisions now made', Felicity told me that:

> some people I've spoken to have said that Occupy is a bit like street theatre and it is. But at the same time, it's not just theatre, it's very real. It is a *performing of an alternative.* It becomes your life and so you sort of … it does profoundly change the way you are in the world and that's a really interesting thing.

For Felicity, Occupy was literally creating an alternative future – one which was more democratic, equal, and just than the one which had been reasserted after the crisis – through its very performance of that alternative in everyday practice. She spoke in romantic terms about this possibility, comparing the movement to the Greek polis:

> Occupy has been able to provide that sort of … like St Paul's from October til mid-December was that sort vibrant city-square, or was like what I imagine Athens was, where you have all the political discussion. Because you need people on the street. And you don't have political discussion just if you go to a public meeting, actually you have them on the street. Unless you link up physically, there's not much you can do really.

Some activists also emphasised the diversity of the movement as anticipating a future society of social equality between genders, ethnicities, races, sexualities, physical abilities, and classes. 'Obviously', Julia claimed. 'Because it was such a great diversity of people … from middle-class people, to working-class people … many issues we wanted to highlight … the timing was really right … this moment when the crisis was starting to feel really strong for the first time'. She then went on to stress the importance of finding space outside of wider structures of power, an autonomous space, in order to showcase and prefigure such diversity:

> To me, basically, since capitalism has always tried to privatise everything, but even more so after neoliberalism started, like, in the 70s/80s …

> started to privatise every square metre of the city. It's only through the use of space that we interact with people and we create identities and we create political alternatives ... And now we live in a very individualistic society and people don't engage with each other, but that's the only way we can create change, by engaging with other people, talking, that sort of thing ... and that can only happen through space.

Others took this need for autonomous interactional space to the extreme:

> I looked at [Occupy] as an experiment that I'd never seen before. I'd never seen a space that was completely isolated from this system, from this world we're forced to live in. No politician, no policemen, could ruin that ... we had to handle everything ourselves. That was interesting. Every time you set up a community, habits and issues come up that you've brought in from the outside worlds and if you resolve it, they you resolve it in the whole of society.
>
> (2014, int. 6)

The problem is that prefiguration presupposes an 'outside' space – free from the structural hierarchies, exclusions, and normative control of the wider police order – which cannot be obtained. As I outlined by reference to Foucault in Chapter 1, while his analysis of modern normative power is often misunderstood as completely closing down the possibility of resistance, he nevertheless shows how resistance and power are co-constitutive, that they always exist in relation to one another, since resistance is necessarily conceived as 'normal' or 'abnormal' – legitimate or illegitimate – in relation to such 'common sense'. The question for social movements therefore should be how to mobilise reverse discourses and *détournement* in order to refigure the police order from within, and yet such ideas of creating a prefigurative autonomous space outside of such power structures (which can then operate with purity and authenticity) continue to be frequently echoed in social movements and social research alike. Social movement theorists, for instance, often talk about 'interstitial spaces' (Wright 2010), 'temporary autonomous zones' (Bey 2011), and the perfect interaction situation of 'the public sphere' (Habermas 1987), ignoring how all space is distributed and has a persistent normative structure. To insist on autonomous space, I will argue in the next chapter, is to risk overlooking (and leaving unchallenged) normative inequalities which do persist within social movements. What's more, the emphasis on creating a space 'outside' of society, from which to establish and prefigure open inclusivity, diversity, and horizontality may seem important for creating and performing a democratic organisation; however, these are not useful principles from which to organise a symbolically efficient appearance that challenges (and intervenes in) an unequal society.

Conclusion: making 'non-sense' appear

When the police order distributes what may or may not legitimately appear or be heard within a given context, the public, semi-permanent, and contextually embedded occupation of space offers a radical potential. In the post-crash context of London – where neoliberalism reasserted its normativity as the only *sensible* use of London's space and the only *reasonable* approach to the crisis – the idea of an alternative was ideologically and aesthetically deemed to be 'non-sense'. And yet occupying space can provide a basis from which to organise an aesthetic intervention in that order and make 'non-sense' appear against its designation as such. As Occupy LSX demonstrated outside St Paul's, the publicity and longevity of the protest camp fulfilled practical considerations of organisation, utilising the design of the space (the regular flow of an audience) to help to spread its message, receive donations, and interact with the public. What's more, the contextual narratives of the cathedral allowed the activists to occupy not only a legal grey area as to the public nature of the space, but also a *moral* grey area, affording them a certain authority to remain and appear despite attempts to 'move them along' as 'nothing to see here'. Yet maintaining the appearance of protest was complicated by the physical challenges of living on London's streets – including the weather, the lack of facilities, an inability to defend themselves against violence – which led to burnout, fatigue, and disillusionment. What's more, the homeless question in the context of wider cuts to public services created difficulties around an ethical and political duty to provide support, while at the same time dealing with addiction or mental illness. Yet despite the challenges of maintaining the image of their appearance, it was argued that there remains a spatial imperative for movements to occupy space in order to refigure wider 'common-sense' distributions.

It was also argued, however, that the imperative to occupy space is *not* based upon finding some 'authentic' space 'outside' of power relations, from which the movement could 'be the change they wanted to see in the world' and literally enact (prefigure) an alternative society into being. Such an argument, as I will demonstrate in the next chapter, not only leads to unaccountable hierarchies and exclusions through a fetishisation of the space as 'structureless', but also extends wider norms of individualism, libertarianism, and symbolic inefficiency. Instead, the occupation of urban space as a tactic of resistance needs to be recognised as democratically important for *organising appearances and voices otherwise distributed as non-sensible and marginal.* Julia offered an honest assessment of Occupy along these lines:

> In reality, I think we made many mistakes and I don't like to think of Occupy as this great thing that changed the world, because it didn't. It marked a point in history, but now the movement has declined a lot. To me, we haven't been able to make a transition from when we were occupying public space – because that creates certain conditions which is so

> much easier to organise around – to now being completely separated and divided across the country or across the city, you know?

The political possibilities provided by occupying space are neither to be found in the unproductive enjoyment of *la fête*, nor in ostensibly 'autonomous' spaces 'outside' of wider power relations. Instead, it lies in the potential for a collective appearance that can intervene and refigure the police order, through an organisation of 'that moment when those who are speaking begin somehow to speak – this moment is only made possible by the prior production of space from which speech can appear' (Chambers 2013: 120–1). Or, as David Harvey has argued, the reason that 'the street is a public space that has historically often been transformed by social action into the common of revolutionary moments' (2012: 73) is because 'the collective power of bodies in public space is still the most effective instrument of opposition when all other means of access are blocked' (ibid.: 162).

Notes

1 https://www.alphabeta.london/ (accessed 16 August 2017).
2 http://www.grantthornton.co.uk/ (accessed 16 August 2017).
3 https://www.bloombergspace.com/about/ (accessed 16 August 2017).
4 As I will outline in the following chapters, it is no coincidence that this agenda sounds so close to the libertarian, openly inclusive, horizontal, and individualistic agenda of the Occupy movement. Florida's website even predated Occupy in quoting Victor Hugo's 'you cannot resist an idea whose time has come' (Peck 2005: 758).

3 We are the 99%

Trafalgar Square, May 2013

It had stopped raining for now, but the paving slabs of Trafalgar Square were awash with water and created a mirror image of the marquee and the sign outside: 'Socialist Worker Party. NO CUTS. FIGHT FOR EVERY JOB. Strike to win. www.swp.org.uk'.

It was May 2013 and there were no longer any Occupy camps left on the ground in London. Many activists were now talking instead about the anti-fracking environmental camp at Balcombe, Sussex, where protestors had managed to prevent drilling machinery and workers from entering the site. I had come across this march at Trafalgar Square on social media and mailing lists connected with Occupy (in) London, yet there seemed to be no direct references to the movement as far as I could tell.

Stepping back to look at the protest from Nelson's Column, the sheer diversity of flags, banners, iconography, and ideologies was clear. Anonymous had gathered in the centre of the steps outside the National Gallery, their hoods up and the V for Vendetta Guy Fawkes masks on, waving a green flag depicting a figure in a suit with a question mark for a face. Another activist wearing a Guy Fawkes mask stood away from them and waved a rainbow-coloured peace flag. Others held up home-made placards:

YOU CAN'T TAKE THE PANTS OFF A BARE BACKSIDE!
ITS TIME FOR CHANGE. ENLIGHTENED HUMANITY DESIRES PEACE, FREEDOM, EQUALITY & SUSTAINABILITY.
Wake up UK. Our NHS is being sold off piece by piece.
STOP THE NEW WORLD ORDER.
GOVERNMENTS LIE, CHEAT, STEAL & KILL FOR PROFIT TO MAINTAIN WEALTH & POWER FOR THEIR CORPORATE MASTERS.

Two signs in particular seemed somewhat contradictory. A group at the back (who appeared to be Black Bloc anarchists) held up a black sign with white text that simply read 'ABOLISH THE STATE', while, to the right, a Socialist Worker Party banner read: 'TORIES OUT. VOTE FOR US'.

It was very hard to discern an overall message. The purpose of the march, what the protestors wanted, and who the protest was being addressed towards, seemed not only unclear but self-contradictory. I returned to the crowd and enjoyed the samba troupe who were trying to build some energy in the soggy audience. Some people danced, a few held up camera phones, and others just stood chatting under their umbrellas waiting for something to happen. To our left, police riot vans had pulled up next to the gathering and an activist I didn't know came up to me brandishing a smartphone with a picture of the Illuminati 'all-seeing eye' that he claimed to have taken in the window of one of the vans.

We began to march towards Downing Street, but there were riot vans in front of us all the way down Whitehall, managing the speed at which the protestors could move, as well as a row of police along our flanks and behind us. The street was lined all the way down with crash barriers, separating the march from bemused pedestrians and tourists taking pictures on the path. We eventually reached Downing Street, but after only a few chants, returned once more to Trafalgar Square to meet up with the rest of the rally (who had clearly not seen the point of marching on Whitehall).

Introduction: a question of organisation

This chapter takes seriously Badiou's (2012) assertion that the question of politics par excellence is one of *organisation*. When the Occupy movement attempted to translate its democratic and egalitarian aims into practical questions of everyday practice – how best to organise the movement's identity and appearance, as well as how to establish a 'we' which was identifiable while at the same time being open, inclusive, and horizontal (leaderless) – it was heavily influenced by notions of prefiguration. The principles which guided its organisational practice were therefore intertwined with the future alternative society that its members wanted to enact into being, one in which there would be no exclusion, hierarchy, inequality, or oppression. However, as I will demonstrate in this chapter, this attempt to bring about the desired change proved incredibly difficult, as wider normative distributions not only persisted within the movement, but were often overlooked and rendered unaccountable because of the idea that their space was 'autonomous' and 'outside' of such structures.

In the first instance, it will be argued that the very assertion that Occupy (in) London was *structureless* which was meant to embody radical democratic aims (i.e. an open, unqualified inclusion with horizontal leaderlessness), unintentionally and paradoxically resulted in the very hierarchies and *pre*clusions (i.e. exclusion in advance) that Occupy was trying to avoid. Adopting a stance of 'inclusivity for the sake of it' made structurelessness a democratic virtue, but ultimately led to a situation in which the movement was collectively unable to address hierarchies and preclusions, or to hold them to account (which Freeman 2013 calls 'the tyranny of structurelessness'). Thus, in the second instance, I will employ activists' self-criticisms to show how such a loose definition of the movement's collective identity and politics also undermined the movement's symbolic efficiency and made it easier for Occupy to be dismissed as 'non-sense'. Insofar as Occupy resembled the loose and unclear organisation which the police order used to dismiss the movement, it was harder to intervene in the distribution of the sensible, and easier to move it along as 'nothing to see here'. Furthermore, I argue, this symbolic inefficiency is indicative of a problematic extension of wider anti-collective norms of libertarianism and individualism, demonstrating a cross-over between anarchist streams within the movement and neoliberal theory, as well as demonstrating the foreclosure of possibility during the post-crash reassertion of neoliberal normativity.

It will be concluded that there is a need for the left to rediscover the symbolic efficiency and authority of collective politics, but that this cannot be achieved as it is on the political right (which can find its constitutive ideas of objectivity in preclusions based upon imagined histories of 'nation' or 'race'). The left simply cannot find its authority in such an undemocratic and authoritarian manner which simply precludes any positions which don't fit into the universal vision, and instead needs to adopt a position of *negotiated exclusion* which would allow movements to remain democratic (i.e. include the multiple inequalities and injustices expressed by 'the 99%') while at the same time being symbolically efficient and acting with collective authority. Part of this involves seeing inclusion less as a *tokenistic* gesture (i.e. a matter of diverse representation of different people and identities) and more a matter of a fundamental principle of democratic formation in negotiating what the movement actually stands for: taking on capitalism and neoliberalism, but also colonialism, imperialism, white privilege, patriarchy, heteronormativity, ableism ... Too often, those who (correctly) identify the problem on the left in complying with postmodern symbolic inefficiency have conflated this list of social structures with 'identity politics'. In contrast, however, I start from the position that there is a fundamental difference between, on the one hand, a problematic individualised performance of political identity – which, I might add, *includes* those Marxists who see themselves as 'above' identity politics – and, on the other, creating an intersectional democratic movement that collectively intervenes in distributions of inequality and injustice (or 'the 99%').

Inclusivity for the sake of it

Arguably the greatest legacy of the Occupy movement has been its popularisation of the slogan 'we are the 99%'. Deconstructing this statement, 'we' can be said to imply a collective politics which might overcome wider individualism and symbolic inefficiency, allowing those drawn to the movement to 'appear to ourselves even if we say "we" knowing there are divisions and differences among us that we express and that the term 'we' expresses' (Dean

2012: 212). By suggesting that the movement was a collective, in other words, 'we are the 99%' gave Occupy the potential to invoke a 'we' in the post-crash moment of 'those of us opposed' (ibid. 2002: 2). The second part, 'the 99%', then defined what this 'we' stands for. It highlights at the same time a profound democratic deficit *and* a socio-economic inequality which had been demonstrated and highlighted by the crisis. It is therefore incorrect to see 'the 99%' as a statistic (as in Dorling 2014), because this was more than 'a sociological statement requiring concrete delineable empirical reference' (Dean 2012: 122) and should instead be understood as an expression of 'capitalism's reliance on fundamental inequality [while it] asserts a collectivity' (ibid. 2011: 88). By declaring that 'we are the 99%', Occupy had the potential to claim a political and democratic authority that challenged post-crash inequality and injustice, while at the same time turning its 'statement into a question: and you[?]' (Holloway 2014: 1072).

And yet despite this potential, there remained tendencies within the movement which began to undermine and ultimately foreclose this possibility. Early signs of a persisting individualism were slippages between using 'I' (*I* am the 99%) and 'we' (*we* are the 99%) and, while Occupy LSX never really adopted the slogan outright, its initial statement (agreed on the first day outside St Paul's) nevertheless attempted to 'define' the movement in similar terms: 'We are of all ethnicities, backgrounds, genders, generations, sexualities, dis/abilities and faiths. We stand together with occupations all over the world' (Occupy London 2015).

Despite starting with 'we', Occupy LSX defined 'the 99%' as a series of ahistorical 'Is', namely, specific groups with specific grievances, which then happened to make up the overall movement. Rather than claiming a collective common identity, instead the emphasis was on the movement being open, inclusionary, and fluid. There were to be no explicit exclusions and no official hierarchies asserting who could or could not be part of Occupy, and this would allow it to prefigure an alternative future society. The movement would be 'outside' of wider structures of inequality and privilege – an autonomous space – whereby its members could organise around principles of disorganisation and structure themselves around principles of structurelessness. Yet, as it slowly became clear, social structures such as class, gender, and race were not only persisting within the ostensibly structureless movement but were collectively being left unchallenged and unaddressed by virtue of this organisational approach.

It was a hot day and Lucy suggested that we hold the interview outside, but our table – which was right next to the railway arches and the bustling Brixton high street – was a very noisy place to try and record our conversation. Yet the setting also seemed to give the conversation an informal and casual air, and Lucy clearly felt comfortable enough to share with me her quite personal experience of joining the Occupy movement from a working-class background.[1] She began recounting to me her perspective on the movement in London:

> We were very good at the beginning of Occupy LSX [at] having a lot of wide representation with a lot of different people. You just have to … look back at the photographs and you can see all sorts of people: people of colour, white people, different genders … so on and so forth. It didn't really happen, so to speak, when it transitioned to 'Occupy London'. The movement was slowly dwindling in London and what you were left with was almost the very middle-class cis-gendered type of environment. And I don't know whether that … I can't judge the intentions … as to whether that's an intentional thing, or whether they were just people who remained with Occupy London and thought it still had some legs to stand on … but sadly that's how it turned out.

For Lucy, while Occupy had certainly not set out to create a 'middle-class cis-gendered type of environment', this had slowly become the case over time, unintentionally extending privileges from wider society. I responded that this was a problem which had been related to me by others as well and asked whether she thought the movement had ever really achieved its aim (as expressed in the initial statement and their interpretation of 'the 99%') of being openly inclusive and horizontal:

> In terms of this idea of 'the 99%' that Occupy Wall Street (and a lot of other Occupiers in the Middle East) has … I think we fall foul of this idea of inclusivity for the sake of it. I think it's probably one of the main problems of Occupy London. Again, although it's espousing great rhetoric, perhaps in practice it was doomed to fail really, because *we were too inclusive*. We weren't equipped to deal with people from all sorts of backgrounds (people who had serious madness problems … mental health problems). We weren't equipped to deal with that. And I think this idea of inclusivity and diversity was a bit of a misnomer for Occupy London. It's a great idea to join and have this intersectional idea of class, gender, race and … you know, whatever else. But it really didn't turn out … that wasn't really the practice of Occupy London unfortunately.

The topic of inclusion and diversity once again sees the return of the 'homeless question' and whether the movement had the resources or capabilities to include and take care of those in need of support; however, Lucy also stretches the problem to what she calls 'inclusivity for the sake of it'. Despite asserting openness as a foundational principle, it simply didn't happen in practice. Despite 'espousing great rhetoric' that Occupy (in) London should be organised on a flexible, open, inclusive, diverse, horizontal, and structureless basis, Lucy explained that it did not succeed in realising these values:

> There definitely was a difference at the time, but I can't work out whether or not these people looked different to me from a kind of working-class background, where I like my Burberry, I like my brands. That's changed

> slowly … but at that point in 2011, when I was someone new coming to these kinds of political organisations, you could see the people were of a particular type. It's going to sound very stereotypical (and I don't mean it to) but the very loose clothes, no branding, a lot of sandals and baggy trousers … but I can't really overgeneralise on that point because there were people there that resembled someone who you wouldn't have thought to have been a devout anarchist or a devout Marxist. People with jeans, sunglasses … There were also people branded in different ways … branded in terms of wearing other protest-activist insignia (May 1968, those types of badges).

On the one hand, then, the fact that Lucy joined the Occupy movement in the first place helps to undermine the broad brush (police order) dismissals of Occupy as a middle-class (petit bourgeois) movement; yet, as she also makes clear, her attempt to be part of the movement was far from straightforward. There was certainly a clash between her identity and the broader collective identity of the movement which, I would suggest, is more than a trivial matter of individual taste (or habitus) and identity politics. Rather, this is evidence of a wider *internal* distribution of voice and appearance within the movement, which would ultimately limit what the movement stood for overall:

> At the time, when we were transitioning from Occupy LSX to Occupy London … a lot of us felt that we weren't being heard or that our views were being excluded and started to break off to have our own meetings about process … 'how the hell do we fix consensus?' … so on and so forth.

Lucy's grievances about the effect of capitalism and neoliberal austerity on the working class should have been one of the central themes of the movement, yet she found her voice and appearance beginning to be ignored and excluded from the broader consensus. As the structureless Occupy movement consolidated and coalesced, it became clear through such marginalisation that it had been unable to gather around the democratic politics of 'the 99%' (as a broad post-crash collection of different grievances, injustices, and inequalities). Instead, some voices and appearances were findings themselves sidelined, while others remained privileged (i.e. were distributed as carrying more authority).

Others also commented on class divisions within the movement, pointing out how those from more privileged backgrounds seemed to possess an added confidence in making their voices heard above others, directly contradicting the ideal that the General Assembly (GA) was a structureless space in which all voices were to be distributed equally:

> The difference is that you have a certain confidence when you're like 'middle class' or something. You've got educated … because there's a

cocky-ness that comes with that, isn't there? Like a confidence within your class: 'oh look, I know how to speak good, you can't fool my lawyer, I've read a few books'. Again, it's arse over tit, because the people who had the money to make the phone calls probably organised it [Occupy LSX] … who already had upbringings which allowed them to have the confidence to make those phone calls to places … probably have contacts from when they were at uni and stuff like this. So, it's completely the other way round.

(Greg)

It's easy for articulate, educationally privileged, middle-class people like me, who actually *enjoy* talking in groups of people.

(James)

Yet this unequal distribution of appearance, voice, and authority within the GA was by no means restricted to class, and this problem perhaps becomes clearer if we focus on gender inequalities and the persistence of patriarchal structures within the movement:

Undoubtedly there was a gender imbalance in the camp. I'm not sure about the movement … but in the camp (I was one of the people who stayed in the camp) by the end, there were five women there. People would argue and debate … then you would realise that there was one person – often a man, but not always – who would just not allow things to move forward. And it would be out of … the most generous thing I can think of it that they would genuinely think they were smarter than you. That 'you would just not understand', y'know? It was very … it's going on until this day with the GA model.

(2014, int. 10)

It was quite hard work, to the extent … I mean, I think it's interesting when one looks at feminism in that context, because I think there is still a tendency for a certain amount of dismissal of women – particularly younger women. It's quite complicated in meetings to get your voice heard … you can sit around waving your hands for ages and the facilitator doesn't notice you.

(Jenny)

A lot of these white cis-gendered men typically tended to be old Marxists, or perhaps people who only give a shit about one cause, which is the idea that these bankers are to blame for everything that's going wrong in the world. And with that, as the movement slowly crumbled, you started to see this concentration of those types of politics and those types of

> 'physicalities' of people … those identities. It's something that's been very difficult to penetrate.
>
> (Lucy)

The problem of gender inequality demonstrates clearly how the very structurelessness of the GA actually made the organisation more vulnerable to unequal distributions of authority and privilege. Men could make their voices and appearances heard and seen at the behest of others and therefore held greater sway over what the movement should (or should not) stand for, using their authority to prevent an argument progressing along a line they did not agree with, and claiming superior understanding while dismissing others in the process. Open and horizontal discussions within the GA were therefore susceptible to subtle exclusions and distributions, with the facilitator sometimes overlooking the contribution made by women within the group. This is not to say that there weren't attempts to address this imbalance through perfecting GA mechanisms:

> I think we were certainly conscious of it. We did sort of try to counter that by effective facilitation. Reflecting on it a bit more, it does tend to be men that monopolise the time and speak for a long time … and there have been occasions where men have been aggressive, even overtly aggressive really (not often, but it only has to happen once to put someone off). Women don't hog the space in the same way as blokes do and they don't take it so personally if the facilitator tries to bring discussion to a close or invite others to contribute.
>
> (2014, int. 1)

Owing to a persistent normative distribution of roles, voices, and appearances within the movement, patriarchal privilege (like class privilege) was inadvertently maintained, relegating women and feminism to the margins of identity cliques. As a statement on democracy, 'the 99%' *had* to include an attack on structures of patriarchy, and yet – while there were certainly feminists within the movement – the unequal distribution within the 'structureless' GA meant that this was never explicitly adopted as part of a collective intervention and resistance.

Relying as I was on snowball sampling, I noticed very early on that the majority of the activists with whom I was put in contact were (more often than not) white men. However, whenever I brought this up there was always a consistent explanation that this concentration had only happened 'over time' and that Occupy in the beginning had not been like this:

> As time goes on, it tends to be the same people. It's a lot less diverse now. For example, it's mainly white (I'm thinking of all the people I see on a regular basis, it's mainly white). It's still mixed up in terms of

> socio-economic … if you can put people in those kinds of categories. It's probably fair to say there is more men.
>
> (2014, int. 1)

> [Occupy London is] very white … but I think, if there's any kind of predominance, that's not to do with the movement but the still remaining patriarchal structures within society which give rise to these unfortunately natural remaining structures.
>
> (2014, int. 4)

Such concerns over the white-washing of the Occupy movement have also been reflected in academic analyses of the movement (particularly in the American case). For example, while not wanting to 'dismiss or tear down what is so importantly positive and requisite about what Occupy represents', Campbell (2011: 42) raises concerns about the lack of inclusion of African-Americans in the movement, and what this meant for the democratic credentials of 'the 99%'. To reiterate, this is a far more important issue than tokenistic diversity; it is a fundamentally political matter of whether the movement identified with black politics and addressed the anti-democratic legacies of white privilege. As Campbell and others have pointed out, however, while capitalism had long been exploiting and oppressing BAME populations around the globe, it was only when middle-class white people began to be affected after the crash that the public seemed to take notice.

What's more, as I briefly touched upon in terms of the language of 'riots' in Chapter 2, the racialised distribution of the sensible within the city means that a movement which is predominantly white can appear and make a noise with relative impunity and with less risk of reprisal than a black movement (such as Black Lives Matter). This means that Occupy as a movement for socio-economic and democratic justice simply had to take on these issues and make a collective assertion that black politics should be seen and heard, but this possibility was foreclosed by the fact that 'black people – and by extension, people of colour – [did] not feel that Occupy Wall Street [was] a safe space for them to raise issues of *internal* white privilege to Occupiers' (Campbell 2011: 43; emphasis in the original). This failure was in addition to a further oversight of colonial legacies of inequality, which was a criticism largely raised by indigenous activists, despite the crossovers between indigenous politics and the Occupy movement, such as a 'broad-based opposition to economic and political marginalisation, strong sub-currents of environmentalism and direct democracy, and antipathy towards state violence' (Barker 2012: 327; see also Brady and Antoine 2013).

Structural inequalities, hierarchies, and preclusions, therefore, not only persisted, but remained largely unresolved within the structureless space of the GA. In addition, whenever there were attempts to address such inequalities – such as the 'Safer Spaces Policy' (Occupy London 2017) brought in to challenge racism, ageism, homophobia, sexism, transphobia, ableism, as well as prejudices based on ethnicity, nationality, class, gender, gender presentation, language ability, asylum status, or religious affiliation – *this remained at the level of interactions between individuals rather than a collective redefinition to address these structures in wider society.* Of course, it was absolutely necessary to insist on these rules as principles of process, insisting that participants should be 'aware of the space you take up and the positions and privileges you bring' as well as the democratic need to 'give each person the time and space to speak … in large groups, or for groups using facilitation: raise your hand to speak'; but this did not go far enough in reorganising fundamental structures that needed to be addressed by 'the 99%'. They remained, in other words, the purview of individuals, the responsibility of identity groups and cliques (which then loosely made up the 'we' of 'the 99%'), rather than structural inequalities and injustices which were inseparable from the movement's collective democratic intervention.

The tyranny of structurelessness

Using one of his characteristic turns of phrase, Greg described to me the persistence of hierarchy and unequal distribution within the GA, pointing out that 'you can tell who the leaders are, they're the ones going around saying there are no leaders!' This diagnosis seemed to bear an uncanny resemblance to what Jo Freeman has described as 'the tyranny of structurelessness' which begins from the premise that there is simply 'no such thing as a structureless group' and that the very *idea* of structurelessness can act as a smokescreen for 'unquestioned hegemony' (2013: 232). For Freeman, the very notion that structures and distributions can be overcome by simply asserting that 'we are now in a structureless space' – i.e. autonomous and located outside of wider societal inequalities – creates a problematic situation in which structures become overlooked and are able to persist with impunity. Subsequently, this creates an opportunity for tyranny, because 'when informal elites are combined with a myth of structurelessness there can be no attempt to put limits on their use of power … it becomes capricious' (ibid.: 237). Without a formal mechanism of checks and balances, self-effacing elites are rendered unaccountable as notions of structurelessness allow them to act freely. This then has a further impact on the movement's overall politics, as any negotiation over what constitutes their collective democratic intervention is 'all too often smothered beneath the frenetic urgency of actions, by the sheer momentum of our inherited structures of oppression, and silence by loud chauvinist voices who took up too much space' (Maharawal 2013: 180).

To put it another way, because of the idea that Occupy had established a structureless and autonomous space, those who couldn't get their politics heard or seen found themselves excluded from the movement and separated out into cliques and fractures. As Occupy (in) London inevitably consolidated, so it also divided and undermined the possibility of a democratic solidarity based upon 'the 99%':

> So many conflicts emerged within Occupy and so many rivalries and so many people wouldn't work together anymore. I kind of think one of the biggest problems is that we should have participated much more with Occupy [LSX] and I think the reason many of us didn't is because we didn't come from an activist background and it was dominated by some of the bigger characters and personalities that were involved in the movement – who were often very good, open-minded people – but at the same time, there was the hierarchical relationship around these characters and these figureheads that drew the movement away from being this kind of horizontal autonomous model it should have been.
>
> (2014, int. 4)

As the activists became disillusioned with the consolidation of the GA (which was seen as being synonymous with Occupy LSX) conflicts and rivalries began to emerge and the movement fractured and split into various political cliques. Contrary to its goal to achieve structurelessness, clear hierarchies began to form around 'the bigger characters and personalities' or those socially distributed as carrying more authority. Subsequently, many became all too aware of the tyrannical contradictions at play in their attempt to establish a structureless organisation:

> Anything that tries to be a horizontal movement is going to give rise to people riffing a bit louder and constructing a narrative out of it or manipulating it for different ends. Because there are obviously a lot of different political factions … you'd be having a General Assembly on, you know, the problem of food at St Paul's or food donation … and it would get hijacked by someone saying: 'you know, we should all be supporting the Socialist Worker Party' … or something like that. So, in terms of its definition there was totally this clash of interests.
>
> (2014, int. 4)

Unwilling to compromise on their own politics, such characters not only made decision-making processes extremely difficult and tiresome, but – by dominating discussion and negotiations – also foreclosed the possibility of 'the 99%' being collectively defined by a politics which wasn't their own. It was also found (perhaps unsurprisingly) that the public simply weren't interested in taking part in dry internal arguments about where the money should be spent, who should run the social media, or where the movement were going to get food. As James put it to me after the impromptu assembly outside St Paul's:

> Activism is theatre and activism is about attracting energy and being entertaining … and if you're going to do something in a public space and attract people in, then you have to put up a tent, a stage, logos … it's all *identity and iconography.* And the problem is, when you start talking about 'finance' and long-drawn-out decisions in public spaces, then people walk away (and we saw that at the end).

It did feel odd that the public was invited to take part in the GA and given a say about what the movement should be spending money on, yet this had to be permitted because of the movement's insistence on open inclusion and horizontalism. The only thing that this achieved, however, was to put people off. Thus, even the mechanisms which had been put in place to facilitate the movement's structurelessness became the target of criticism, including 'jargon' – such as 'working groups' or 'general assemblies' which 'make us feel part of the group but it also excluded other people' (Ollie) – and 'process' – like the gestures being used at the assemblies 'where everyone was doing 'wavy hands' and all the rest of it … which appeals to some and feels exclusive to others … a circle which is very inclusive to those in it can feel very exclusive to those outside of it'(2014, int. 3).

In addition to practical and internal decision-making preventing an extension of the movement, however, it also led to smaller working groups claiming the authority to make strategic decisions without accountability to the movement as a whole. But as Jenny described it, this was less of a power-grab and more of an organic transition driven by a pragmatic urgency to actually make some decisions:

> I was on both the Finance Working Group and Process Working Group (both of whom were roundly disliked and both of which were considered to 'control' the movement). Where, in fact, most of us on it thought quite the reverse, that we were *serving* the movement, that it was quite a thankless task … [a] painstaking job with quite a lot of responsibility. It's fine, I don't mind about it, but it's the opposite of taking control of things … it was trying to get things into some sort of coherence that people could gather around.

As the movement fractured, such groups took it upon themselves to make decisions on behalf of 'Occupy London', feeling the need to try and pull the movement together around some sort of centre, before it dissipated completely. Thus, for all the desire to avoid 'being controlled' by others and to form a disciplined organisation, the tyranny of structurelessness and the attempt to establish an autonomous organisation that could prefigure horizontality, open inclusivity, equality, and democracy resulted instead in the emergence of exclusions and hierarchies that were able to assert themselves with impunity. The structureless GA, in other words, became just as exclusive and hierarchical as a more formal movement might have, yet without any process of accountability. So, while it may seem virtuous to open up decision-making 'to all' or establish a set of mechanisms to facilitate unqualified openness, these also become exclusive and in this case prevented the qualitative extension of the movement beyond itself. The upshot was that, as well as simply failing to establish a structureless 'democratic' movement of 'the 99%', Occupy (in) London also failed to achieve 'some sort of coherence that people could gather around'.

As many Occupys as there are occupiers

Yet many within the London movement expressed a clear commitment to the unqualified openness and fluidity of their organisation, arguing that 'one of the strengths of Occupy was the diversity of voices and the diversity of opinions' (2013, int. 2), taking this as evidence of their democratic credentials. Subsequently, individualism and symbolic inefficiency was linked directly to the movement's politics:

> It's like, all down to *individualised opinion* … but I think that gives us a wider branch. Like, technically we kind of spread across every audience. In a sense, like, we have ex-bankers who are here, we have my kind of age group (like young people) and we have, like, the 'older white male', the 'older black male', we have 'older women' … we technically could branch out to pretty much anyone.
>
> (2012, int. 5)

Evidence that the movement was 'democratic' was therefore tied to the tokenistic inclusion of diverse individuals and the diverse cacophony of voices within the GA. In particular, the 'Occupy Nomads' at Mile End were especially defensive of these principles, and they certainly were more diverse than the activists at Finsbury Square, having a range of nationalities (including individuals from Ireland, France and the Ivory Coast) as well as ethnicity and race. There was also a wide span of political ideologies at Mile End, as revealed by one activist when I asked him how he got into activism in the first place:

> Well, I first got involved in politics when I was 18 … I was anti-Europe/European Union … I found myself getting involved in the BNP and things … I ran a few council elections for them in the south-west region … and I was the leader of their youth group whilst I was at uni.
>
> (2012, int. 10)

Having been an active member of the populist and racist right-wing nationalists of the British National Party, it seemed clear to me that his politics must have taken a dramatic turn given that he then joined the ostensibly left-wing Occupy movement. But when I suggested that the BNP was the complete opposite of Occupy, he looked puzzled:

> I don't think it is. I think when you get down to it … as a nationalist you're not very pro-establishment … and nationalists favour distributionist policies … We're all affected regardless of our ideological leanings. Our economics change everything: it's under everything and controls everything. And Occupy just struck me as a movement that was, I don't know, willing to accept that fact.
>
> (2012, int. 10)

In this extreme example, the movement's open inclusivity and insistence that it did not define an overall collective identity meant that a right-wing nationalist could join with impunity and claim their racisms to be those of the Occupy movement (something which is clearly at odds with claims for equality, justice, and democracy, but *not* with aims for structurelessness).

It was becoming quite a struggle to talk to the other activists at Mile End. No one seemed to be interested in getting up to go somewhere private for an interview, meaning that – sitting around the campfire – conversations were often interrupted by the others. The group became particularly fired up whenever I asked questions about who should or should not be included within the movement. From the perspective of this group (which had allowed a member of the BNP to protest with them), Occupy should be considered a melting pot of all ideas and identities:

> This movement is not a properly organised advertisement of one idea, its everybody's idea and nobody's idea at the same time, so it's a big pot, like a big soup.
>
> (2012, int. 13)

> Occupy is not standing behind one single issue, it's standing behind overall corruption and deception and non-transparency, so it doesn't care … Occupy's not caring what it's looking at, it's looking at everything, so everyone and anyone can bring information to Occupy and find some groups.
>
> (2012, int. 9)

> If someone gave you a description, Occupy is a *movement of ideas. No one can speak on behalf of Occupy, no person can represent Occupy* … Because you see some people who have been at St Paul's have been asking us to vote for a candidate, but we're not a political party. No one can represent Occupy. Occupy is a movement, it's an idea that's completely abstract. So basically, it does not exist … anyone can claim to be an occupier.
>
> (2012, int. 12)

Complete fluidity and a lack of any collective definition meant that 'anyone can claim to be an occupier' and therefore that this movement was radically democratic. Yet, as I outlined in the previous section, not only was it far from the case that this approach prevented 'anyone from speaking on behalf of Occupy', but such a celebration of structurelessness was precisely that which made unwanted exclusions and unaccountable hierarchies inevitable.

Subsequently, not everyone agreed that such a lack of definition was something to be celebrated about the Occupy movement. Shaun, for example, despite coming across as a friendly and approachable guy, clearly experienced painful feelings of remorse and regret whenever he recalled the Occupy movement. As our interview moved onto the challenges of organisation, therefore, his face visibly dropped – he knew exactly what I was talking about and had experienced this first-hand as part of one of the working groups:

> We had a second round of funding which … it was in the middle of this big fight and this guy said: 'well, if [he] is involved, I'm blocking it!' It was five grand which we could have done a lot from, but we didn't do it because of an internal scrap. So, the problem is not with money, the problem is with us not taking the opportunities which are presented to us because of rather petty internal politics.

Shaun paused before offering another example in which such internal divisions had undermined the movement's ability to affirm and manage their collective appearance. Because social media platforms, as 'neoliberal technologies of the self' (Mirowski 2013: 328), tended to be designed for single administrators (or small groups of administrators), individuals who were unaccountable in the structureless movement could problematically wield greater control than others over the overall identity that was being conveyed online:

> Like, we had a real problem with Twitter, because one geezer from our gang … used [our working group] name, he said … well it was when Julian Assange went into the Ecuadorean embassy and some people, some occupiers, were in favour of him (I thought he was alright, I didn't have any strong views). But some guy from [our working group] just had a real issue with him and used … made a really stupid comment on Twitter about 'we at [working group] are not rape apologists'. And you know, with Twitter, you've got about 121 characters and you can do it in 20 seconds … and we lost half our hits in one day. You know, that was kind of the beginning of the end really, when I look back at it.

The problem I want to highlight here has less to do with who was 'right' – whether Assange, who was accused of rape but had yet to be convicted, should or should not have been advocated by the Occupy movement – and more about the ability of individuals within a structureless space to see it as a democratic virtue to allow individuals the liberty to do what they want, and to wield unaccountable control over the movement's appearance and political stance.

The next time we met, Shaun invited me back to his house and the conversation once again returned to the subject of collective organisation. I was keen to see if the two years which had passed since his altercation with the working group had softened his bitterness towards the movement. 'I don't know what *Daily Mail* readers think about when they hear the name 'Occupy', he answered indirectly, 'when I hear it, it arouses very contradictory emotions because it was so *impotent* in some ways. As a great big movement that fractured so quickly, it was such a microcosm of … all the stupidity of human being came out in Occupy. All the really stupid fractionalisation and finger-pointing and pettiness'. He gave me an example:

> Someone friendly who had been involved in the past said: 'Oh, how's things going with Occupy London?' and one of the people on our team said: 'I don't have anything to do with "Occupy London"'. And the way she was using the term was a little group of people – six people or something – who she'd had a personal spat with (with her group of six or ten people). From outside of those two groups, that was just a completely mindless thing … people outside are asking about Occupy London not 'Occupy London TM'; but she was so buried in her own little thing … and that's kind of when I gave up hope.

Such individualism coupled with a libertarian aversion to committing oneself to a collective disciplined organisation which might be able to appear with symbolic efficiency, did not lead to a radically democratic movement, but to factionalism and a lack of definition:

> I think Occupy has spurred off a lot of different groups and you get people saying they're 'Occupy' … but then other people within the movement will go: 'No! You're not Occupy!' … and then other people again will go: 'No! You're not allowed to say that!' or 'No! You're not', you know?
>
> (Felicity)

> Because we've basically … there's 40 Occupys around the UK, they have their conferences … and I'm just getting really fed up of how people have become really like: 'we're Occupy London' … and some people are like: 'They're not!' I bring all these contacts from different organisations, and I'm like: 'we need to work together' and they're like 'oh, they might try and co-opt the movement' and that's not what it's about!
>
> (2012, int. 16)

> I think Occupy is a bit of … not really defined itself properly. And I think that the potential it's got is quite good and I think that all this other … the impression it gives the public is probably not a very good one.
>
> (Nick)

While not wanting to deny the democratic importance of being part of a diverse movement, therefore, these activists were becoming increasingly frustrated with a tendency for those within the movement to resist being included within an overarching identity that didn't perfectly fit their current worldview. There was a tacit agreement that Occupy should avoid 'defining themselves properly' and that there should be 'as many Occupys as occupiers' which undermined their ability to act and appear collectively:

> Diversity is difficult. It's difficult because … it's important (and I'm really up for diversity) but it's also quite hard at times to make things happen. Because people will take their opinion of, like: 'but this is *me* and I don't want to go further than that, and I don't want to sometimes compromise'. And I think it's because we were born into a society like that … [which is] very individualistic.
>
> (Julia)

Such individualism was directly detrimental to Occupy (in) London's symbolic efficiency, and ultimately made it easier for the wider police order to designate them as incomprehensible 'non-sense'. In such a context of disorganisation and in-fighting, it became much more straightforward for commentators (politicians, experts, journalists, etc.) to normatively claim that Occupy didn't know what it stood for, didn't know what it was doing, and that the activists were just facetious kids. And yet symbolic inefficiency continued to be seen by many as a democratic virtue of the movement, with inconsistency being championed as a clear indicator of the movement's commitment to inclusivity and horizontalism.

Rather than intervening with a degree of collective authority, therefore, the activists complained that Occupy (in) London eventually became 'more a battle of personal identities and personal wills' (Lucy), with fracturing and division as people 'gravitated towards each other in little cliques, and two years on they have … people have stayed together in little sections' (Greg). Greg felt particularly strongly that the insistence of avoiding solid definitions was detrimental to the movement.

While sitting on a log in the woods outside the Cat Hill environmental camp, he explained:

> This is the problem. 'We are the 99%' … but the 99% don't agree on what needs to be done to overcome the 1%. The very least is to agree to have lots of different ways to oppose the 1% … but that wasn't something that was kind of suggested.

The goal of the Cat Hill protest camp was to protect the woodland from a housing development which was threatening to encroach on the boundaries of its planning permission. Every now and then, a builder would pass by on the other side of the barriers which separated the housing estate from the trees and the blockade. The camp itself was criss-crossed with 1-foot-high blue fences in a bid to keep the endangered Great Crested newts from wandering onto the construction site:

> I mean, I never heard of this 'Deleuze and Guattari' (everyone's name-dropping them at the moment). And it's like: 'yeah, it's all about not defining and just being really fluid'. It's like, this is just an apologist … an apology for a lack of commitment, you know? No surprise that people within a recession are using them as a crutch and not committed as much to the movement as you'd wish. In fact, the irony is they're there doing lectures on the definition of people who said: 'Let's not be defined'!

He laughed before explaining further that this didn't necessarily mean he was in favour of the collective name of 'Occupy London' which, as he had made clear in previous interviews, was a specific former St Paul's group that he despised. Because of the structurelessness of the movement, this group had been able to monopolise the name 'Occupy London' and this had given its members a certain amount of undemocratic control over the movement's appearance:

> When you have that umbrella name of 'Occupy London' that was going to mediate on behalf of the two camps, you're suddenly taking all the space between those two camps as well. I mean, if it was Occupy *City of* London, it would mean Cheapside and Moorgate were not part of that … but it was *Occupy London*.

And yet, while this experience had made Greg cautious of collective identities which could be hijacked by small groups of self-nominated vanguards, he nevertheless insisted that some sort of collective symbolic organisation was necessary (even if this meant a certain level of exclusion):

> Towards the end of Occupy I was saying: 'you've got to get your identity right first'. You work out who's 'in' (whatever 'in' is) then, once you've worked out who is 'in', those people can decide the process that is being used. It doesn't have to be written down, it can be done very organically. Then, once you've decided process, you can decide on things like finance (how we spend our money depends on that organic use).

For Greg, getting the identity 'right' by deciding 'who' and 'what' is 'in' should have given the movement a constitutive base upon which to establish collective authority and decision-making. While this would have made the organisation exclusive, it would then at least have been in a position to claim a shared authority as well as to define the movement properly, enabling it to appear with consistency and symbolic efficiency.

The decline in symbolic efficiency, as I outlined in Chapter 1, is argued by Žižek to be part of a wider trend in postmodern society of encouraging individualism and flexible identities which never have to compromise to accommodate wider, collective ideals. The individual can hold fast to their own views, changing and altering their identity only when they see fit to do so, never having to relinquish their identity project or beliefs towards a collective cause. The libertarian streak within anarchism, which has been adopted by new social movements more generally, therefore precludes a disciplined collective definition of a movement's politics, opting instead for the symbolic *in*efficiency of open inclusivity and horizontality. Not only does this make it more difficult to make their politics appear consistently, but it makes it easier for their resistance to be foreclosed, dismissed, marginalised, and policed as 'non-sense' – irrational, unreasonable, chaotic, disorganised, naïve, idealistic – by the wider distribution of the sensible. Their symbolic inefficiency is showcased as 'proof' by normative champions that there can be no alternative and that they, in comparison, have clear and careful, strong and stable plans to address the crisis.

Symbolic inefficiency

Such individualised anti-collective norms that view politics simply as a matter of individual whim and choice – rather than as collective commitment to an Idea – share their libertarianism with a neoliberal doctrine that also sees individual choice and flexibility as permitting greater liberty than do collective institutions or organisations (which, no matter how progressive, are framed as necessarily oppressive and leading down the road to serfdom (Hayek 1979). Thus, not only did symbolic inefficiency create the organisational difficulties described in the previous section, but it also extended post-crash norms and presuppositions, re-establishing them as 'common sense'. Occupy (in) London shared some of the central premises of neoliberalism that seek to undermine collective institutions in favour of individual freedom, foreclosing the possibility of the movement to not only organise *against* such norms, but even extending their redistribution after the crisis. The organisational problem of symbolic inefficiency, as one activist put it, was that individuals within the movement simply 'didn't want to be told what to do about anything' and, for him, this could be directly linked to:

> the whole postmodernist nonsense [that] has driven the overwhelming majority of people into *hedonism* … a libertarian narcissistic approach that has historical strands within some forms of anarchism … and therefore people are very, very reluctant, it would seem, within the progressive political groups, to commit to anything.
>
> (2013, int. 7)

This lack of commitment is characteristic of Žižek's dual definition of postmodern capitalism (outlined in Chapter 1), which involves an injunction for individuals to 'enjoy!' while at the same time keeping them sufficiently supple and flexible as individual identities for future opportunities to consume. Such a decline in symbolic efficiency played out within the Occupy movement via calls for unqualified and open inclusivity, horizontalism, and structurelessness, coupled with an individualist and libertarian insistence that personal beliefs and choices should never be challenged, changed, excluded, or forced to compromise by wider commitments to a collective organisation. One activist encapsulated this attitude perfectly:

> To be honest, I haven't got any political kind of viewpoint, I think that … I am not a socialist, I'm not a communist, I'm none of that … I just don't agree with it. I think we need a *new thing*. I just don't agree with any of it.
>
> (2012, int. 4)

Such a lack of ideological commitment appeared to be rife within the Occupy movement in London, but one of the central themes which really highlighted this animosity towards collective definition and organisation, was a heated disagreement about whether Occupy should accept its designation as an 'anti-capitalist' movement. For some, such a label was problematic, because despite being a *very* loose and flexible signifier, it risked excluding people who did not personally identify as anti-capitalist:

> not everyone in the movement will label themselves as 'anti-capitalist' and also I think fundamentally saying that 'we're anti-capitalist' disenfranchises a lot of people.
>
> (Felicity)

Others were adamant that they themselves were *not* anti-capitalist, but that this didn't contradict their inclusion in the movement, because one's politics was simply a matter of personal preference:

> So, we have been described as 'anti-capitalist' protestors … personally, I'm not anti-capitalist. But I believe there are flaws in the system and those are those which personally I am addressing.
>
> (2012, int. 12)

Even something as broad and apparently relevant to the post-crash egalitarian and democratic politics of 'the 99%' as 'anti-capitalism', therefore, was deemed too restrictive, thus once again demonstrating the unwillingness of individuals to compromise or alter their personal beliefs in order to commit in the direction of a collective organisation. This impasse was described by many as frustrating:

> We need to appreciate that there are going to be people with widely different theoretical and practical views as to how to challenge the state and capitalism. Occupy London may have mentioned the words 'anti-capitalism' a couple of times ... but it really wasn't an anti-capitalist movement. So, people like me, who slowly over time became more about: 'hey, actually there's this great ringing thing called "capitalism" and we're not challenging it' ... we were kind of excluded from that.
>
> (Lucy)

> Like, the thing that struck me is the amount of people that will say: 'yeah, we know capitalism is flawed, but what's the alternative?' You don't have to convince them its flawed, they *know* it's flawed, it's just: 'what's the alternative?' And when you say, 'well, we're not here to say we've got an alternative, we're here to say, look, can we find an alternative then? You know: and then you talk to us, we talk to you, everyone talks to each other ... it's not like we have the answer!' And some people get that ... but then they lost it really quickly because ... I don't know, if it's something to do with human nature, or if you can say its *consumeristic culture*, but certain people talk about it like they're going to change their electric or gas supplier: it's like, 'so, what's your rate? What's your policy? Yeah ok, I'm behind you, yeah, yeah'. Like, fucking completely consumeristically!
>
> (2012, int. 3)

Rather than a collective solidarity and commitment around an idea which the movement could cohere to, anti-capitalism – as feminism, as class politics, as anti-racism, as decolonisation – were seen to be individualised identity choices among others. Thus, activists were not only hesitant to commit to this politics as part of a collective project, but to *any* wider politics which might limit their individual choice or liberty.

This problematic aversion to collectivity has been identified in social theory. As Butler has argued in the past, for instance, the problem with establishing collective 'universal' identities – i.e. an identity that is assumed to represent everyone in a group – is risky for the left because it presupposes that there is some essential characteristic shared by those involved (which risks excluding people who do not fit into that category). Therefore, while recognising that collective identity 'has its purposes', Butler argued that it 'denies ... internal complexity and indeterminacy' and only 'constitutes itself through the exclusion of some part of the constituency that it simultaneously seeks to represent' (2006: 194). We might think, for example, of attempts to assert what 'the 99%' stood for as excluding those who suffered most from democratic deficit and socio-economic inequality (e.g. the working class, women, BAME groups, etc.).

Yet in her 1999 foreword to *Gender Trouble*, Butler appears to soften her aversion to universal identities:

> I have been compelled to revise some of my positions in *Gender Trouble* by virtue of my own political engagements. In the book, I tend to conceive of the claim of 'universality' in exclusively negative and exclusionary terms. However, I came to see the term had important strategic use precisely as a non-substantial and open-ended category … I came to understand how the assertion of universality can be proleptic and performative, conjuring a reality that does not yet exist, and holding out the possibility for a convergence of cultural horizons that have not yet been met.
> (2006: xviii)

So, while maintaining a certain prefigurative flavour, Butler nevertheless suggests that such collective identities can be useful, insofar as there are *performative* and hold a strategic use for democratic movements. This may be to risk a certain level of exclusion, but so long as such boundaries of exclusion remain flexible – 'non-substantial and open-ended' – then the possibility remains that such exclusions can be *negotiated*. In her own words, 'without the presupposition of a goal of unity, which is, in either case, always instituted at a conceptual level, provisional unities might emerge in the context of concrete actions that have purposes other than the articulation of identity' (2006: 21). Through concrete organisational actions (such as occupying space) a collective organisation can be created, without *precluding* (excluding in advance) those who should (democratically) be part of it. Žižek agrees, arguing that the universal can 'simultaneously open up and sustain the space for questioning these inclusions/exclusions, for renegotiating the limits of inclusion/exclusion as part of the ongoing ideologico-political struggle for hegemony' (2000: 101). Or as one activist put it:

> There's this whole kind of slow process of actually learning about everyone's background and sort of getting together on our common goals – what we want; the common causes – the causes that bring us together.
> (2012, int. 16)

Conclusion: negotiating exclusion

In order to be a democratic movement representing equality and justice, the movement of 'the 99%' had to include many different politics: anti-capitalism and environmentalism, sure, but it also had to collectively address histories of structural privilege (e.g. class, race, colonialism, patriarchy, heteronormativity, and ableism). Occupy needed to explicitly consolidate around these politics in order to create a clear intervention and provide the basis for a collective authority, but as it was, the attempt to address these structures by insisting on structurelessness, instead led to a *undemocratic and unaccountable consolidation that precluded many politics which make up 'the 99%'*. In order to be symbolically efficient, organisations inevitably reach the point where they become exclusive, but for movements on the left, this must happen in a *democratic* and *accountable* manner, rather than simply insisting that open inclusivity and horizontality will prefigure the change they want to see in the world.

What the discussion above demonstrates, is that this simply cannot happen when activists insist on structurelessness as a democratic and egalitarian organising principle. Not only does this render the movement unable to make decisions and easier to dismiss as 'non-sense', but it allows the very inequalities and social structures it was attempting to challenge to persist anyway, rendering them unaccountable and unaddressed. By repeating wider societal distributions of who possessed the ability to speak and to be seen, much of the politics of 'the 99%' – as I demonstrated through the examples of class, gender, and race – remained marginalised within the movement's overall politics. Such resistance was instead reduced to cliques and identity groups, who were freely allowed to choose between what they believed in, rather than committing to a central and collective political ideal of 'the 99%' which directly incorporated these politics. Yet this is a subcultural tendency that some have traced back to the alter-globalisation movements of the late 1990s, pointing out how 'activists in the USA have yet to effectively incorporate many lessons from global justice activism including the need for a global analysis and strategy as well as greater sensitivity to how consensus practices can exclude people most harmed by the structures the movement opposes' (Smith and Gidden 2012: 288).

What's more, the persistence of wider norms of individual liberty, anti-collective libertarianism, and symbolic inefficiency, although a source of frustration for many within the movement, also indicated a problematic extension of the presuppositions of neoliberal capitalism. Committed to non-commitment, the libertarianism of the neo-anarchist left extends the common sense of the libertarianism of the neoliberal right, who use such ideas to justify rule by the market and plutocracy. Thus, the aim of Occupy to 'change the world without taking power' is an approach than can only lead to foreclosure, as this process is 'facilitated by significant ideological resonance between neoanarchism and neoliberalism' (Taylor 2013: 729). Situated and distributed by their context, it was simply too 'easy to recognise individual interests as the only 'real' ones' because 'the social world has been stripped of the institutions on which the possibility of collective affiliations and futures depended' (Boltanski and Chiapello 2007: 533).

As has been argued by Jodi Dean, 'a politics that includes everything and everyone … in my view, this is not politics … politics involves division' (2006: xxi). Therefore, rather than attempting to incorporate 'everyone and everything' – but also recognising that the left cannot draw on the populist racism and nationalist preclusions that underpin authority on the right – it is my contention that such movements would be better off adopting *negotiated exclusion* as an organising principle. Drawing collective boundaries and disciplining their aesthetic appearance, such an approach also avoids *pre*-cluding often marginalised voices and politics by remaining open to negotiation over where exclusions should be made. Instead of a tyranny of structurelessness, such an organisation could then qualitatively extend through reflexivity and accountability, going beyond relying on the willingness of individuals to alter their personal views. Or in Lucy's words:

> If we're ever going to achieve in a struggle, it can't just be a single issue for the people who are fighting it – it's got to be expanded somehow – but central to that is the idea of checking privilege.

Such alterations *can* bring about the collective authority and symbolic efficiency needed to make 'non-sense' appear, while also maintaining democratic principles of justice and equality. As the same time, this means moving away from the popular 'anti-institutional style of participatory democracy and self-expression for both real democracy and radical capitalist critique' because this 'undermines political power – and ultimately results in less progress towards participatory democracy as the movement becomes less relevant and less able to bring about social change' (Kreiss and Tufekci 2013: 164). While the left quite rightly ties itself up in knots over questions of equality and democracy, the argument that these aims require structurelessness risks placing such politics in a position of ineffective, easily dismissed, marginal authenticity at a time when what we really need is an empowered common movement for change. We cannot think about organisation without thinking about identity (and vice versa); furthermore, the tactic of occupation – in order to force through a 'non-sense' alternative – simply cannot be endlessly open and instead must be backed by a consistent identity and aesthetic. As Occupy (in) London demonstrated, insisting on 'inclusivity for the sake of it' will not bring about progression towards democracy, justice, and equality, and cannot simply prefigure an alternative society into being.

Note

1 For more detail on the use of public interview settings, see Sinha and Back (2014).

4 This is what democracy looks like

Rochester Square Gardens, September 2013

I pulled on the rope which was strung between the main building and the firmly locked gates, upsetting a group of cans suspended next to the front door, which clattered into one another and loudly announced my arrival. After a while, a collie ran out to meet me as a face appeared around the corner of a door-frame which had been roughly cut out of the wall. Once I had introduced myself as a researcher interested in the Occupy movement, she unlocked the gates and invited me in with the caveat: 'you won't find many activists here – we're all hippies'.

The disused garden centre in Camden was situated in the middle of Rochester Square. Before the squatters had acquired the property, the derelict space had mostly served as an impromptu site for shelter and occasional drug use, but they assured me it had been empty when they moved in. Having only recently founded the centre as a community space, there was still much to be done. The long glass greenhouses were mostly smashed up and overgrown with a lot of rubbish strewn about, and yet they had already managed to grow some food even in the short time they had been living there. I witnessed the excitement as they discovered their first tomato.

It was hard not to be filled with admiration. Here were around ten people living permanently away from society and attempting to be as self-sustaining as possible: growing their own food, recycling the water (I was given a demonstration of how the washing-up water was funnelled back into the flushing toilet) and repairing the broken-down buildings, greenhouses, and flowerbeds. One of the most pressing tasks was to move everyone inside and out of the tents dotted around the ground before winter set in, and the plan was to build new walls inside the large main building in order to make the interior smaller and more efficient to heat.

Despite being directed here by Occupy activists, there was very little evidence of political organisation, apart from a newly acquired printing press and a couple of the squatters who told me that they had been involved in the Occupy movement. There were a few acoustic guitars with missing strings, a set of bongos, sofas, a projector screen (for community film nights), a bookcase containing radical literature, posters advertising forthcoming events (Yoga, horticulture, meetings, etc.), some broken-down bikes and gardening equipment, as well as an impressively functional kitchen area. They had given up on wider society, and instead decided to resist *indirectly* by establishing the square as an autonomous space that could facilitate more 'authentic' and 'non-conflicted' lifestyles, beyond corruption by the state and capitalism, as well as large organisations like Occupy. They wanted to enact and prefigure an alternative, more sustainable way of living, while opening up this previously wasted space to the local community.

They kept the gate locked for security reasons, fearing both an unexpected police or bailiff eviction and an unsustainable overload of squatters. Some were maintaining full-time jobs outside the square and donating some of their wages for food, while others (who had been there the longest) focused more on developing the space: building, cooking, gardening, cleaning, fixing bikes, considering insulation over a joint or two. There were some migrants from Southern Europe also staying there who told me about being involved in similar squats back home. Two women (one of whom was pregnant) appeared to be performing most of the domestic duties, offering tea to visitors, and preparing vegetables from the garden for dinner.

When the squat was suddenly evicted in June 2016, the activists attempted to reaffirm their outsider status through the media coverage of the event. On 4 July 2016 *The Guardian* reported, sympathetically, that 'about 30 people have been left homeless from a squat that had transformed a derelict plant nursery in the heart of London into an off-grid, sustainable living hub' before quoting one squatter 'who gave his name as "∞just-rob©ofearth" that 'whatever the claims of the lawfulness of whatever eviction they have done today, what they have actually done is expelled a nature tribe who are outside the English law'. Having chosen to become 'free men of the land' and rejecting 'corporate law used to govern people of the UK by fraud', the squatters had seen themselves as an autonomous and authentic community, 'with the aim', according to their Facebook page, 'of promoting sustainable living, growing organic food, nurturing wildlife [and] cultivating free artistic spaces'.

Introduction: the pursuit of authenticity

This chapter will build on the normative foreclosures discussed above by considering the cultural logic of *authenticity* in the context of postmodern capitalism. As well as the problematic extension of individualist and libertarian norms outlined in the previous chapter, it is argued that the pursuit of authenticity within contemporary activism provides both the basis of a further tyranny of structurelessness *and* a normative extension of the very market dominance that movements like Occupy were attempting to challenge in the post-crash moment. By 'authenticity' I mean the attempt to establish a critical distance from (what is perceived to be) complicity with the corrupting and stifling influence of capitalism, the state, or other large institutions and organisations which might discipline their actions. Those deemed to be 'more authentic' are considered to be far from the instrumental rationality or *co-optation* of the market or state, while the 'less authentic' is considered to be symbolic objects, cultural signs, or identities which have 'sold out' and become incorporated into consumerism or parliamentary limits. While, at first, it may seem entirely logical that activists would attempt to withdraw their resistance and adopt a distance from that which they are attempting to change, I will use the idea of the 'new spirit of capitalism' to argue that this very pursuit of authenticity has become part of the cultural logical of consumerism itself.

Tracing the 'new spirit of capitalism' back to a cultural turn in the 1960s, Boltanski and Chiapello argue that ideas of authenticity were adopted by the market in order to appeal to cultural changes in the global north-west. While the industrial organisation of early 20th-century production emphasised uniformity and mass consumption, this new post-industrial organisation was instead based upon principles of:

> autonomy, spontaneity, rhizomorphous capacity, multitasking (in contrast to the narrow specialisation of old labour), conviviality, openness to others and novelty, availability, creativity, visionary intuition, sensitivity to differences, listening to lived experience and receptiveness to a whole range of experiences, being attracted to informality and the search for interpersonal contacts … taken directly from the repertoire of May 1968.
> (Boltanski and Chiapello 2007: 97)

While the 1960s were certainly a crucial period for the emergence of new social movements and politics which had historically been marginalised by a traditional (white, working-class-centric) left; it was also, uncoincidentally, the point of emergence for a new type of capitalism which took criticisms of a lack of diversity and heterogeneity to heart. Western economies adapted and companies began to produce products and subcultures which appealed to individual expressions of difference and authenticity, signalling an attempt to move away from the perceived oppression of capitalist mass production and produce a new vibrant individualism that would directly contrast with the dull, grey uniformity behind the Iron Curtain. Addressing such criticisms, therefore, there was a cultural turn in the west which made authenticity (i.e. a perceived distance from capitalism) *part of capitalist accumulation itself.*

As I will demonstrate below, the pursuit of authenticity is also a preoccupation within contemporary activism and was expressed widely within the Occupy movement in London. Like the Rochester Square squatters, emphasis was regularly placed on the need to pursue autonomous space from which to authentically organise, equating 'proper' activism with purity and adopting the moral high ground, attempting to establish spaces that were uncorrupted, untainted, non-compliant, non-complicit, and 'outside' (or at least at a distance from) wider social structures and institutions (e.g.

capitalism, parliaments, cultural inequalities). Often, the navigation of authenticity was inconsistent, self-contradictory, and complex, but underlying all narratives remained a common presumption that authentic withdrawal, as much as possible, was ideal for effective resistance.

The pursuit of authenticity created a number of problems for Occupy (in) London. In the first instance, it provided further grounds for a tyranny of structurelessness within the movement, as a number of activists simply saw their resistance as 'more authentic' than that of others (usually newcomers and/or younger, unseasoned activists who were dismissed as naïve, stupid, or inexperienced). This created a basis for an internal distribution of the sensible which partitioned some activists as 'authentic' and others as 'inauthentic', creating further preclusions along these lines that denied the possibility of democratic negotiation of an exclusive collective identity. It also provided the fuel for further unaccountable hierarchies to develop within the movement, between those who considered their resistance as more 'authentic' than that of others.

In the second instance, the problem with the pursuit of authenticity was that it played into the same *external* police order distribution of the movement which was attempting to dismiss their appearance and voice as 'non-sense'. By taking seriously accusations of their inauthenticity – that they were hypocrites who needed to go away and take a long, hard look at themselves before criticising anyone – Occupy inadvertently accepted those normative co-ordinates which dismissed their politics as 'nothing to see here'. Using the stigma that surrounded Starbucks coffee and V for Vendetta Guy Fawkes masks, I will show how the very concern over whether the movement was rendering itself inauthentic by using such cultural items, played into wider claims that the movement was 'non-sense'.

Finally, I will argue that the pursuit of authenticity allowed a problematic extension of market norms *at the very moment that they were attempting to challenge the ideological hold of capitalist realism*. It will be argued that myths of co-optation (i.e. that resistance culture is authentic at first but is then incorporated into consumerism) plays into wider market norms of obsolescence, competition, and product development. Rather than pursuing authenticity – which creates preclusions and hierarchies; plays into wider distributions of their appearance as 'non-sense'; *and* extends market logics at the very moment they are attempting to challenge them – it will therefore be my contention that such striving for authentic distance is not only structurally unachievable (and therefore a waste of valuable activist time and energy), but a dead-end for resistance and a foreclosure of possibility.

An activist identity

In order to broach the topic of authenticity and find out whether activists considered co-optation of their resistance to be a problem, I often asked occupiers about the notion of an 'activist identity'. More often than not, this had the desired effect of implying a collective subcultural conformity within the movement, tapping into concerns that libertarian left-wing activists might be creating an 'inauthentic' target market of lucrative rebel consumers. Thus, asking about an activist identity steered the conversation towards criticisms of consumerism within social movements and subcultural identities within activist circles, reflecting upon the apparent paradox that cultural signifiers of dissent might be commodified and rendered inauthentic or tamed by commodities that carried (and sold) sentiments of protest. What I hadn't anticipated, however, was the pre-existing sensitivity towards such a view, which manifested itself in sophisticated defences and arguments that interviewee appeared to already have at their disposal in order to defend the authenticity of their activism against the implied criticisms of an 'activist identity'.

Harry, for instance, who had attempted to join the movement late in the day and was faced with the difficulty of trying to become part of the 'in group' (not least because he was distrusted for fear that he might be undercover police, see Chapter 5), was particularly candid about his thought process about what clothes he should (or should not) wear to Occupy meetings:

> You do kind of … we do I suppose in some way purchase goods that help us feel part of something, that connectivity with other people … so I guess it's part of it. It's just, I don't think it should be that important. Yeah, I don't think it should be that valued 'cause you know … when I go to these meetings, it's like 'well, should I wear my more baggy jeans? Or my ripped clothes to feel that slight kind of original activist look?' It's like no, it's like no, bollocks. I'm just going to be myself.

Wanting to fit in and identify with the movement, as well as develop 'connectivity' with the existing members of the community, Harry weighed up what he (sarcastically) called 'the original activist look' – baggy jeans, ripped clothes – with the authenticity of 'just being myself'. The activist look, he concluded, was the inauthentic option and not a price to be paid for belonging, while the individual liberty of being true to himself was seen as the authentic decision (i.e. distancing himself from the consumerist performance of an activist identity).

He then continued by reflecting back on the styles, fashions, and trends which he had adopted in the past, as well as to the fact that he used to belong to alternative subcultural groups:

> I guess you'd call me part of the 'alternative spectrum' (although I don't know how actually meaningful that word is anymore … *I think the 'alternative' really has become 'mainstream'*). But if you go back to the early 1990s/2000s, I was … I suppose you could call me a 'grunger'. I used to have hair down to here!

Despite appearing to encapsulate a distance from the 'mainstream', the authenticity of the alternative, for Harry, was now problematic because it had become co-opted into consumerism and was therefore no longer 'meaningful'. Referring to the grunge scene of the early 1990s – a subculture which was continually tormented by the balance between popularity and authenticity, as detailed in Kurt Cobain's suicide note – is indicative of this. As more and more people pursue an identity which demonstrates authentic distance, it is quickly considered too popular – too mainstream, too profitable, too trendy – and therefore no longer authentic.

Harry was not alone in expressing concern for the authenticity of his resistance being jeopardised by a consumerist co-optation into some sort of shallow popular subcultural fad. As one activist who had travelled around to some of the other Occupy protests in Europe observed, for instance, 'the German occupiers look *exactly* like Finsbury Square … the same lingo, the same movements, the same … every bit of detail was the same … like they've created some kind of subculture … the way they rolled their joints, the way they were talking' (2014, int. 6). This implies that this similarity was a clear sign of inauthenticity – these individuals weren't being 'true to themselves' (to use Harry's phrase) but were simply buying in to a subculture and following a trend.

For many, it was therefore important to defend their activism and the Occupy movement from the criticism implied by an activist identity, because this would suggest that they had been co-opted and turned into a mainstream popular subcultural trend. One activist, for example, sought to play down such subcultural characteristics as simply pragmatic or inadvertent results of direct action:

> With anarchists, army surplus is very popular because it's very cheap and very hardwearing. So, this creates an identity by itself as well … it's always the case when they say 'bunch of crusties … get your hair cut you bunch of hippies'. Unfortunately, you just don't have a choice sometimes.
> (2014, int. 3)

Attempting to downplay elements of the movement which resembled some sort of fashion statement or sign of conspicuous consumption, the argument was that individuals were justified in buying army surplus gear, or growing their hair long, because these were practical decisions and simply by-products of direct action. They weren't doing this just for the sake of fashion or to belong to a subculture (which would be 'inauthentic') but because the pragmatic demands of living on the street or in a protest camp meant that they had 'no choice'.

Another defensive narrative used to downplay the charge of an inauthentic activist identity was that such attempts to belong through purchasing signifying items were part of a natural human inclination to belong and identify with others:

> It's not that I'm second-guessing you, but when I hear question like that [on activist identity] I kind of feel like people search for excuses not to do things, y'know? Now, yes, there are some people who have that identity, and people also … in a way, a lot of people who are more into that identity are more into it than formulating a more sophisticated critique. So, its fashion really. And it's not totally superficial, but it is in a way a fashion that appeals to certain people who I imagine are jobless a lot of the time – or 'creative' – and it's an avenue for them to express themselves. I've never really had a problem with it, but I've been a part of that, so I've never been intimidated by it. Doubly so, I've never needed to put it down. It's generally people trying to do the right thing and bonding … human cliques … it's very ordinary.
>
> (2014, int. 10)

> 'But I'm wearing black and red and I look like I've just stepped out of Camden … I *have* just stepped out of Camden … I bought this hat in Camden, I've got dreads … and certain people will look at me and … It's all uniforms: that's the way identity works'
>
> (James)

Signifiers of resistance – the black and red of anarchism being incorporated into a hat to be sold at Camden Market (itself a cathedral of rebel consumption, with the appearance of an authentic marketplace at street level, but with glass towers above) – might be co-opted by capitalism, but ultimately such items are defensible as merely being ways of belonging and a natural process of identification. What's more, for the former activist, people who buy into such an 'activist identity' simply lacked a more sophisticated critique, insisting that while 'some people' might be like that, it didn't characterise Occupy as a whole.

Even with the more sceptical activists, there remained a desire to be unconflicted (and therefore authentic) even if it wasn't always considered to be possible. The overriding concern remained to establish an authentic politics by creating a distance, as far as possible, from a life conflicted with consumer capitalism, either by avoiding certain goods that contradicted their politics (boycotting) or by obtaining more ethical options and alternatives (or what we might call *buy*cotting, a term I first came across in Albinsson *et al.* (2010). Speaking via Skype, Ollie made it particularly clear that he disagreed with the artificiality of consumerism, outlining his distaste of capitalism and defence of authenticity in relation to what he would or would not purchase:

> I'm really against this marketplace which I've tacitly agree to be part of. Every time I purchase in that marketplace, I am tacitly saying this is a good thing to do. So more and more I try to buy second-hand stuff, build my own kit. I'm in the process of building a bicycle generator, second

> hand solar panels, second hand batteries … that's still benefitting from the market that's there, but at least it's withdrawing.

While recognising the ubiquity of the market and his complicity with it, Ollie nevertheless sees the answer as withdrawing as far as is possible and pursuing some sort of authentic distance through exercises of individual consumer choice. By purchasing second-hand stuff and building his own kit – including generating his own energy in order to be off-grid – the argument was that he was no longer being inauthentic and 'tacitly saying that market is a good':

> That's the kind of world we live in. It's a world full of contradictions. And if there was a fair trade-type phone, I'm going to migrate to that. You know, I love my Converse All-Stars … but the same thing applies. I would love to live an unconflicted life where every item of clothing I wore was not made at the expense of someone's health or poverty.

In an ideal world, the 'unconflicted' life would allow Ollie to avoid hypocrisy by maintaining his desire for products (such as his Converse) or the need for technology (like mobile phones) without having to compromise his ethical or political authenticity. I asked whether this meant he was an advocate of Black Spot branded trainers (which look very similar to Converse but are produced by Adbusters as an ethical alternative):

> For instance, Black Spot … if I was able to entirely dress in 'right-on' stuff, I could stop at any point because I'm not living a conflicted life. I can wear hemp, my trainers were made by people who were given good wages, etc. … But if I use that as a way of saying: 'well, I feel good about myself, so I don't need to worry about anything anymore'. I'm much more interested in somebody that's alive and active and seeking … and wearing Converse … than I am about a self-satisfied smug git who's wearing an anarchist t-shirt, an Anonymous mask and 'right-on' sandals.

Here, then, Ollie adds another level of complexity to his argument. Not only are consumer goods themselves conflicted, but even *buy*cotting 'non-conflicted' goods could be seen as inauthentic, because such a distance prevents activists from being 'active and seeking' in their politics. In other words, the argument appears to be that a certain level of hypocrisy is necessary to motivate resistance.

Such a careful and elaborate navigation through the field of authenticity involved many layers of argumentation which sometimes appeared self-contradictory – e.g. why is purchasing a fair trade phone as an ethical buycott any different to someone opting for 'right-on' sandals? – but the underlying point here is that activism should always pursue authenticity. It's therefore less my suggestion that these arguments are simply either right or wrong, and more my intention to highlight the presupposition of such ready-made sophisticated defences that were deployed at the mention of an 'activist identity'. Such arguments, I suggest, indicated a persisting, underlying discomfort with possible accusations of authenticity and hypocrisy. Those who were deemed to be pursuing an activist identity, who lacked a sophisticated critique and who simply treated Occupy as a subcultural trend, were either dismissed outright as 'inauthentic' or were defended using pragmatic or pseudo-social psychological arguments that such cliques were 'natural'. Either way, what was considered to be at stake was the authenticity of the Occupy movement, and whether their resistance was clearly distanced from the shallow, trivial, and corrupting influence of consumerism. Such rapid defences of authenticity suggested that the ideal position for activists was not to be incorporated or to comply, and instead to locate purer autonomous positions from which to express one's resistance. However, this preoccupation and anxiety within the movement, as I will now argue, created numerous problems and foreclosures for the Occupy movement in London.

More authentic than others

The first problem that the pursuit of authenticity caused for Occupy (in) London is that it became yet another source and basis of hierarchy and preclusion – another 'tyranny' within the 'structureless' (inclusive and horizontal) democratic space. Like Harry's dilemma over what to wear to a meeting or Lucy's concern with her purchase of Burberry-branded items in the previous chapter, the 'core' of the movement sometimes gave the impression of an exclusive subculture which saw their resistance as more authentic than others. In particular, such hierarchies and preclusions developed around those who were deemed to be impure activists, because they had mistakenly bought in to signifiers of dissent offered by the market:

> Che Guevara T-shirts man! They make me laugh! You know, it's this whole: 'oh, it's cool to be left wing' thing. That sort of thing does my head in, y'know? Those people, they're not into any *cause*, they just want to be part of the 'gang'. And people like that, in my opinion, should just be avoided.
>
> (2012, int. 10)

Those who purchased goods – like Che Guevara T-shirts – in order to be 'rebellious' or 'dissenting' just 'didn't get it' and therefore should simply be avoided as facetious, inauthentic, and not truly into the cause. Such an attitude seemed to develop into a mechanism that caused newcomers to the movement to be thoroughly judged for signs of inauthenticity, as well as a method through which cliques became stigmatised as 'less authentic' than others:

> In Occupy it was so obvious … because Anonymous is a very diverse group (anyone can call themselves 'Anonymous') and then there's this

> really good part of Anonymous that are like the hackers and doing a really good job. And then just like a bunch of people that are really just trying to create trouble. And they are really confrontational. They don't have a strong politics. They're lost really, they don't know what they're doing.
>
> (2013, int. 10)

This, I argue, is indicative of that distribution of the sensible which developed within the Occupy (in) London movement of whose voice and appearance was considered to be legitimate and whose was not. For this activist (above), for instance, the Anonymous group at the campsites were not the real, authentic, proper Anonymous, but just some confrontational group in Guy Fawkes masks who didn't really know what they were doing:

> And then they really just like pose with the mask to the camera, so they would just stand there … but in the camp, there was never any energy given to them to improve, or to participate with what's going on, they would never engage with us. They would just sit there in the tent with the flag waving around and as soon as the media arrived they were like posing. But they never worked for it, they didn't believe in the idea.
>
> (Julia)

While a more disciplined organisation might have been able to draw lines of exclusion and inclusion with such groups, the structurelessness asserted at Occupy meant that they were automatically precluded as inauthentic, without democratic negotiation. Interestingly, the same activist who criticised Anonymous as inauthentic then went on to blame the symbolic inefficiency of wider society for encouraging such people to join movements at such a shallow level:

> And I think there's a problem within activist circles sometimes and more mass movements (like Occupy was at some point) are that people become … They're maybe more, like, *excluded* from society, and they see social movements as: 'be part of something like a community'. Because activist groups are like that, you don't just go to your protests then go home, there is a sense of family, we're really close to each other, we support each other in our everyday life. And I think people are really attracted to that … but maybe don't engage in the politics so much (and that's really a massive problem).
>
> (Julia)

The result was that some activists considered themselves 'better' or 'more authentic' than others (who were deemed to be engaging at a shallow, non-committal level, and were subsequently dismissed as 'non-sense'). Those who were considered to be left wing because it was 'trendy' or 'cool' or 'fashionable' were considered not to have 'strong politics'. They should only be considered 'posers' who have never really 'worked for it'. Once again, my point is not so much that these arguments are necessarily inaccurate, but that the problematic logic which they represent (a preoccupation with pursuing authenticity) continues an unaccountable tyranny of structurelessness (creating un-negotiated and undemocratic hierarchies, distributions and preclusions in the movement's organisation).

Another way in which this distribution manifested itself was on a meta-level: those activists who recognised the problems of pursuing authenticity, and subsequently saw their politics as 'more authentic' than those who were naïvely concerned with being authentic:

> 'People have this – even if they don't realise they have it – a lot of them have this stupid idea about purity. We're never going to get anything that is completely black or completely white. We're never going to have anything that's completely good or completely evil. That's not going to … in the real world, that just does not happen, y'know?
>
> (2012, int. 14)

> You know, initially, when my politics were more liberal and unseasoned, I really would have bought into this idea of cultural capitalism. I would have boycotted things, particularly the Israel-Palestine thing at the time (boycott Marks and Spencers). At the time, I would have given into that.
>
> (Lucy)

> I think a trail of thought that emerged – the idea of 'purity' – this emerged within activist movements and activist mentality as well, and it kind of goes along the terms: 'unless you're living out of … unless you're a freegan living out of dumpsters, unless you're squatting or not paying rent, unless you're not buying things from a commercial store … then you're not pure and that's problematic'. This is a real extreme idea of things and I think its foundation is the idea that an individual can change society by changing their behaviour and things like that. I don't really buy into that. I think this stuff is hypocritical because we're so like entrenched and locked into the market system that you can't just make a clear break from it, whilst trying to actively critique it or participate in an alternative of it … I think it's quite true that there's no real alternative to what Mark Fisher calls 'capitalist realism' as a dominant imaginary. And I think it's a dominant imaginary because *the market is reality*. You can't just step outside that market, I don't think, I think it's a really unfair idea.
>
> (2014, int. 4)

The problem here is the way in which these activists criticised the pursuit of authenticity by other activists, assuming that they had become aware of the 'truth' behind the pursuit of authenticity and purity, overlooking how their criticisms also presupposed their own distance from complicity. For these three interviewees, purity was an idea pursued by the 'stupid', for the 'liberal and unseasoned' activists that they themselves 'didn't really buy into', asserting their expertise and authority on this issue by positioning themselves as above such trivial activities. There is no democratic presupposition of 'reason between equals' here (see Rancière 1991); instead there is a presupposition of inequality, in that some activists 'know better' than others how to create an authentic movement and protest.

Rather than extending the movement and democratically negotiating organisational lines of collective identity, therefore, such 'unseasoned activists' were dismissed and marginalised within the movement. This also played out in activist biographies, with those newcomers who didn't have a background in activism and therefore were without experience, understanding, or expertise, treated as second-class members of the movement. Some occupiers distanced themselves from such newcomers by boasting about their involvement in previous movements:

> I'm not here personally for Occupy … but I'm here with Reclaim the Fields, Reclaim the Streets. But this is what I am as a home. Occupy is home for me.
>
> (2012, int. 1)

> I think it's true that a number of people who were active in the sixties – such as myself – will have a different view of what is happening because we've seen a lot more. And we've also seen … we were opposed to what was happening in the sixties which was much more progressive than what's happening today. Now we never expected it to go back, but what we had from '45 to '75 was probably an aberration.
>
> (2014, int. 11)

> Like, one of the things that pissed me off at St Paul's was just how short-sighted so many people were. Like, I could see some article by some guy being like … saying: 'those of us who learnt our politics in 1999' like 'Seattle protests' or whatever. And you think like, it's not like 1999 was significantly different from the sixties. Like we have the internet … but like, the world is still recognisable. Even life today, the world is still recognisable to what it was, y'know, sixty years ago.
>
> (2012, int. 14)

Belonging to a previous movement or era, especially if it already had some kind of legendary status attached to it (such as Reclaim the Streets), provided a certain claim to authenticity for longer-term activists above those who had perhaps come to activism for the first time. Those who had already earned their reputations and social capital as being committed activists were subsequently distributed as possessing a more 'sensible' voice and appearance within the movement, able to assert their opinions and views on authority within the 'structureless' space. As the frustration of the last activist suggests (see above), the hierarchies which then developed off the back of this – between seasoned activists and those deemed to be unseasoned newcomers – developed into further divides and fractures, as the newer activists became fed up with the condescending attitudes and unequal distribution of voice afforded to them.

In an apparent echo of Freeman's tyranny of structurelessness, one activist even described to me what he called 'the tyranny of the founders', or 'a sort of inner circle that were "experts" in activism, teaching us "how it's done"', sarcastically adding: 'I suppose if I was an expert on activism in London – and I'd been around and I'd earned my spurs and my credit rating was high – then I could probably meet these people and they could vet me… but one phrase that appeared at the end was the 'circle of trust' and it became an identity thing: them and us' (Burgum 2015b). Those who claimed to have founded and started the movement, who had 'been there since the beginning', laid a certain claim to Occupy (in) London as more 'theirs' than any newcomers, creating preclusions that foreclosed the possibility of a democratic negotiation over the boundaries of the movement. In particular, those who attended Occupy LSX at St Paul's seemed to use this as a 'go to' reference for their personal claim towards representing the *authentic* Occupy London (in contrast to the trivial, inexperienced, and shallow engagement of late arrivals).

In addition, claims to being an 'original occupier' which provided authenticity and authority over others, were also expressed in terms of a willingness to put oneself at personal risk, either through direct violence (e.g. altercation with the police) or via personal sacrifices (e.g. 'holding the fort' by staying in the tents):

> We're sort of family, we are a community, I mean we started as a community in St Paul's churchyard and we … somebody referred to us this week actually as diehards … and I think that's about right. Those of us who are still active, as much as they can be, are diehards … they've decided to stay because … a few people I know say it's a way of life for them.
>
> (Sally)

> Direct action, physical work, direct action is needed. I'm not denying the amazingness of the internet, but we need more than just signing petitions and talking about it. You have to talk before you do action, but you know … to me you feel *alive* when you do direct action, you feel alive, like you're doing something, like you've made some change.
>
> (2013, int. 9)

> The consumeristic model is so much easier … 'cause you just … you buy your T-shirt and you buy your mask and *of course* [speaking sarcastically] you're part of it, 'cause you've got the T-shirt! You got the mask! But you didn't have to spend any time in the tent or in the mud protesting to feel like you're then part of that thing.
>
> (2012, int. 3)

The 'diehards' who were willing (or, at least, had a reputation for being more willing) to risk their safety through direct action, or who made personal sacrifices by spending time in the mud, were deemed more authentic than those who were imagined to be only belonging to the movement at a superficial level (and therefore were not far enough removed from the mainstream). Even the inhospitality of the steps of St Paul's Cathedral was celebrated as being *beneficial* for the movement in performing such sacrifice:

> and the space itself was so *unhospitable*. That alone made it quite perfect! … I think because people just look at it and think: 'how extraordinary that these people are actually living here', y'know? Actually creating a life there, they've got a kitchen and a library and … it's all functioning!
>
> (Jenny)

For Jenny, the very challenge and adversity of camping in the city streets was a 'perfect' way of demonstrating the activists' authentic commitment to the cause. Yet she was also no stranger to the problems of hierarchy and preclusion which could be created by such authenticity through sacrifice, drawing links between her experience at St Paul's and similar ideas which had circulated at the Greenham Common women's peace camp in the 1980s:

> I think there is an 'activist identity' and, again, it happened at Greenham and needed squashing. It becomes an accidental hierarchy of the people who are deemed to have done most. The difficulty of Greenham was that those of us who had been to prison were given a lot more respect than people who hadn't. And I think the same thing applies – or did apply at one point – in Occupy. There was a notion that you, kind of, if you'd been arrested you'd kind of got your colours. And if you camped in the camp, compared with visiting, then you were more of an activist. And if you spend a lot of time online rather than physically attending meetings, then you're less of an activist.

Being willing to put oneself in harm's way or to have altercations with the police was seen as endowing some activists with an aura of authenticity, performing their activist identity that they were at a clear distance from capitalism and the state, but also above others who were considered 'less of an activist' for not doing so. While on the face of it, such commitment to the cause seems to adhere to Badiou's (2012) argument for fidelity; in a disorganised and structureless movement like Occupy, there was simply no overall idea for which this commitment to risk and sacrifice was being performed. Thus, these acts only achieved in the development of individual kudos and authority for some at the expense of others, developing unnegotiated exclusions and unaccountable hierarchies between those deemed more or less 'authentic'.

The pursuit of authenticity was yet another blockage to the movement's ability to organise collectively, once again deepening divisions, fractures, preclusions, tyrannies, and an undemocratic distribution of voices along the lines of who were considered to be the heroic vanguards of the movement versus the facetious newcomers. Rather than organising a basis from which to make a collective intervention and refigure the wider police order, therefore, there was instead a preoccupation with purity and authenticity – whether seeing oneself as 'authentic' or as 'more authentic than others'. The Occupy movement in London inadvertently created further unchecked distributions of power within its horizontal and structureless space which meant that, when it did inevitably coalesce and become more exclusive, it did not do so under conditions of acknowledged and reflexive negotiation, but upon presuppositions of who was (or was not) considered authentic. Those who were able to claim expertise, knowledge, originality, and authority – or at least demonstrate their commitment through physical risk or sacrifice – were seen to carry more authenticity, thus creating a situation in which some were able to claim authority over the movement at the expense of others.

Attempting to avoid hypocrisy

In addition to the problem of creating further preclusions, unaccountable hierarchies, and unequal distributions within the movement, the concern and preoccupation with pursuing authenticity can also be an issue for the wider distribution of the movement as a whole. In pursuing authentic resistance, the concern was to avoid criticism that the movement was somehow hypocritical, by acting in ways which demonstrated its secret reliance on capitalism while loudly announcing its criticism of it. By taking such dismissals seriously, however, the activists inadvertently played into the normative co-ordinates that positioned them as 'non-sense', despite the problem of hypocrisy being relatively inconsequential. It is not necessary, I argue, to adopt a pure, authentic, non-hypocritical 'moral high ground' before making an intervention or criticism of the status quo, yet such anxieties were widespread within the movement and flared up around a few key examples.

The first was the question of whether Occupy activists could remain 'authentic' while drinking coffee from the global corporate chain Starbucks. What is particularly interesting about Starbucks as a case study of authenticity, is that the company originally fashioned itself as a buycott by positioning its fair trade products as an ethical alternative to other coffee suppliers, offering an opportunity on the market to 'have your coffee and drink it too' (i.e. consume without ethical guilt towards the exploitation of coffee farmers). Yet the corporation's in-store employment practices, tax avoidance, criticism of the limit of fair trade schemes, as well as its sheer uniform ubiquity in every major city, has led Starbucks to attract the same alter-globalisation scrutiny as did other worldwide corporations in the 1990s (e.g. McDonalds, Microsoft, Nike). In the centre of major cities like London, Starbucks coffee had become so common that it is often the only choice for hot drinks, Wi-Fi and toilets, as more 'authentic' independent cafes struggle to compete. Both the camp at St Paul's and at Finsbury Square had a local branch of Starbucks nearby and, while trying to keep their protest going during the coldest part of the year, the activists visited them regularly.

Yet this caused great tension within the movement, with some questioning the authenticity and hypocrisy of buying coffee from such a global corporate entity and consumer-capitalist flagship as Starbucks. For some, it was clear that Occupy should be boycotting the chain:

> Well, obviously it's kind of hypocritical to our whole message if we're buying Starbucks or stuff like that. It's not the perfect look if we have people from Occupy sitting outside Starbucks drinking frappuccinos. But it's all down to choice and at the end of it … it's kind of difficult in this day and age not to consumer those things. Like it's pretty hard to survive when we're not getting donations unless someone pops into Tesco's and gets some reduced food … it's better to boycott, but there's not much you can do sometimes.
>
> (2012, int. 5)

> Well I was just walking past Starbucks and one of my gripes with the whole thing was how often we're in Starbucks and pubs and things to use the internet … and now I'm using the stuff in the Barbican a lot (which I think is 'better' just about, using the Barbican, even though it's City of London). Again, me going in the Barbican and being followed around and questions about what I'm doing is … y'know, I'm not going to call it 'Occupy'. This is the thing. I consider this stuff [the tents] to be 'occupation'.
>
> (Greg)

Once again, we encounter the palpable discomfort of consumption associated with the activist identity. The activists were concerned that, through consuming coffee from Starbucks, they were contradicting and undermining their cause, rendering the movement's resistance inauthentic and hypocritical. While admitting that it is difficult to avoid complicity altogether, we also encounter the argument that it's 'better to boycott' or that some contradictions are better than others (e.g. using the Wi-Fi at the City of London-sponsored Barbican instead). The overriding issue, however, was how activists drinking coffee at Starbucks portrayed and distributed the movement, arguing that it wasn't achieving the 'perfect' appearance for occupiers to be sitting outside a branch of the chain.

This controversy came to a head when right-wing commentator and ex-Conservative Member of Parliament Louise Mensch condemned the movement publicly on the satirical BBC news programme *Have I Got News For You* (YouTube 2015). For Mensch, the activists were clearly hypocrites for buying coffee from the chain, arguing that 'if they prop up a corporate titan like Starbucks, they've got to ask themselves how much of capitalism they really don't like'. While her suggestion that the activists needed to adopt the moral high ground before pointing any fingers was excellently refuted by others on the game show panel – such as *Private Eye* editor Ian Hislop who stated that 'you don't have to want to return to a barter system in the Stone Age to complain about the way the financial crisis has affected huge numbers of people in the world, do you? Even if you're having a cup of coffee and you've got a tent!' – Mensch's comments clearly hit a nerve:

> There's a slight contradiction and people who do it recognise it's a contradiction. But it's so minor, it's not even worth giving much time to, there are so many more important things. And if you're out there camping and you're cold and there is a Starbucks literally right next to your tent … I don't think it's worth [Mensch] having a go at people for that.
>
> (2013, int. 6)

> Yeah quite a lot of people criticised … there was that person on *Have I Got News For You* who came out complaining that Occupy were drinking coffee in Starbucks. If you've got a choice of two different coffee shops, it would make sense to boycott and buycott, but in central London where we didn't have much choice … in terms of pragmatics, I'm not sure how much weight that has.
>
> (Shaun)

> I'd rather see my mates drinking Starbucks [coffee] and fucking with the heads of the system. Coffee is as important as coffee, that's it. And it's just a cheap shot, it's just a cheap shot … y'know, not to talk to a member of the public or scorn them because they're drinking Starbucks. No, there's more to their choice of being than their choice of coffee.
>
> (2012, int. 9)

Similarly to the wearing of army surplus clothing and long hair, the insistence on the practicality of drinking Starbucks coffee suggests a deep-seated feeling that the activists needed to defend themselves against such an attack on their authenticity, making it clear that, while drinking Starbucks coffee may seem contradictory, it was simply a pragmatic decision. The problem is that simply by addressing such comments, it was clear that they had considered this dismissal of the movement as important and consequential enough to be taken seriously. In other words, it suggested a normative agreement that Mensch had been correct to suggest that drinking Starbucks coffee undermined their resistance and rendered their whole appearance 'non-sense'. She had tried to designate the movement as inauthentic, but by attempting to protect the integrity of the movement against such an accusation, the activists' response extended the same normative distribution which she was appealing to (i.e. that authenticity matters).

In addition to Starbucks, another focal point around which defences of authenticity were quickly deployed was the infamous Guy Fawkes mask lifted from the graphic novel and Warner Bros' film *V for Vendetta*. First used by Anonymous in a protest against Scientology in the USA, the mask has quickly become a popular image for resistance all over the world, and yet it remains a copyrighted plastic commodity, mass-produced in the Far East by multi-national toy companies (Sheets 2013). Thus, while some insisted that the mask were simply a symbol of belonging – with one activist commenting that 'I thought I had found my people because of the Guy Fawkes masks' (2014, int. 6) – others felt conflicted over the mask's authentic credentials for activist purposes, comparing it to Che Guevara T-shirts:

> 'I will *never* buy a T-shirt with Che Guevara on because if it becomes fashion it loses its real meaning. There was a great picture of this factory producing all these Anonymous masks in a massive factory, and to me, it's like we should give an example of the sort of society we're trying to create, and you're basically supporting this consumerist culture while you're trying to oppose capitalism and the exclusion it creates. So, to me it's completely wrong. I mean it shouldn't be done. It's good for the media, but then just maybe I think it's because of the visuals (the visuals are very good).
>
> (Julia)

> You've got the mask, people covering their faces, this whole Anonymous thing along with the tents, the banners … the iconography and the visual symbols and logos gave the movement identity and these are important. I mean the masks … people don't wear it to the [General] Assembly anymore … that has become a cliché. People in the movement are upset with a lot of people who have used that image. I mean, who was the famous house DJ from Radio One who did a DJ set inside Parliament and he wore that mask – 'I'm occupying Parliament!' – and most people are never going near that mask again. It's like when you see hipsters turning up to fancy dress parties and [it gets] hijacked in the same way as Che Guevara's face did.
>
> (James)

> I think popular culture can be useful, but after a while things become cliché, don't they? So, I think wearing the mask is almost a cliché now. But if that's what people want to do, I don't have any problem with it.
>
> (2013, int. 6)

The concern here is that the mask has become too mainstream, too popular, and therefore too much of a cliché, to be used as an authentic activist tool. Despite having some potential for the movement's collective appearance and identity, therefore, the argument here is that the mask had become co-opted by consumer culture and rendered an inauthentic commodity, thereby contradicting the movement's aims and 'the sort of society we're trying to create'. The references to mass consumption – sweatshops, mainstream DJs – was therefore seen as damaging the mask's symbolic potential. James' reference to hipsters is also striking. For him, the mask had become hypocritical because it was being worn for non-activist purposes of enjoyment (e.g. fancy dress parties) and yet if we define the term 'hip' as attempting to avoid cliché – as being 'concerned more with advanced knowledge about the illegitimate and staying one step ahead of the consumer crowd than with any ideology of good community faith' (Frank 1997: 30) – then James' criticism of such products becoming hip seems to suggest a certain 'hipsterdom' in staying one step ahead of co-optation.

Perhaps one of the clearest examples of the pursuit of authenticity with regards to the Guy Fawkes masks came from my very first interview at Finsbury Square. Sitting at a table in the kitchen tent that morning, I noticed that the activist I was talking to was wearing a Slipknot T-shirt and a raver 'smiley face' pin badge. He told me about the music he was into (rave music, mostly, he wasn't really into Slipknot although had seen them about five times) and that he enjoyed going to 'hippie gatherings' (in fact, as it turned out, he was leaving the protest to go to a festival that very afternoon). As the conversation turned towards the masks, I asked whether he thought it was problematic that they were essentially a commodity:

> Well … Anonymous brought out their own mask. It was only a little adaptation, but it has little rosy cheeks, so it wasn't V for Vendetta masks. So, the people can't make money off it. It was more a case of: 'if you buy the mask, that's how much it costs to make'. Down at St Paul's, they were selling them for a pound each. Just 'cause that's how much it costs to make them. So, no one was making any profit.
>
> (2012, int. 1)

By producing their own 'authentic' alternative product, it seemed that Anonymous were attempting to circumnavigate hypocrisy altogether by competing with the V for Vendetta mask. Suggesting a certain entrepreneurial spirit, therefore, the movement had opted for innovation: activists didn't have to buy the Warner Bros' trademark, they could buycott a more ethical version:

> Well, the V for Vendetta masks … I used to know a few of the Anonymous here, like proper hardcore Anonymous that used to live in here. But they don't even wear the V for Vendetta masks. The true symbol for Anonymous is a man in a suit with a question mark for a face. That's what the true thing it. But because it's been adopted and it went viral, that way it got adapted into it. And I've spoke to the guy who made *V for Vendetta* the book, he was on a protest march with Anonymous, and he says he does not feel the mask should be used like that. But at the same time, it's not the mask itself, it's the symbol it represents. And it's more symbolism than the mask itself.
>
> (2012, int. 1)

Having met the original author of the graphic novel – presumably Alan Moore who had visited Occupy (in) London on a few occasions (Occupy London 2012) – this activist *knew* what the real (authentic) used of the mask should be. But even beyond that, his argument was that 'proper hardcore' activists didn't even use the masks anyway as they had their own un-corrupted logo.

The activists of Occupy (in) London demonstrated varied and relatively sophisticated reflections upon their complicity with consumerism, which demonstrate how both the pursuit of authenticity and the attempt to avoid hypocrisy were clear preoccupations within the movement. The problem, I have suggested, is that such a logic indicates a conformity and extension of wider norms, which inadvertently play into the police order distribution of their protest as 'non-sense'. As demonstrated by Louise Mensch's attempt to dismiss their appearance and voice on the basis of their (apparent) hypocrisy for drinking Starbucks, the attempt to defend themselves against such criticisms only indicated that they shared the same idea (that authenticity was an important thing to establish). This distribution of the sensible was also reiterated by the V for Vendetta masks, demonstrating a clear market logic: 'don't like the status quo? Then innovate and release your own authentic product, a competing consumer choice which is more ethical and 'right-on.' In other words, both the persistent concern with authenticity and the approach of producing more 'authentic' imagery and cultural products, indicated yet another extension of (and foreclosure by) the very system they were attempting to challenge.

Myths of co-optation

Activist concerns that their protest might be rendered inauthentic or hypocritical through an immersion and incorporation into capitalism need to be understood within a wider context, and in particular, the notion that we (in the over-consuming societies of the global north-west) live under a 'new spirit of capitalism' (Boltanski and Chiapello 2007) in which 'authentic experience matters' (Žižek 2009a: 54). Beginning with the move away from alienating and stale uniformity of mass consumption in the 1960s – driven as much by Cold War competition and the perception of grey uniformity behind the Iron Curtain, as by the cultural turn – Boltanski and Chiapello argue that western capitalism adapted by incorporating and commercialising criticisms of the mass market as disenchanting, inauthentic, standardised, regimented, and destructive of beauty. For them, because capitalism is an inherently amoral economic system, with no notion of the 'common good', it always has had to look outside of itself for cultural justification, which (from the 1960s onwards) created a convergence between economic ends and emerging trends of individualised cultural freedom. The argument is that those who opposed the mainstreaming tendencies of the market, therefore, counterintuitively extended the new spirit of capitalism by supplying the moral support and cultural material from which 'authentic' alternatives could appear. Liberating 'people's aspirations to mobility, to multiply their activities, to greater opportunities for being and doing [that] emerge as virtually boundless reservoirs of ideas for conceiving new products and services to bring to the market' (Boltanski and Chiapello 2007: 437). Consumerism appeared to become more diverse, more exciting, and more *authentic* by apparently accounting for its own critique, developing normative principles of difference, creativity, and individual freedom that both mass production and collective conformity (whether the market, state or party) were said to stultify.

For Boltanski and Chiapello, this subsequently led to a seemingly paradoxical situation in which a commodity, in order 'to earn the label authentic … must be drawn from outside the commodity sphere, from what might be called 'sources of authenticity' (2007: 443), endowing products with a value 'that cannot be equated with the commodity and would be destroyed if they were introduced into the commodity circuit' (ibid.: 466). Through such co-optation, we end up with a capitalist consumerism that can sell its own criticisms via commodities that appear to offer an authentic distance from profit, monotony, or a de-individualised lack of freedom and choice. Liberated consumer-citizens are offered endless innovations and options on the market, with each round of boycotting and buycotting creating further opportunities to be 'hip' and get ahead of the inauthenticity and cliché of the mainstream. In other words, the new spirit of capitalism is one that actually 'needs its enemies, people whom it outrages and who are opposed to it, to find the moral support it lacks and to incorporate mechanisms of justice whose relevance it would otherwise have no reason to acknowledge' (ibid,: 27).

While I agree with the overall argument, and especially the centrality that Boltanski and Chiapello afford authenticity within this new spirit, I would argue that they somewhat overstate how much anti-capitalist criticism comes from 'outside' of the market. Instead, the *pursuit* of authenticity, something which is beyond the instrumental ends of consumerism, is often itself an idea that is '*pre*corporated' into commodities via 'pre-emptive formatting and shaping of desires, aspirations and hopes of capitalist culture' (Fisher 2009: 9), with commodities sold with their self-critique already built in (like 'prefaded blue jeans' (Hall *et al.* 2008: 110). While capitalist consumer culture is clearly operating through a cynical self-distancing, therefore, we should also recognise that this doesn't mean that there is some 'authentic space' to be located outside of capitalism which then becomes corrupted. Instead, we might describe the existence of a 'myth of co-optation' (Frank 1997), in which the very idea that capitalism or other oppressive institutions (like the state) will incorporate authentic resistance and critique, that it will corrupt and soften dissent, and *is also part of the new spirit.* And yet the idea of co-optation was widespread within the Occupy movement in London:

> A lot of rebelling got co-opted though, didn't it? I mean, the whole thing of revolution: it's just the same sixties stuff, you know? It's the fact of … where are all the people from 1968 who were throwing bottles in France? Where are they? And where are all the hippies?
>
> (Greg)

> Icons of resistance, like many of these totems of resistance, they've been sort of monetised and captured by and perverted by the forces that we're seeking to overturn. I mean, I'm a child of the sixties, which was another period of great hope when we thought we would change the world, love, peace … and within less than a decade it was monetised and bastardised. Our heroes become tax exiles and financial whiz-kids rather than artists (I mean, not all of them …) but the whole thing was sucked into the money machine and created accordingly.
>
> (Brian)

> There is a danger in the activist scene of the commodification of some of these ideas – anarchism or something like that – it can be easy to package up these ideas and sell them to people, rather than explore them in a more honest way.
>
> (2014, int. 4)

> Well, if you want to look at the ways in how capitalism can swallow up its own contradictions, it does it very effectively, y'know?
>
> (Nick)

As Gitlin (2012) has argued, the Occupy movement might even be described as having suffered from a 'co-optation phobia' with a popular fear of commodification, monetisation, capture, perversion, bastardisation, and anxiety that its authentic resistance might be packaged up and swallowed by that which it was attempting to resist. But such a fear of being rendered inauthentic only added to the *myth* of co-optation, which actually indicates an extension of market norms. As Hall *et al.* explain:

> manufactured and mass-marketed rebellion must be passed off as 'co-optation' in order that the perpetual cycles of competition and obsolescence in which the subject feels trapped can be blamed on the oppressive 'system' rather than the true source in the underlying code of bourgeois individualism manifested in the competitive consumption of positional goods that signify individuality.
>
> (2008: 109)

The preoccupation with authenticity and the fear of being co-opted and rendered inauthentic, in other words, plays into the drive for individual freedom, flexibility, symbolic inefficiency, and the postmodern injunction to 'enjoy' which define the new spirit of (consumer) capitalism.

Once again, this has an added effect of undermining collective organisation. The pursuit of authenticity, supported by myths of co-optation, promotes norms of individualism as 'conformity quickly became the new cardinal sin in our new society' (Heath and Potter 2006: 31). In place of commitment to any collective, disciplined identity, rebel consumers are instead encouraged to opt for the freedom and authenticity of individualised and unique identities, without realising that 'it's the non-conformists, not the conformists, who are driving consumer spending' (ibid.: 106). With each apparent act of non-conformity, including attempts to be 'off-grid' or to establish autonomous spaces, the myth of co-optation extends market innovation and norms through boycotting and buycotting, and demonstrating how 'the eternal urge for escape has never enjoyed such niche marketing' (Klein 2001: 64). The problem, therefore, is not necessarily consumerism itself, but an activist tendency to simply 'identify consumerism with conformity … [and] as a result they fail to notice that it is rebellion, not conformity, that has for decades been the driving force of the marketplace' (Heath and Potter 2006: 102). Or as Frank puts it, in 'resistance, obsolescence [has] found a new and more convincing language' (1997: 31) as 'consumer capitalism did not demand conformity or homogeneity, rather it thrived on the doctrine of liberation and continual transgression that is still familiar today' (ibid.: 20).

Ideas of authenticity as an attempt to avoid hypocrisy and co-optation by (as far as possible) establishing a cultural distance from the market, are therefore a central mechanism of symbolic inefficiency and postmodern consumer capitalism. By criticising all conformity as co-optation, activists problematically extend the normative distribution of the market, and it is in this way that the 'critique from the left not only accepts the basic terms of neoliberal capitalism, but actually promotes 'alternatives' that ultimately advance its cause' (Hickel and Khan 2012: 206). By framing political action as a matter of boycotting or buycotting certain commodities, such an approach plays into the planned obsolescence of product turnover, allowing our 'anxieties over consumption' to create 'niche markets' (Littler 2009: 1), ultimately revealing 'the scale of our collective failure to deal with these problems on any significant level other than through small palliative measures orchestrated through lifestyle choices of the sufficiently privileged' (ibid.: 14). Building upon the libertarian distrust of conformity as dampening individual free will, the new spirit of capitalism and the myth of co-optation directly promote 'many of the individualistic and libertarian ideas that have always made neoliberalism and free-market ideology' (Heath and Potter 2006: 72). The possibility of collective solidarity and organisation is, therefore, once again, foreclosed by norms which filter cultural desires for change 'through individual lifestyles' with the 'organisation of individual actions in terms of meaning assigned to lifestyle elements (e.g. brands, leisure pursuits and friend networks) [which] results in the personalisation of issues' (Bennett and Segerberg 2011: 771).

Conclusion: being politically responsible

On the one hand, it is problematic that resistance has become a lucrative cultural resource for consumer capitalism, as this raises a number of important questions about the possibility of actually undermining or challenging such a system. Rather than a homogenising force, the new spirit of capitalism thrives off symbolic inefficiency, encouraging heterogenous, unique, undisciplined, and perpetually unsatisfied libertarian, non-conformist identities, which are always in search of a more authentic experience and in the process of moving on from those deemed co-opted clichés. Thus, this is a consumer market which is always (seemingly) able to overcome its own cultural limits, and remains popular by appearing to address its shortcomings, creating a culture where 'not only resistance but even our distaste of the artificiality of consumerism itself has for a long time been incorporated into marketing strategies' (Hall *et al.* 2008: 100). And yet, on the other hand, we need to be careful that our argument that capitalism 'incorporates' its own critique, doesn't lead us to mistakenly situate resistance as something which is authentic and outside such normative structures, as this would itself feed into the perpetual pursuit of authenticity and myths of co-optation. We also need to recognise that this very pursuit of distance from capitalism is already an extension of market norms which underpin such a system.

As I have argued above, through all the twists and turns in logic and argumentation, the pursuit of authenticity – such as through boycotting and buycotting, through being original members of the movement, or through self-sacrifice and risk – was a prominent underlying principle within Occupy (in) London. It has been my contention that this is problematic, as insofar as we find evidence for the pursuit of authenticity, purity, and the 'moral high ground', we also find evidence of a certain normative foreclosure of the movement, unintentionally reiterating the normalcy of the very distributions it was attempting to resist. There is even some evidence that a few activists were allowing such norms to directly limit the horizon of their own politics:

> I want to make it perfectly clear, *I am not an anti-capitalist at all.* I buy cigarettes, I buy tobacco, I buy clothes … we live in a capitalist world! I think it's personally *impossible to be anti-capitalist in a capitalist system.* You can avoid the system as much as you like but I mean … even nowadays … if you are making your own clothes, you are buying the fabric off someone, you're buying the sewing machine off someone … there's no possible way you cannot be capitalist in this world I don't think.
>
> (2012, int. 4)

Prelimiting her resistance, this position suggests that if her protest cannot be authentic and free from hypocrisy, then she simply cannot adopt that political stance. The possibility of anti-capitalism is therefore foreclosed to her by the very police order that reasserted capitalism after the crash as the only sensible (rational, reasonable, possible) socio-economic system. Not that this is a problem unique to Occupy, as 'even in the case of the most radical movements, it shares 'something' with what it seeks to criticise … [which] stems from the simple fact that the normative references on which it is based are themselves in part inscribed in the world' (Boltanski and Chiapello 2007: 40).

It is concluded that activists need to avoid such tendencies of pursuing an authentic, pure, autonomous identity from which to adopt the moral high ground and must try not to get caught up in the games of hypocrisy and co-optation. Rather than fearing the inauthentic, movements should simply accept the Foucauldian double bind that there is 'no outside to power' and instead concentrate their energies on refiguring wider normative distributions through symbolically efficient collectivity and making 'non-sense' appear. Or in Jenny's words:

> Capitalism is so pervasive that I think it's exhausting to try and do it 'right' all the time. Sometimes you just have to say: 'we're all contradictory'. We're contradicting sitting here, right now, this minute, having a conversation about it!

Instead of playing into police distributions of the sensible/non-sensible, movements like Occupy should avoid making unwinnable defences against claims that they are 'inauthentic' or 'hypocritical' ('nothing to see here, they drink Starbucks!'). Such an approach can only play into the idea that this is a legitimate ground from which to marginalise and designate their appearance and voice as 'non-sensible' and 'powerless', while perpetuating ideas of marginal righteousness where movements decide 'not to take the risk of winning [when] … defeat, at least, can't be co-opted' (Foucault 1989: 106). The pursuit of authenticity creates a culture of resistance that aims to be 'always morally correct and never politically responsible' (Dean 2009: 6) in that, by locating 'authenticity' in a 'distance' from the mainstream and powerful institutions, activists are led to celebrate powerlessness and marginality. In order to intervene in the distribution of the sensible and force the appearance of two worlds in one, the 'non-sense' idea that there could be an alternative needs to be asserted through a collective aesthetic, democratic authority, and political responsibility.

5 They owe us

Docklands, September 2013

Our rendezvous point was the Prince Regent stop on the Docklands Light Railway line. While we were standing around and waiting for something to happen, Police Community Support Officers (PCSOs) had begun circulating among the crowd, saying hello and trying to make casual friendly conversation with the assembled activists. As two approached us, however, the protestor I was talking to warned me not to speak to them: 'you know these Smurfs are forward intelligence officers, don't you?' Mockingly known as Smurfs for their baby-blue vests, these outwardly affable PCSOs were immediately treated with suspicion for fear that they might be harbouring hidden intentions. 'They' were not on 'our' side.

We were there to occupy the world's largest arms fair – the DSEI (Defence and Security Equipment International) – which boasted a guest list which included countries on the UK government's own human rights watchlist (e.g. Colombia, Iraq, Pakistan, Saudi Arabia) as well as the world's largest arms companies, including manufacturers of illegal tear gas, and suppliers to the Saudi and Israeli militaries. A press release on the Campaigns Against Arms Trade website (CAAT 2017) explained the motivation behind the protest:

> The weapons companies and militaries responsible for the civilians killed on the streets of Bahrain and Egypt, for those killed in drone attacks, and even for arming Assad, will be in London. We're taking action to stand in their way, to bring down the government support for the arms fair and to take on those who profit from conflict and repression.

Suddenly, there was a shout for everyone to follow and we moved quickly around the corner to the entrance of the ExCeL centre. The plan had been agreed in advance but kept to a small group so that the police couldn't anticipate the activists' movements. Green pop-up tents adorned with anti-war slogans sprang up on the roundabout leading to the entrance, although there was no sign of other resources needed for a long-term occupation (e.g. sleeping bags) which suggested these were a symbolic gesture. The drums started up. One protestor, who had created a fantastic costume of the grim reaper, was dancing on stilts just as the 'bike bloc' arrived and everyone cheered as they did a lap of the roundabout. Other activists lay down in front of the trucks as they arrived and chained themselves together in front of the entrance gates. In a clever example of artistic *détournement*, they had even printed out the admission policy for the arms fair, underlining the pertinent sentences:

> DSEI Admission Policy
>
> Any person in possession of non-permitted items will be refused entry to or ejected from the venue and site. Prohibited items include knives, fireworks, explosives, smoke canisters, aerosols, airhorns, noisemakers, flares, weapons, dangerous or hazardous items, illegal substances, laser devices, bottles, glass vessels, cans, poles, or any article that may compromise public safety or which may pose a hazard or nuisance to any other person, or any article to be used for a commercial or a charitable purpose.
>
> (See www.dsei.co.uk/page.cfm/Link=16/t=m/goSection=11_52)

I spotted Shaun who, clearly remembering our conversation about undercover police earlier that week, came straight over to me and without saying hello, pointed out someone he thought was a plain-clothes officer. He commented on the way this individual was moving around the protest and the suspicious manner in which he seemed to be walking between the police and the protestors. But most of all, Shaun told me, the biggest giveaway were the black boots.

Introduction: conspiracy theories

Labelling someone a 'conspiracy theorist' is usually taken as an insult. It suggests that they have no capacity for reason or rational thinking, it questions their sanity, and insinuates that their grievances should not be considered 'sensible'. The more elaborate the theory the more distance people try to put between themselves and it, with some speculations (for instance, that movements have been infiltrated by undercover police) deemed more 'reasonable' than others (say, pan-historical and international networks of power operating beyond our imagination). To speak of the Illuminati, for example, as an underground network in pursuit of a New World Order and responsible for major historical events (from the French Revolution, to 9/11 and the financial crisis) is to risk inviting mocking laughter and raised eyebrows. To mention the Rothschilds and Freemasons who are thought to control global finance, the mainstream media, and governments, is to risk dismissal as 'nonsense'. And yet we also live in an era in which many so-called conspiracy theories have actually proved to be true. Take, for instance, the invasive state surveillance of the US National Security Agency (NSA) and the UK

Government Communications Headquarters (GCHQ) through communications software and mobile phones (as revealed by Edward Snowden); the mountain of secretive state actions revealed by Chelsea Manning and WikiLeaks; and right down to the elite education and social clubs of British politicians and corporate executives (fast-tracked from Eton to degrees in Philosophy, Politics and Economics at Oxford and thence to Downing Street via Bullingdon Club swine-based initiation rituals).

Whether something counts as a conspiracy theory, in other words, should not be simply a judgement on its *truthfulness.* Whether the theory is that the Queen of England is a shape-shifting reptilian overlord (following David Icke) or that there are undercover police officers at an anti-arms rally, I argue that what we should focus less on determining the accuracy of such theories, and more on *how such theories construct self-understandings of power and resistance.* This allows us to understand the possible foreclosures that such narratives create for resistance, rather than speculating on the policing of movements by secret forces. By definition, arguing whether a conspiracy theory is true or false is unwinnable, as they speculate on the *known unknowns* of power – things we 'know' that we 'don't know' – and therefore cannot be proven. Even in cases of revelation, the conspiracy itself retreats anew ('you think that was the truth? That's what they *want* you to think'). But how such narratives frame power and resistance is clear. Power becomes constructed as something which is secret, controlling, top-down, centralised, hidden, and operating behind appearances, meaning that a conspiracy theory could include any 'narrative that has been constructed in an attempt to explain an event or series of events to be the result of a group of people working in secret to a nefarious end' (Birchall 2006: 34). Thus, conspiracy theory could be said to apply to a wide range of ideas about power: from the often-mocked explanation of global networks like the Illuminati, to more widely accepted ideas of shady collusions between state and market (the 1%) and operations carried out by undercover police in surveillance and espionage.

Taking this broad definition, I will demonstrate in this chapter how conspiracy theories and cynicism were central to the way in which Occupy (in) London framed its resistance in relation to the power the activists understood themselves to be up against. We will begin with an outline of the prevalence of conspiracy theory within the movement, as well as activist defences of such narratives as useful for organisation, disruptive of normative discourses of knowledge, and simply 'accurate' in capturing the 'nature' of power (if not the truth itself). Such arguments find their parallels in social theory, but it will be my contention that, while these defences are not necessarily wrong, the political potential granted to conspiracy theories actually overlooks many limitations. First, against arguments that such narratives might be useful for organisation, Occupy (in) London demonstrated that the idea that fellow activists might be undercover officers and representing a powerful conspiracy actually fractured and undermined solidarity. The distrust that such narratives caused, it will be suggested, actually did *more* damage to the movement than any potential information that infiltrators may or may not have gathered. The second idea, that conspiracy theories might disrupt the normative order of knowledge, is limited insofar as this creates further libertarian cynicism towards collective organisation and authority. The post-crash UK Parliament, which was suspected of colluding against the democratic interest, was not in any way challenged by snide and cynical criticisms, with such cynicism precluding the possibility of intervening into a central and crucial site of influence.

This model also plays into the third and final limitation. Far from providing an 'accurate' intuition about the nature of power, framing it as centralised, top-down, cynical, and hidden *overlooks* structural critiques in favour of a more revelatory mode of resistance. When the truth of power is always considered to be behind appearances, then the aim becomes to 'reveal' that truth and show it for what it really is (hence ideas of 'waking up the people' or the well-worn Anonymous phrase 'what if I told you …'). Yet not only does this play into a certain modernist conception of truth and a postmodernist cynicism in which all appearances cannot be trusted, but it also automatically pre-positions the protestors as the weak and powerless and 'them' as the all-powerful and insurmountable. Furthermore, whenever this self-definition of powerlessness intersects with ideas of authenticity, movements risk playing into a 'cunning of impotence' (Nietzsche 2008) and a 'siege mentality' (Brown 2001) in which that weakness and marginality is celebrated as a *virtue*. It will be concluded, therefore, that movements should avoid accepting (and championing) their designation as marginal, weak, inconsequential, and without authority, and instead assert positions of collective democratic authority and political responsibility.

Mobilising conspiracy theories

Because designating someone a conspiracy theorist can be used as a way for the police order to designate grievances with power as 'non-sense' – as well as draw a normative line between the rational and the irrational, the sane and the insane – I have tried to be careful about the way in which I portray conspiracy theory within the Occupy movement in London. This does of course depend on how we identify conspiracy theory (and I have taken a particularly broad definition, which I argue will be useful in highlighting the limitations such narratives present movements in a problematic framing of power and resistance). Yet I do not want to overstate the prevalence of what we might call the 'popular understanding' of conspiracy theories, which might add to policing labels of the movement as naïve, unreasonable, and irrational. The majority of Occupy activists in London were not conspiracy theorists in the popular sense of the term. Ideas about 'the 1%' varied in sophistication and depth, from outright pathological dismissals of individuals to more complex narratives of systematic and ideological collusions between state and market, and while ideas about undercover agents were widespread, they were based on a precedent of previous cases when undercover police have been outed (see Evans and Lewis 2013).

Having said that, popular conspiracy theories were nevertheless sufficiently prevalent within the movement to be part of everyday conversations:

> I worked at the info-tent at Occupy London [LSX] for a long time and I'd have people coming to me (thinking I was some kind of authority because I was standing behind a desk) saying: 'I've got some YouTube videos for you' – Great, what are they about? – 'Well, did you know that 9/11 didn't actually happen?!' You got it *all the time.* And I can't just say that that's down to ignorance, this idea of Rothschilds, Illuminati, the 'all-seeing eye'… just because there was an icon somewhere near the camp in Occupy London, everyone being like: 'yeah, we've been infiltrated'.
>
> (2014, int. 8)

Although this is the experience of just one activist, this interaction suggests that such narratives of all-encompassing hidden power networks were quite common occurrences and were considered by many to be a common-sense understanding of the way in which power operates. It demonstrates that there were certainly some occupiers in London who promoted and spread what are commonly understood as conspiracy theories about the Illuminati, the Rothschilds, or 9/11 being an inside job, and that the activist who had shown me a picture of 'the all-seeing eye' at Trafalgar Square (see Chapter 3) was not a one-off.

Some activists expressed despair at the popularity of such theories, arguing that those who believed in such rubbish were exhausting, mad, or just ignorant; on the other hand, others (while ensuring that they were still distancing themselves from such narratives) mounted reflexive defences of conspiracy theories. For instance, some argued that such narratives might actually be considered useful for organising resistance, putting it to me that such discourses of power could be mobilised as part of Occupy's consolidation of collective protest:

> There's a collective narrative that goes on as well … about how we take shit for so long and then we rise up against the dictator or the evil king or stuff like this … To that extent, this can be part of what Occupy is doing. It's, y'know, for it to go around the world so quickly, there must be something like a collective meme or something … I mean, what does 'conspiracy' mean anyway? If two people get together to agree a plan on something, that's a conspiracy!
>
> (Greg)

> Questioning the status quo, looking for alternatives, looking for one that's more positive so the outcomes effect the general public (as far as they're

> not the 1% you know?) Being really critical of the way that … it seems that governments are lobbied and these think tanks exist by corporations and there's things like that influence government … well, government seems to be influenced by corporations.
>
> (Harry)

While Greg and Harry don't necessarily 'believe' in such narratives they argue that they might form the basis of a movement if used as a pragmatic organisational tool and a method for encouraging the wider public to be critical and look for alternatives to the status quo. Such a defence of conspiracy theory as useful for spurring collective organisation and critical consciousness finds its counterpart in political theory. As Dean has argued, for instance, conspiracy theories might be considered as bestowing a certain symbolic efficiency on 'us' as opposed to 'them', drawing the lines in the sand through 'the fantasy of a "we" [which] is held open through the suspicion that there are secrets' (2002: 97). For Dean, conspiracy theories can also help to draw connections between different powerful groups as part of a critical approach to society and politics, because 'insofar as practitioners can link together varieties of disparate phenomena to find patterns of denials, occlusion, and manipulation', then 'conspiracy theory, far from a label dismissively attached to the lunatic fringe, may well be a vehicle for political contestation' (ibid. 1998: 8). Such narratives, in other words, could become the basis of a collective self-recognition and collective critical identity, defining 'us' in comparison to 'them' (who are the cause of our grievances) and providing cohesion in a context of symbolic inefficiency, or as Dean puts it 'the so-called distributions and imaginative leaps of conspiracy theory may be helpful tools for coding politics in the virtual relations of the techno-global information age' (ibid.: 144).

While this organisational and critical potential of conspiracy theories might seem convincing in theory, I argue that the experience of Occupy (in) London suggests that such narratives – insofar as they are based on the perpetuation of a fundamental *distrust and cynicism* – actually have the opposite potential to undermine solidarity and collective organisation. As I will demonstrate below, the conspiracy theory that there were undercover police and agents infiltrating the movement proved to be a fracturing and divisive narrative that, far from creating a helpful tool for coding politics and becoming a vehicle for political contestation, actually helped to dissolve and break the movement apart.

And yet, as Birchall has argued, conspiracy theories might instead be thought of as useful for challenging the normative distribution of the police order. By pushing the limits of what counts as 'reasonable' knowledge and subsequently demonstrating the *contingency* of those limits, she argues that conspiracy theories can advance marginalised and dismissed 'folk knowledges' while at the same time illustrating how 'all knowledge is only ever "theory", that the relationship between the sign and its referent is necessarily inflected by imaginary processes, and that any transcendental truth claims rely on contingent strategies of information' (Birchall 2006: 73). Conspiracy theories, in other words, might be defended on the grounds that they highlight normative orders of *knowledge* and hierarchies of *authority*, and these police that which may or may not be considered 'sensible'. Or, in Felicity's words:

> [Conspiracy theory] is that feeling that something's wrong and that you don't like the current system. Yet because you are in the current system, you're so engulfed in it, it's very hard to find a way to resist it or to you know … 'cause in a way it's not really enough to resist: you have to start tearing its logic apart.

By illustrating that there is a police logic at play, the argument is that conspiracy theories break through foreclosures of resistance and instead 'start tearing the logic apart'. By demonstrating where the distribution is being drawn between the sensible and non-sensible, conspiracy theories allow activists not only to discern that line but to see it as contingent and un-fixed (i.e. challengeable).

And yet the evidence from Occupy (in) London, once again, suggests that this doesn't seem to work in practice. Rather than pushing activists to challenge police order logic and distribution, instead such conspiracy narratives add to the libertarian *cynicism* of power and collective authority, seeing all authority as something to be avoided. Theories of the state colluding with the market ('the 1%'), for instance, foreclosed alternative possibilities of what government or political parties could be, instead framing them as *necessarily* corrupted and corrupting of authentic resistance and change. Faced only with cynical and snide ridicule, politicians and experts felt emboldened by neoliberal normativity, and able to simply dismiss the idea of alternatives as 'nonsense'. Not only did this dismiss the state in advance as a crucial arena of post-crash struggle, but it also defined politicians and experts as those in possession of legitimate 'authority', while the protestors, in comparison, were the ones without authority.

Crossing over with this cynical approach to the state is our third and final defence of conspiracy theory, which argues that – while such narratives of power might not necessarily be 'true' – they nevertheless capture something about the nature of power, oppression, and democratic deficit:

> If you can easily suspect a government of doing that sort of thing, then it's bad enough. If you can imagine them doing it, then it's bad already because it means they have the *capability* of doing it.
>
> (2014, int. 6)

> The other thing I think about this conspiracy thing is that, it's contemporary myth, if you like, it's always rooted in something. I looked into

> this a while back. I looked into rumour and the sociological functions of rumour and urban legends always point to something … some kind of instinctive truth. For example, there is an urban legend of crocodiles in the [New York] subways, and sociologists look at it and say: 'there is a clear mythical perspective that there are *great powerful forces under the surface that are dangerous and moving around*'. And I really think that's got some weight to it, the kind of narrative we come up with – the reptilian overlords, the bloodsucking aristocrats – I mean, that's very symbolic.
>
> (Shaun)

The argument here is that if people can imagine elites acting in such a way against the public interest and with unaccountable impunity, then the situation has already got 'bad enough'. There is a 'grain of truth' to all theories, there is no smoke without fire, even if the theory itself might seem a little unbelievable or far-fetched. For these defenders, therefore, conspiracy theory not only tells us something about the truth that power is unequally distributed in an (allegedly) democratic society, but also that power is something dangerous, that is operating 'beneath the surface', and which more people should wake up to and become aware of.

To reiterate, it is not the intention of this chapter to take a stance on the accuracy of conspiracy theories of power, but to critically elaborate on how such narratives develop problematic constructions, framings, and understandings of the relationship between power and resistance. The problem with this final defence, therefore, is not that all conspiracy theories are simply false understandings of power, but that *they encourage the construction of power as something which is, by its nature, top-down, nefarious, and operating behind appearances.* This model not only extends modern narratives of truth and postmodern narratives of cynicism, but also pre-positions activists as the 'powerless' and the 'marginal' when faced with all-encompassing and secret powers which can never be reached or challenged. When this intersects with ideas of authenticity, the problem is then further amplified through a cultural tendency to then *celebrate* this powerlessness and marginality as a virtue and sign of authenticity.

Conspiracy theories may well have some political potential in certain contexts – such as facilitating critical organisation, challenging normative distributions, and capturing part-truths of power – but it is my contention that they perhaps do more harm than good, by spreading distrust, libertarian cynicism and foreclosure, as well as pre-positioning activists as 'the weak'. Conspiracy theories are a direct result of a disenchanted and cynical political climate, characterised by profound disillusionment, disconnectedness, and alienation felt towards collective institutions, as well as a sense of powerlessness, helplessness, and anxiety brought on by a decline in symbolic efficiency. As has been argued elsewhere, in this climate, conspiracy theories might well be considered a predictable part of any movement, which 'symbolically takes to task the political leaders of the most powerful nation-states' as 'this can go hand-in-hand – visually, rhetorically and analytically – with the depiction of world leaders and their associates as secretive, undemocratic conspirators trying to take control of economic processes' (Schlembach 2014: 18). But I argue that effective resistance is not, in fact, something prevented by secret and nefarious powerful interests which are opposing activists from behind the scenes; but by a normative structure and foreclosure that was actually maintained through such cynical models of power and resistance.

Infiltrators and saboteurs

One of the more sinister explanations given for the eventual fracturing and dissolving of the Occupy movement in London was that a number of activists were in fact undercover agents who had infiltrated the movement in order to corrupt and sabotage its resistance from within. Such a suspicion that their fellow protestors could be part of a conspiracy against the movement in some capacity – be that the police, the security services, or the Illuminati – was widely shared within the movement, as indicated by a number of high-profile cases which demonstrated how police in the UK do not consider it beyond their legitimate capabilities to infiltrate even peaceful movements (with perhaps the most famous example being 'Mark Stone (Kennedy)' who went undercover in environmental movements for seven years (see Evans and Lewis 2013). For some, while such infiltrations were clearly an abuse of power, they were also evidence that their protest was morally right and presented a real political challenge to the establishment. After asking outright if I was undercover police, for example, James explained:

> They're all over us! They're studying hard what we're doing. They're studying Occupy and they're infiltrating the squats and they're spending multi-million pounds to get inside our heads, our motivations, and find out what it is we want to do, how we plan to do it, and the dangers of how that could spread (because if it does spread, they're in real shit!) And they know this because they know how much they're going to cut and they know how desperate people will become, they're going to increasingly pump money into security and politicking and military and surveillance to quell further unrest.

Who exactly 'they' were was not always made completely clear, but 'they' were understood to be worried about the potential impact of the Occupy movement, or at least concerned enough that they were attempting to directly police and oppress the protest using surveillance and intelligence, pre-empting direct action in order to organise against them, and disciplining the protest from spreading further. For James, it was clear that what the movement was doing was important, otherwise why would 'they' be trying to stop it?

The overall effect of this particular conspiracy theory within the movement, however, was not one of self-designated pride for having created something important, effective, and worthwhile. Instead, speculation and rumour hung in the air, with accusations beginning to circulate about who the 'agents' were. This soon developed into clear organisational problems of who should (or should not) be trusted:

> Well, I mean there's probably infiltrators on the site – obviously we can't know who it is – but I have more respect for people … the infiltrators who actually have to sleep in tents and stuff and live on hardly any food. It was funny at St Paul's, you know, people with no money somehow got fuller of face … seemed to be getting wider.
>
> (Greg)

> I think there is a possibility that capitalism may try to infiltrate this to cause problems and things like that, but if that happens, I am absolutely certain that we'll seek them out and send them on their way.
>
> (2012, int. 8)

> But Occupy was certainly infiltrated by this. I wouldn't have much problem naming who they were, but there might have been one that I missed. And they're always good fun doing the work, we feed rubbish information to take back [laughs]. No, I mean, there's always been undercover police in every left-wing organisation. Even the right-wing organisations (even though they'd be more sympathetic to the right-wing organisations).
>
> (2014, int. 11)

> You know there was infiltrators at various levels. You've got MI6 around the corner you know, because of the Anonymous being there as well, there was CIA (and it was actually mentioned in court, CIA involvement).
>
> (2013, int. 13)

It was taken as read that there were definitely infiltrators within the movement, with 'clues' including something as innocent as activists 'getting fuller of face' despite a lack of food, and 'slips' being as innocuous as those who turned up at the camps with expensive, brand-new tents and sleeping bags (or even those who simply arrived in pairs, including two men who had apparently arrived wearing matching socks and black boots). Despite a lack of clear and direct evidence, however, the activists were certain that there were spies and saboteurs among them, as if the very fact that it was difficult to know who they were was itself an indication that there was a conspiracy afoot to try and bring down the movement.

Given this atmosphere in the background, James wasn't the only interviewee who was somewhat suspicious of whether I – with a voice recorder, notepad, and official consent form – was trying to infiltrate and gather intelligence on the movement for the police. But I was by no means alone in being treated with suspicion and distrust simply for being a newcomer. As Harry explained:

> I mean, even the same way you got in contact with me, I thought: 'ok, maybe they've [Occupy] sent this guy to me to find out if I'm kosher?!' because it does make you start to think like that … When I went to the actual meeting, these people who were facilitating the meeting I found very cold. I felt there was a real wariness towards me. I voiced my concern saying: 'look, I think some of these people might think I'm some sort of undercover agent, they might think I'm press, you know? I've come from nowhere, I've turned up, I've said can I get involved … yeah, maybe they think I'm police or press or … you know?' And he said … I can't actually remember what he said, I can't remember whether he said 'maybe' or 'not sure'.

Distrust towards newcomers brought on by the fear of infiltration created clear preclusions and hierarchies within the movement, making it less easy to welcome people to the movement and to qualitatively extend to others. This wariness created a debilitating doubt within the organisation, and some activists expressed dismay at the growing paranoia within the movement:

> I think there's a lot that goes on that we have no knowledge about … I think that undercover policing thing … people are bound to get paranoid about that because there have been so many revelations and a lot of … I mean people's trust has been destroyed.
>
> (2014, int. 1)

> Sometimes when you get too well known, then people start accusing you of being a police officer and that is damaging as it can land you in trouble sometimes. If they bad-mouth you to other people, then you're going to be suspected.
>
> (Dan)

Accusations of people being saboteurs became more and more common as the movement began to fracture and break apart, with cliques even formed by those who shared reservations about certain individuals, in order to keep them out of decision-making. Newcomers who wanted to join in or learn more about Occupy (and therefore asked 'too many questions') were treated with immediate suspicion, while long-involved personalities who had become 'too well known' within the movement were accused of being agents trying to take over, co-opt, and steer Occupy in an ineffective direction. This meant that those who were simply trying to join the movement of 'the 99%', or just to speak up and offer an alternative point of view at the assemblies, started to be viewed sceptically:

> For me, there's a very strong discomfort in being distrustful. We want to be a movement of the 99% and include people who look a bit different and don't really turn up to these kinds of things. But if we immediately treat them as coppers, then they're not going to feel welcome, etc. … It's the threat of those things more than the reality that does the damage. I mean, if anyone could be a copper, then as soon as you see anything that anyone is doing as 'counter-productive' to the movement (as per your vision of it) – 'hang on a minute, you're a cop! That's why you're doing this because you want to fuck everything up!'
>
> (2014, int. 3)

By creating a 'zero-level' argument in open debates, theories of infiltration allowed people to hang onto their individualised views of the movement and dismiss the views of others merely as 'sabotage'. Thus, through such 'simplifications of power to be found in paranoid rhetoric', a minority of activists were able to simply 'produce knee-jerk reactions to anything that threatened their belief system' (Birchall 2006: 89). Unfalsifiable arguments that people were only disagreeing because they were trying to create division and break the movement apart were utilised by individuals in order to maintain their previously held positions and beliefs, never having had to be prepared to compromise or to be reflexive in the direction of collective solidarity, and even using such accusations as a last resort in order to supply stubbornness. Subsequently, raising alternative ideas which went against wider consensus became treated less as evidence of democratic vibrancy and more as an attempt to manipulate and destroy the movement.

It could be argued, therefore, that there did not actually need to be undercover agents within the movement for the damage to be done. This is not to say that there weren't infiltrators, but it seems that the theory itself was enough to spread just enough insecurity and distrust among the activists to cause them to eventually split and divide. Once again, Jenny provided a valuable insight into how the theory of conspiracies can, by itself, dissolve movement solidarity, making further comparisons with her experience at Greenham Common. She recalled that at the peace camp 'there was certainly an inordinate amount of conversation about undercover agents and such … some people were obsessed with it and many people were accused of being one'. One theory in particular – which was initially brought to the group by an activist returning from arrest – was that the Russians (in collaboration with the British) had developed a weapon that could make the activists in the camp suddenly fall ill:

> The nickname for this microwave bombardment was 'zapping' and she [the informant] said 'zapping' was going on at Greenham. Within short order, numbers of women started leaving the camp and becoming ill … and I used to say: 'well, I haven't been zapped!' It was supposed to happen … you'd be sitting around the fire and somebody would say: 'I've been zapped'. And I'd think, really?

For Jenny, the *rumour* that the camp was under attack was enough to begin tearing it apart. It therefore didn't matter whether 'zapping' was real or not because, after the conspiracy had been spread by this 'double agent', it was able to act as a *meta-conspiracy* or a rumour started by the police in order to disrupt their protest. Continuing with her story, Jenny then told me that she was invited to take part in a Channel 4 documentary on the Greenham Common protest in the early 1990s, which was also going to include a former intelligence officer. However, the programme was cancelled at the last moment:

> to a huge amount of disturbance on behalf of TV critics who said it was going to be a great programme and why was it being taken off the air? And certainly, in my own mind, it's because this guy was going to say it's an exercise in psychological warfare. And I think that's quite interesting in terms of conspiracy theories … because it's a double-bluff, isn't it?

Whether or not 'zapping', or the sudden cancellation of the programme, is evidence of conspiracy is beside the point. What this story demonstrates is the power of conspiracy theory in creating distrust and division within the movement, a narrative that is perhaps more effective than any infiltration in destroying collective organisation. Conspiracies of infiltration have the potential, it seems, to cause more damage as myths and rumour, than they might as surveillance, espionage, or sabotage. Such paranoia creates situations of fracturing and division, breaking apart efforts to organise collectively as well as democratically negotiate the movement's collective identity, appearance, and actions.

Frustration, stress, sleep deprivation, extreme weather, paranoia-inducing drugs, as well as the inability to care properly for those suffering from mental illness, surely did nothing to alleviate the distrust which developed between members of the Occupy movement in London. As things began to fragment, and people became ever more exhausted, accusations of who was responsible for compromising the movement (and all the effort the activists had invested into it) became rife. Disagreements were no longer seen as the hallmark of democratic negotiation, but instead as evidence of a conspiratorial plan to undermine and sabotage their resistance, leading to the development of exclusive cliques and hierarchical circles of trust. In other words, the problem of conspiracy theory here is that it *foreclosed* the possibility of collective organisation and solidarity, instead lending itself to further preclusions and unaccountable hierarchies.

'The 1%'

As the group which was imagined to be directly opposed to 'the 99%', 'the 1%' became an empty container for many post-crash grievances and summed up Occupy's anger and indignation at neoliberal collusions between ostensibly 'democratic' governments and plutocratic demands to socialise the crisis through bailouts, quantitative easing, austerity, tax relief, and tax avoidance. What is particularly at stake in the idea of 'the 1%', is that corporations are seen to be operating against the democratic will of the electorate with a disproportionate sway over the policy and decisions that representatives make. The implication being that there was a consistent 'elite' conspiracy across state and economy, with the power to make far-reaching decisions of global significance despite merely being 'the 1%'. This powerful, anti-democratic ruling class was, in the aftermath of the crisis, considered simply to be maintaining inequality, injustice, and democratic deficit for its own mutual benefit:

> Let us be under no illusions that the ruling class and their executives in government have got an armoury that they will use against us: we've seen that in various countries around the world.
>
> (2012, int. 8)

> I think Occupy is against exclusivity, yeah? Occupy's promoting inclusivity … but I think that's where we left with the 1% … I think we can be pretty sure that the 1% who are in power are not going to give up, not in the short term. I think it's a lot of things going on at the moment that they won't give up lightly, and as far as I'm concerned, they can fuck off to the Cayman Islands and suck it.
>
> (2012, int. 9)

> Clearly the very powerful do conspire in their mutual interests – and that's why they are the 1% – but it's because they conspire very effectively and they get together in Davos to work out some specific elements of that.
>
> (2014, int. 3)

> The stock exchange hosts and supports all these disgusting corporations that are harming us in so many different way and are basically controlling our lives. We have so little say in stuff that affects us and international trade is something that affects us all … the whole global capitalist system is something that affects us all.
>
> (2013, int. 6)

Considering themselves to be 'under no illusions', these activists had seen the 'truth' behind 'the 1%' as an international ruling class supported by powerful national governments and their armoury, ready to conspire and act towards their mutual protection of power, status, and wealth during the crisis. The notion of 'the 1%', therefore, expressed a suspicion of powerful and wealthy individuals acting in cahoots, purposefully exploiting democratic loopholes and corrupt parliaments in order to get their own way. Collective formal politics (such as political parties), as well as democratic governments, were simply fronts for much more closet operations and interests:

> Because that's the arrogance of politicians, they think they can do whatever. They call it 'democracy' … how is it a democracy when two million people go on the streets and say: 'we're totally against sending troops to Afghanistan/Iraq'. They go on the streets … and they totally ignore them. And this is called a democracy. I think democracy is a name for tricking people right?
>
> (2012, int. 8)

> [Austerity] is a deliberately designed programme to slaughter your public services, to sell them off to people-in-power's mates who run the utility company and the private services or whatever, and you know, funnel money out of people … and keep them so fucking hard at it, working, paying rent, being able to afford the bus, the food, everything else, dealing with all the other shit that's going on.
>
> (2013, int. 9)

Elected politicians, as part of 'the 1%', were a cynical and deceptive group, guided by selfish and instrumental principles of serving their own careers, as well as others in their class. Members of Parliament were understood to be abusing the trust placed in them by their electorate in order to simply further their own interests (rather than social justice or democracy) and subsequently – rather than seeing the '1%' as a group which had been legitimised by the continuation of neoliberal normativity – instead such narratives made a *pathology* out of individual actions. Whenever a politician broke a promise or defended corporate interests over democratic interests, this was simply an inevitable part of what is, in essence, a shady, immoral, and untrustworthy state.

This framing of power, therefore, extended a profound libertarian disillusionment towards the state (as a central and influential arena of struggle) and, by extension, any formal collective organisation or project (such as a party). Central government was seen as *inherently* flawed and beyond repair, a corrupted and corrupting system that will always be systematically exploited and abused by 'the 1%':

> And then, you know, in the news we see: 'oh yeah, politicians, MPs, we're going to give ourselves possibly ten grand [pay rise] because we think

> we're worth it!' And you think: 'You cunts! You fucking wankers!' There's all this ... all this kind of poverty going on (and we all know the Cabinet is supposed to be full of millionaires anyway). It's just greed looking after itself.
>
> (Harry)

> And the stuff in Westminster, that's not politics. That's not politics. And I'm bored of saying 'politicians lie' I mean we know that. I mean, in a sense, why are we still surprised by that?
>
> (2013, int. 4)

> Look what's happened with the Tories and the Liberals and stuff. They'll change these things and hope we kind of forget by the next time around. And even if an MP loses ... the lobbyists aren't going to care, are they? They'll hedge their bets and they'll bribe and lobby the next person who comes in, and the system itself can't really change that.
>
> (Greg)

It was reasoned that even seemingly idealistic and trustworthy politicians, as soon as they were elected, were susceptible to lying, spin, and becoming part of 'the 1%'. They were bound to collude with corporate interests eventually, and it was an easily predictable outcome of this system that MPs would, at some point, break promises to the electorate and let them down. They would sooner give themselves a pay rise or abuse the expenses system (even when so many came from already privileged and wealthy backgrounds) while the rest of the country were told to put up with austerity, than actually challenge corporate interests on behalf of the democratic post-crash grievances of the people. *And nothing was going to change that.*

Central to this cynical framing of 'the 1%', therefore, were debates about whether Occupy (in) London should or should not engage with the parliamentary system, either by forming its own party or by advocating support for existing organisations that resembled its views (such as the Green Party). The debate grew in the last days of the campsites when they were facing eviction, but became an extremely hot topic when counterpart movements in Greece (Syriza) and Spain (Podemos) appeared to be having limited early success in working alongside political parties. For many, however, entering the dark halls of power would necessarily lead to co-optation and therefore corruption of their authentic resistance, making them complicit to a system that only worked for 'the 1%':

> I think Occupy as a whole didn't want us to be a political party. I think the point was that the political system is part of the problem and I think that's right.
>
> (2014, int. 1)

> In terms of anything that veers towards reformism or complicity with the status quo of the state organising … these aren't models that solve the problems that Occupy was initially trying to address (or trying to address from my point of view). So, I don't think these reformist notions are productive, no.
>
> (2014, int. 4)

> Why would we choose to work within the frameworks that are fundamentally, by their own structure, inherently causing these problems? Why would we choose to engage on that platform?
>
> (Lucy)

> The brand is big enough that Occupy is perhaps the only name that could challenge UKIP or challenge the major parties and say there is a different way to do this. But then again, if we went into electoral politics, it would lose an amount of innocence and the innocence as seen by the public, the simplicity of the 99% and the 1%.
>
> (2014, int. 11)

When 'government' and the formal organisation of politics is seen as the problem, then any hint of reformism or developing a radical model of the state – or even simply viewing the state as a central and crucial arena of struggle and the distribution of possibility – is dismissed in advance as inauthentic complicity. Occupy (in) London's extra-parliamentary status was taken as evidence of its authenticity. Anything to do with the state or formal parties subsequently became the object of libertarian suspicion and rejection, thereby denying the protestors the possibility of using the state as an influential platform of resistance. This isn't to say that Occupy should have in any way limited itself to *only* engaging with the state, nor that it should even have necessarily become a political party, but that to not see the state as one major site of resistance *among many others* was a profound foreclosure of their ability to make their appearances seen and their voices heard.

In contrast, there were others within the movement who saw forming a political party or supporting an electoral alternative as crucial to changing the system from within and affecting wider societal change. Thus, many regretted the fact that Occupy (in) London never developed into something along these lines:

> But I think at heart it needs to be a political party that people can have faith in. And parties without spin doctors. A party where you have just got people to be brave enough just to be honest about shit.
>
> (Harry)

> The more level-headed and mature people … I mean, ok, you have rebellious people and a few good people can actually make changes, but

> unfortunately for that rebellion to succeed, you really need to actually have the majority of people. Suffragettes and the civil rights movement didn't do it by themselves, they ended up with politicians and unions and everybody else got involved. So, you can say: 'oh yeah, we're here, we're radical, we're special … *you can't join'*. It's like no, that's ridiculous.
>
> (Jenny)

> Well, when Occupy was happening, I was dead against it. When it was a camp, it seemed really poisonous to go down that track. But now we're trying to do things differently … well not differently … we're trying to promote ideas rather than just be against other ideas. It seems immature to discard the state. But having said that, I'm not sure I'd want to engage with the state via political parties … I don't know if there is another way because this is actually a huge hole in my activism … it's a big hole and I'd like to address it. I kind of think the Green Party has some very positive things it wants to do.
>
> (2014, int. 10)

Adopting a much less cynical position on organised politics and the state as an arena of resistance, these activists argued instead that it might be possible to create a 'different sort' of party, one which was more transparent and without the tendency towards spin, double-bluffs, secrecy, or conspiracy. For these advocates, while cautious, it might be possible to change the system from within and use the state as one platform from which to make an alternative appear.

And yet the lack of movement in this direction meant that Occupy (in) London only ever saw formal organisation and the state as limited to its current form:

> We say 'fuck you, government, what you are doing is wrong'. We try to do here altogether, the people together (because you're so fucking useless, government). We try to do it here in a way that's a little more sensitive or sensible.
>
> (2013, int. 8)

> This [Occupy] is the disenfranchised of this country. And the whole campaign for 'none of the above' would work by saying that a vote for anything else is a vote for the 1% … which of course, in truth, is what it is.
>
> (Jenny)

That the activists had allowed themselves to be positioned and defined in relation to this (neoliberal) normative insistence of the state's incapacity for direct democracy and radical justice, the police order which justified post-crash intervention of the state into the market, as well as 'unavoidable' and 'regrettable' austerity measures, was simply accepted. The state 'couldn't' (or 'shouldn't') do anything but rescue the wealthy, manage the budget through austerity, and provide national security against terrorism.

What's more, by positioning themselves in opposition to all things to do with the government, when the politician and economist pronounced their *authority* on the matter – that this was the only thing they could do – this was mirrored only by an implicit activist acceptance of their own *lack of authority* in comparison. Cynical, snide criticisms and insults aimed at politicians did nothing to fundamentally challenge this dynamic, and only foreclosed the possibility of a democratic authority and intervention in this distribution of the sensible. The decision not to engage with the state and stick to a cynical mocking of 'the 1%', in other words, only had the effect of reducing and restricting the possibility of their resistance to, in effect, 'asking for the political leadership of the country and the corporate financial system to change, to clean up their act and be less beastly to the global poor' (Winlow and Hall 2012: 10). Or as one activist put it:

> We're basically rationalistic, dualistic, and reactive. We're all inheritors of this kind of *distorted culture.* And I think … 'we're not hierarchical, so we're horizontal'… as if just being anti-hierarchy and trying to enforce horizontality just gives us solutions automatically. And as if organising things in participatory groups (as opposed to engaging with the centralised political system) … I think that's our biggest problem. The system is very happy that movements appear radical – like Occupy – [but] don't have any means or political levers. I think that fits capitalism quite well!
> (2014, int. 3).

Although 'the 1%' may form a group with a collective interest that acts to its mutual benefit, they can easily ignore criticisms that accuse them of 'not really being democratic' or that they are 'only in it for themselves'. This does nothing to undermine their normative authority on the situation, nor assert the authority of democratic alternatives, and instead problematically accepts 'common-sense' limits on what the post-crash state and collective politics could achieve. By addressing grievances 'upwards', Occupy (in) London was 'reinforcing rather than subverting the master's authority' (Dean 2009: 84), positioning itself in relation to 'the 1%' and therefore accepting its own designation as 'the one without authority' (i.e. 'non-sense'). Or as Butler puts it, through 'the effort to identify the enemy as singular in form', activists risk 'a reverse discourse that uncritically mimics the strategy of the oppressor instead of offering a different set of terms' (2006: 18). Through such a construction of power, the state was seen as something which belonged to 'them' and that 'we' cannot ever hope to change, resembling the type of cynical paranoia found in popular culture where 'the enemy is 'the system', the hidden 'organisation', the anti-democratic 'conspiracy' (Žižek 2011b: 170). In comparison to what is perceived to be a corrupted and corrupting system, resistance is rendered futile as the desire not to become 'one of them' by being 'co-opted' into the state apparatus encourages further cynicism, rather than an organised intervention into the normative structures of the police order. Or in Birchall's words: 'if I choose to read an event through the discourse of conspiracy theory, this will determine my agenda … I will find sinister rather than structural reasons for unanswered questions' (2006: 49).

The powers that be

At another level again from undercover police and 'the 1%', are theories of international pan-historical conspiracy networks. These are the narratives which are commonly understood to be conspiracy theories and, for their proponents, they captured the nefarious and secret organisation behind all appearances which was deemed to be in control of everything – from politics, to the economy, to the mainstream media. As *the* example of conspiracy theory par excellence, speculation about 'the powers that be' demonstrates a common theme running across all conspiracy theories: the cynical distrust of appearances. Whether a theory of undercover agents, state and corporate collusion, or international networks: they all rely on a model and understanding of power as being hidden, nefarious, and acting in secret behind appearances. Thus, they share a certain position of aiming at unaccountable and coercive agencies which are deemed to be 'out there', preventing or limiting change and operating against our will.

Following Sloterdijk, we could argue that such cynical narratives are themselves a product of a wider postmodern cynicism, in which the modern pursuit of 'un-concealing the truth' has created a situation in which 'a twilight arises, a deep ambivalence' (1987: 22). If the European Enlightenment project was a search for objective reason and truth via rational thinking, it is Sloterdijk's contention that, in practice, it produced the opposite, by rendering all appearances as potential screens to truth. Subsequently, because truth is understood as something hidden and concealed (rather than something normatively constructed), 'a new form of realism bursts forth, a form that is driven by the fear of being deceived or overpowered … everything that appears to us could be the deceptive manoeuvre of an overpowering evil enemy' (ibid.: 330). Rather than bringing about 'consciousness' or 'illumination', modernity brings about an 'enlightened false consciousness' that creates a disabling sphere of confusion, suspicion, distrust, cynicism, and symbolic inefficiency. Once power has been constructed in this mode, then the aim of resistance becomes to try and reveal the ultimate *truth* of power, to 'sort of peel back the curtain or try and peel back the Monopoly board and seeing if there was … if there is anything underneath' (Harry). Denying the structural operations of power, instead cynical activists set about findings clues for the 'real' power behind appearances, creating a debilitating situation in which the 'truth' of power can actually 'hide out in the open'. Through an 'emperor's new clothes'-style double bluff, Žižek has criticised the way in which such cynical resistance, with 'all its ironic detachment … leaves untouched the fundamental of ideological fantasy, the level on which ideology structured the social reality itself' (2008d: 27).

In other words, the distribution of the sensible, as a police order which needs to be challenged at a structural level, is unaffected and uninterrupted by efforts to try and find some power beneath it. No one believes the truth in front of their eyes. The objective structural violence of the status quo – extreme socio-economic disparity, war, violence, the international and historical exploitation of labour, the democratic deficit of market-driven policy – is *not* considered to be the *true* source of the problem – the truth of power must be deeper. This is why, for Foucault, 'the political question … is not error, illusion, alienated consciousness or ideology; it is truth itself' (1980: 97) because 'the mask is not simply hiding the real state of things, the ideological distortion is written into its very essence … that is why we must avoid the simply metaphors of de-masking, of throwing away the veils which are supposed to hide the naked reality' (Žižek 2008d: 25). For the postmodern subject that no longer trusts their eyes, the normal distribution of power (the emperor is naked) is overlooked in favour of going after some deeper conspiratorial truth and aiming for that final moment of revelation when all the workings of power will finally be exposed.

This construction of power is particularly debilitating, because such pan-historical and international networks, like the Illuminati, the Rothschilds and the Freemasons, were by definition broad, deep, and secret powers that could never actually be fully known or challenged. Conspiracy theories could never be fully revealed and instead would have to be pieced together through snippets of revelation and traces of evidence. Some, for example, found clues for these all-powerful agencies in popular culture:

> [The public is] being subliminally programmed through this stuff already, so when the 'change' happens, the thoughts are there. Films like *Avatar* are out there and whatever, that's put there by the Illuminati obviously and the truth is in it. Like that's their way of telling us … like … well putting the truth in front of our eyes (like *The Matrix*) and there's loads of other films like that that are like, you know, it's blatantly put in front of your face, but most people see it as sort of like, you know, it's just a film or whatever. Behind 'V' [*for Vendetta*] there's a good message and the people who have made those films which are controlled by the Masonry or whatever … they put that out there for a reason.
>
> (2012, int. 6)

Despite being the theories most at risk of being dismissed as 'non-sense', for this activist, the existence of such vast powerful networks was blatantly obvious and he chided the public for falling for it. For him, the truth of power was there to be uncovered if people only opened their eyes to the flagrant clues and how we have been subliminally programmed to accept 'their' domination. While most people would not notice such clues, this activist has seen through such appearances to the power hidden beneath.

Describing international conspiracy networks in such a mundane and 'obvious' manner, however, was not the most common way in which they were invoked. For others, there was a clear attempt to be a little more cautious in describing the secret workings of power. Wanting to avoid being designated as 'non-sense', instead this group downplayed the 'obviousness' of the theories, by adding appeals to common sense and evidence in order to bolster their credibility:

> And you start to think ... ok, you thought it was a 'conspiracy theory', but then you find out 'actually ...' And you only find these things when people start talking and a number of things like Bilderberg, and the 147 corporations that control the economy of the world (and actually it's been *proven* each time). And unfortunately, some of our guys go for the 'conspiracy side' – like the Bilderberg or the Rothschilds and everything else – you find out that the conspiracy side of Morgan Chase, Warburtons, Rothschilds ... they're not listed in the Forbes magazine. The 147 corporations have been proven by *New Scientist* in an article back in 2011. So, you start to think: 'ok, there's actually a bunch of people that are hidden out there, maybe?' I don't *know* but at least we know *something*.
>
> (Jenny)

Jenny's biographical appeal to knowledge is designed to show how she became convinced that there was 'something' going on behind appearances in an appropriately rational manner and through careful consideration and investigation. By referring to authoritative empirical sources and research (e.g. that something was in the *New Scientist* but missing from *Forbes*) she also attempts to appeal to 'reliable sources' of empirical evidence to make her point.

Such use of journalistic sources, however, was inconsistent with other arguments that the mainstream media were simply not to be trusted. Large media corporations and mainstream journalism were taken to be secretly on the side of the conspiracy, and were therefore covering up or spreading misinformation on behalf of the powers that be:

> Right, obviously the public's ideas are shared by what's in the newspapers or on the radio, on television and everything like that. So, there's always a campaign against, you know, dissent, alright? I don't know who leads these campaigns, but crooks, thieves, and liars (and I think Rupert Murdoch is one of the biggest of those).
>
> (2012, int. 8)

> Not that there is any 'one brain' of capitalism, but the powers that are out there to protect themselves were able to use that [media] as a means

> of defence. To show them in a bad light – *occupy* – to show them in a bad light.
>
> (Harry)

> I think one of the geniuses of the modern information deluge system is that the real conspiring that goes on and is operative in the world is diluted in a sea of so many stories of conspiracy that the actual conspiracy is very difficult to distinguish.
>
> (2014, int. 3)

Pre-empting the recent epistemological panic surrounding post-truth, alternative facts, and fake news, these activists were already struggling with the symbolic inefficiency and confusion caused by the information deluge in 2012–14. The problem is that it becomes impossible to say which information might be trusted and acted upon, which information is the 'truth', and which contains a bias or secret agenda. Yet once power is assumed to be something that is hidden behind appearances, then any appearances will simply become part of the cover-up and all sources of information rendered suspect. Cynicism becomes the automatic reaction.

Brian, in particular, demonstrated the sheer difficulty of navigating this field. Pointing out evidence of conspiracy at the Bilderberg conferences, he began (like Jenny) by attempting to add to the credibility of his theories by using empirical sources, as well as appeals to the authority of common sense:

> We're being fed a lot of lies. If you know that a lot of the plans for wars we've seen over the last decade were laid in the previous decade, then there is a plan … things don't just happen. Are you familiar with Bilderberg? The annual meetings? Well, two years ago, if people mentioned to me 'Bilderberg' I'd say you don't need to talk about Bilderberg or the Illuminati or whatever, you just need to look at the system, because if you mention the word 'Bilderberg' people regard you as a conspiracy theorist. I would actually say this is changing. And this year, for the first year, the mainstream media actually did serious reporting from outside Bilderberg.

He then continued by describing Bilderberg as a coalition of interests – financial, political, industrial, as well as the military and mainstream media – who were colluding in order to make decisions of global significance in their own interest. In order to provide further evidence of this, he cited the attendance list of the 2012 conference:

> But if you look at the sequence of events, the people who are involved, last year, who was at Bilderberg in Chantilly? Kodmani, Bassma Kodmani, who was part of the Free Syrian Liberation Movement. So, clearly, what was being organised in Syria, she was being brought in to talk about that. So, these things are orchestrated. People imagine they just

> happen, that the Arab Spring just happens or whatever it may be, but these are carefully marshalled.

That the attendees included a member of the Syrian National Council was enough for Brian to conclude that events in that country were being centrally controlled, with the implication being that his understanding of power was more than speculation: he had reached the hidden truth of Bilderberg through the smallest details, clues, slips, and pieces of evidence:

> The world of misinformation is very complex. Alex Jones rants on about Bilderberg and a few other things, as does David Icke, both those people also say a lot of other things which may or may not have credibility to them. So, does that undermine the whole rationale of what they say about Bilderberg? No, it doesn't. But you know, we live in a very high-impact information age, so trying to separate out messages which are cloaked within stuff that may not be true is quite difficult. Just because Fox News says one thing doesn't make it untrue, but a lot of other things they're saying may be untrue.

Given that he (like many conspiracy-driven activists) saw mainstream journalism as part of the same conspiracy, Brian's appeal to such sources of evidence directly contradicts his theory of power, with the reference to 'serious reporting' seeming to be an attempt to pre-empt criticism of his theory by referring to an 'authoritative source' of information. The way in which evidence for such conspiracy theories is utilised is directly relevant to the framing and foreclosure of resistance which follows. For many, the mainstream media could not be trusted to report on hidden interests and, even in cases of apparent revelation – such as when Jones, Icke, or Fox News did actually portray the truth – these were taken as further proof of an even deeper and wider conspiracy. There was a consistent and perpetual retreat of the 'truth' of power, which in turn made the activists' self-appointed task to uncover it never-ending.

By relying on a never-ending search for empirical evidence and clues to corroborate claims, as well as reiterating the modernist idea that truth is something that needs to be 'un-concealed', conspiracy theories overlook reflexive and normative critiques and instead sustain the police order of what 'counts' as an authoritative source of knowledge. Or, as Dean argued in her research on UFO theorists, believers 'tended to reinforce official assumptions about who or what can be credible because ufology wants to convince political and scientific authorities of the claims' (2002: 42). In the drive to avoid being designated as 'non-sense', activists inadvertently support the very co-ordinates that distribute them in the first place as marginal and without authority. Such appeals to narratives of endless and untouchable secret power networks, in other words, extend a police order that marginalises activists in the first place, by accepting what counts as legitimate or sensible knowledge.

Constructions of resistance as faced with an all-powerful, insurmountable and hidden agency, become evacuated of all democratic authority, and some occupiers subsequently criticised such an approach, describing this as an 'easy philosophy of opposition':

> So, I get the feeling that they aren't really sure about what they believe in and will gravitate towards an easy philosophy of opposition. You know: 'I'm unhappy, it's just gone wrong, where's the problem, who is it, oh it must be Thatcher, oh it must be this, it must be that', you know?
>
> (Sean)

> We should stop talking about ourselves as 'the resistance'. You're already giving a position of inequality in which the other part is much stronger and is sort of oppressing you, and you're just sort of trying to resist that, rather than trying to create a situation where you are equals.
>
> (2013:10)

> I think this is the thing, not allowing yourself to become a victim. If we're talking about resistance, it's never seeing yourself as a victim, that is when you're being controlled. If you think you're resisting against a higher power, then they've already controlled you. So that's why I'm not so keen on this 'resistance' … it's like, connect with your own power.
>
> (2013:13)

> The other side of the paranoia is it kind of *romanticises* protest, it kind of romanticises organisation somehow, because you feel like you're operating outside of the status quo somehow. And: 'oh, look at me, I'm going to do something illegal here, and I'm doing it in secret and in solidarity with a small clique behind me'. There's lots of social capital that can be born from that.
>
> (Julia)

In conspiracy theory, power and resistance are constructed as binary opposites. 'The powers that be' are understood to be something hidden that is acting with bad intentions, but also as something all-reaching, all-influencing, all-knowing, and ultimately, untouchable, unaccountable, and unchallengeable. In contrast, resistance is structured in relation to this power, as something marginal, powerless, ineffectual, 'outside' of influence, and without authority. At the point where this self-marginalisation intersects with authenticity, we also get 'an easy philosophy of opposition', or a narrative which argues that 'we may be marginal, *but at least we are righteous*'; 'we may be ineffectual, *but at least we are authentic*'; 'we may be powerless, *but at least we have the moral high ground*'. Powerlessness subsequently becomes a sign of authenticity, celebrated as 'an election and a distinction' (Nietzsche 2008: 31), with accusations of a 'cover-up' [acting] as a homogenising agent to present the image of a corrupted "them" and a "romanticised and radical us", as well as a lived socio-political reality' (Birchall 2006: 46). With conspiracy theory, power is not understood as something normative and structural, but as something totalising, insurmountable, and unchallengeable, while resistance is fetishised in comparison as authentically marginal and righteously impotent.

Conclusion: avoiding the cunning of impotence

Rather than dismissing conspiracy theories outright and playing into wider designations of the movement as 'non-sense', I have sought to recognise such narratives as a direct outcome of the kinds of issues that Occupy were attempting to address: grievances with the unaccountability and distances of government; disillusionment; the democratic deficit of post-crash neoliberalism; the unaccountable social and environmental impacts of global corporations; historically entrenched distributions of structural inequality; and the inauthenticity of capitalist culture. What's more – while in some contexts conspiracy theory well may act as an organisational tool (Dean) which can present folk knowledges and challenge distributions of knowledge (Birchall) as well as capture 'something' about the nature of power – it has been my contention that a rise in distrust, a lack of authority, a foreclosure of alternative models of government and collective organisation, as well as a binary understanding of 'secret power' versus 'impotent-but-authentic-resistance' within Occupy (in) London did more harm than good.

Regardless of their empirical accuracy, I have argued that conspiracy theories are problematic as constructions of power and resistance. In the first place, they break apart solidarity and limit the possibly of a democratic and negotiated collective organisation by creating distrust and uneven distributions of power. When any fellow activist could be an undercover agent, suspicion and scepticism reign, fracturing and dissolving any chance of solidarity, democratic negotiation, or a qualitative extension to newcomers. Second, such theories play back into a libertarian logic that extends neoliberal cynicism towards the state, foreclosing the presentation of an alternative of what democratic governance or collective politics could be, as well as pre-denying themselves the state as one crucial arena of appearance and voice among others. When 'the 1%' are met with snide and cynical criticism, then the state is not only rashly dismissed as a crucial and influential site of struggle, but protesters also accept the police order limitations of what the state could possibly achieve within the post-crash context beyond austerity and socialising the crisis. Finally, ideas of conspiracy play into distributions of what counts as 'truth' (something to be unconcealed and revealed) which extends the confusion, uncertainty, and contradictions of symbolic inefficiency. When the truth of power is considered to be something hidden behind appearances, then this extends modernist conceptions of truth as well as postmodern cynicism, lending itself to a situation in which power can 'hide out in the open' without being challenged (the 'truth' must be deeper!). It is for this reason that Žižek has argued 'the enemy today is not the fundamentalist but the cynic' (2008d: xxiii).

In comparison to the hidden and nefarious conspiracy, the cynical activist overlooks structural criticisms in favour of searching for clues, slips, evidence, and the final moment in which the truth of power will be revealed. Intersecting with ideas of authenticity, this then can give rise to a certain *enjoyment* in marginality and exclusion, seeing their powerlessness as demonstrating their righteousness, moral superiority, and the underdog authenticity of their actions. Adopting a 'siege mentality', in other words, resistance becomes characterised by 'a stubborn clinging to a certain equation of truth with powerlessness, or as acting out of an injured will' which is 'susceptible to growing rigidly defensive and brittle out of a sense of their imperilled existence … [tending] to preclude their addressing deep sources of injustice' (Brown 2001: 23). Clinging to powerlessness and injury, the cynical activist celebrates their 'imperilled existence' and grows 'rigidly defensive', instead of addressing deep structures of injustice. This is a bizarre situation, in other words, in which 'suffering lives as an identity rather than as general injustice or domination' (ibid.: 39). Pursuing authenticity in powerlessness, a self-understanding of resistance develops in which 'resentment prompts actions that [are] codified as just, and in which righteousness and inferiority act to ramify each other' (Littler 2009: 9).

Movements, therefore, must therefore avoid such a 'cunning of impotence' in which:

> the oppressed and downtrodden and violated tell themselves: 'let us be different from evil, that is, good!' [But] when listened to coldly and without prejudice, this actually means nothing more than 'we weak are, after all, weak: it would be good if we refrained from doing anything for which we lack sufficient strength'.
>
> (Nietzsche 2008: 30)

This construction of resistance is one that accepts (and champions) the police order designation of activists and alternatives as the marginal, weak, inconsequential, and powerless without authority. Instead, activists must take political responsibility by asserting their collective democratic authority, even if they are being distributed as 'non-sense'. Through an aesthetic and reflexive intervention into normative structures of power, one which avoids the pitfalls of pursuing authenticity and the cunning of impotence while being backed by a collective, symbolically efficient organisation, it become possible to make 'non-sense' appear against its dismissal as such and directly challenge wider foreclosures of possibility.

Conclusion

This is not a protest, it's a process

We began this book with a puzzle.

On the face of it, the financial crash and credit crunch of 2007/8 was followed by a crisis which directly challenged and undermined the normativity of both mainstream economics and neoliberal political doctrine, which had argued for a state which *supports* the 'free' competition of the market while extending such principles of competition into all governmental institutions (privatisation) as well as rendering society and culture subject to the laws of supply and demand. Rather than the supposed inevitable tyranny of all centralised state projects – which, however democratic or socialist they claimed to be, always ended up in totalitarianism – neoliberalism advocated a turn towards the promises of individual, libertarian free will. Yet despite such promises of prosperity – through loose guarantees of wealth trickling down and creating a 'rising tide to lift all boats' – the financial crisis appeared to have sincerely rocked the boat by turning Thatcher's firm assertion that 'there is no alternative' into Cameron's cynical plea that 'we're all in this together'.

But the crisis did not, in the end, appear to challenge or disrupt the fundamental principles of neoliberal capitalism which advocated a turn towards anti-democratic plutocratic measures of bailouts, quantitative easing, and austerity in order to reaffirm the viability of market competition. As Paul Mason (2017) puts it, it's almost as if 'liberal democracy had a death wish', responding to those now suffering under austerity or advocating change by reaffirming that there was simply no alternative. In the gap, movements on the left and the right emerged, fighting for a fairer distribution of resources and socio-economic justice, yet even with the global pressure of such movements fighting for democracy and equality from 2010 onwards, it hasn't been the left who have (so far) emerged victorious.

Walter Benjamin once wrote that 'every rise of fascism bears witness to a failed revolution' (see Žižek 2009a: 73), and the rise of nationalism and racist populism in the global north-west appears to have fulfilled this prediction. The crisis did not lead to a swing towards a politics of equality, nor to a democratic revolution that would address historical injustices and inequalities, as left movements were instead simply dismissed as 'non-sense' – naïve, irrational, unreasonable, impossible. The post-crash movements were placeholders for the very possibility of an alternative future which was different to the present, yet they became normatively foreclosed given that the dominant response to the crisis was not change, but conservatism, dominated by the attitude that the status quo needed to be returned and business needed to 'get back to normal' as quickly as possible. 'The market will find its equilibrium again', insisted the rich, as their risks and shortfalls were socialised and placed upon the collective shoulders of society: 'everything will return to pre-crisis conditions'.

As capitalism marches on, the position of neoliberal states remains unchanged – low taxes for the rich, austerity, cuts, changes to the built environment to cater for the wealthy – and has led to unprecedented levels of socio-economic inequality, mirrored only by the continuing democratic deficit for those most suffering from such 'common sense' ideology. Rather than a radical change, we have instead witnessed what Brown has dubbed the birth of a 'neoliberal Frankenstein' (see Burgum *et al.* 2017), or a state which has ignored pleas for voice and symbolic reassurance from the people, and instead pieced together a monster of nationalism, racism, bigotry, xenophobia, and self-denying privilege. Preying on the symbolic inefficiency felt by white, post-industrial working class – who have long since lost the roots of its collective identity but have been unable to find a replacement in the structurelessness of the left – right-wing populism has once again raised its ugly head. Meanwhile, those who have for some time suffered from the objective violence of capitalism's 'smooth' functioning (including normative structures of racism, sexism, ableism, heteronormativity, etc.) have only seen their conditions worsen under post-crash austerity and oppression. Like the white working class, these groups are also unable to make their voices and appearances heard and seen within the left's structurelessness, and instead these activists turn towards their individual identity groups, seeing such issues as 'their' problem to address (rather than the responsibility of society as a whole). Despite attempting to be inclusive and horizontal, structures of inequality – classism, patriarchy, race – ultimately remained unchallenged and unresolved by post-crash collective movements, as the more privileged reiterated their structural position within the unaccountably 'structureless' space in order to make their voice, appearance, and vision of the movement dominant.

Thus, Occupy – which evolved in response to the injustices and democratic shortfalls highlighted by the crash and as the movement of 'the '99%' – was ultimately unable to perform a truly democratic intervention in the post-crash moment, one which might have collectively and reflexively included all structural injustices and inequalities, and made the most of this moment of crisis. Their failure to do so, however, was not simply a matter of organisational problems, but also demonstrated the power of a wider police order which was being reaffirmed and reasserted during the crisis – a distribution of the sensible which foreclosed the possibility of any alternative by designating such calls for change as 'non-sense'. This distribution, which operated through assertions of what did or did not count as 'legitimate' politics, played out through an aesthetic policing of who may or may not be heard or seen in the post-crash context, and was problematically extended through the normative assumptions of those very movements that were attempting to mount a challenge. Educated in the ideologies of individual free will, the sanctity of personal opinion, and libertarianism, the activists inadvertently extended such presuppositions and principles which guide contemporary markets and governments. The approach that Occupy took to resistance – asserting open inclusivity, horizontality (structurelessness) and diversity as prefigurative democratic experiments – ultimately did not challenge neoliberal normativity, but instead reasserted that these were the baseline co-ordinates for the distribution of sensible politics.

Finally, the Occupy movement not only problematically maintained post-modern trends of symbolic inefficiency that distrusted and undermined any attempt to move towards a disciplined collective organisation or authority, it also upheld a distinctly *modern* cynicism about appearances which played into ideas that its powerlessness and marginality were indicators of virtue and authenticity. Playing into cultural norms perpetuated by both the new spirit of capitalism (which seeks to promote authenticity and distance from the market *as drivers of the market*) and the myth of co-optation (which keeps the momentum of this spirit going through a perpetual pursuit of authenticity), many activists inadvertently found themselves being complicit with such consumerist logics *through their very attempt not to be.* Beyond playing into hierarchies, preclusions, and distrustful divisions, however, this cynicism also provided support for widely held views that it is better to be 'non-hypocritical' and 'moral' in one's activism than politically responsible. Rather than pursuing power and authority, a cynical framing of power and resistance instead pre-positioned their protest as marginal and powerless 'non-sense', 'leaving the head on the king' and presuming that what they were up against ('the 1%' or global conspiracy networks) was an insurmountable and ultimately unchallengeable centralised power.

The potential of Occupy

In addition to demonstrating the limitations and foreclosures of the Occupy movement in London as an explanation for the lack of change, I also set out at the beginning of this research to highlight the lessons and potential they demonstrated for future movements. While I did not want this project to become another addition to the pile of abstract empirical work on the movement, nor an overly romantic and naïve celebratory account of a movement that had faced obvious problems and challenges, I was also concerned that my own critical reading of the movement should not fall into cynical dismissal and add to the normative distribution and policing of Occupy as 'non-sense'. Given the activists' initial bravery of taking the risk of organising and protesting in the post-crash era, as well as their admirable belief that another world was actually possible, I therefore attempted to highlight at least two potential legacies of the movement which (notwithstanding other lessons) might actually take the left forwards:

1 The occupation of space is a powerful tactic that can provide a much-needed authority for 'making non-sense appear'

In relation to the police order's distribution of the sensible, that normative foreclosure of alternatives which reasserted the status quo during the financial crisis, the very *possibility* of a more democratic and just society is designated as fantastical 'non-sense'. As well as a symbolic bordering of possibility through the normative assertions of politicians, experts, and journalists, such a 'common sense' distribution can also be found in the material aesthetic and design of the city. For example, what post-crash London (as a hub for global capitalism, finance, neoliberalism, and colonialism) could and could not be used for was reasserted through a policing of its physical space. Paternoster Square, the home of the London Stock Exchange, was not a space for democratic protest. Finsbury Square, the home of innovative spaces for corporate sharing and leisure, was not a space for debating alternatives. London's public spaces were not to be a realm of civil unrest and disobedience, nor of riots or the appearance of the poor or threatening ethnic minorities, but instead areas designed for the smooth flows of capital, labour, and communication, as well as a playground and entertainment complex for the appropriately wealthy.

Directly in contrast to this normative distribution of the city, the activists I spoke to argued strongly that occupying space offered a radical resistive potential. First, the protest camps set up in the middle of such cities, were *public*. Not only did this cater to the movement's practical needs – donations of money or equipment, leafletting, communicating with the public – but it also underlined their democratic aims by directly contrasting with the buildings and spaces around them. What's more, the legal designation of the space outside St Paul's (in comparison to Paternoster Square) allowed the movement to take advantage of a grey area in the police order, claiming a certain legal authority to be there. This legality also benefitted the second advantage of occupying space, in granting their protest – their appearance and voice – a certain semi-permanent longevity. *Semi*-permanent, because the aesthetic of the tents juxtaposed with the cold, hard steel, glass and concrete institutions that surrounded them, made the movement appear more flexible, negotiable, and democratic. Furthermore, they also denoted *longevity*, in providing the physical and material centre around which the movement could be easily located and gathered around.

Finally, the benefit of occupying public urban spaces was the ability to tap into contextual narratives. If the need is to 'make non-sense appear' – as well as avoiding attempts to 'move them along' as 'nothing to see here' by the police order – then the ability to twist, refigure, and détourne this distribution is important. What's more, such narratives offered by St Paul's Cathedral offered a *moral* grey area (in addition to the legal one) which could be incorporated into the movement's appearance and make its 'non-sense' appear against those ready to dismiss it. In other words, by virtue of their context, they were able to play on the contradictions of the church and extend these well-known moral coordinates outwards (such as poignantly asking the church and, by extension, the post-crash public, 'what would Jesus do?') Such a *détournement* allowed their resistance to appear, staging an intervention in the post-crash distribution of the sensible, and refiguring this space as the space for the appearance of democratic and egalitarian principles.

2 'We are the 99%' indicated a step in a progressive direction by attempting to assert a collectivity around problems of democratic deficit, historical injustice, socio-economic inequality, and the objective violence of capitalism.

Prior to the financial crisis, it was common for theorists to claim that we lived in an era of 'post-politics'. Citing the postmodern decline of symbolic efficiency and certainty, as well as the related pervasiveness of individualism, some thinkers declared (or tacitly accepted) that we had reached 'the end point of mankind's ideological evolution and the final form of human government and as such the end of history' (Fukuyama 1992: xi). (Neo)liberalism had simply won outright and was now the only political option. Writing at the end of the 1990s, Bauman offered the following diagnosis:

> We tend to believe … that there is little we can change – singly, severally, or altogether – in the way the affairs of the world are running or being run, and we believe too that, were we able to make a change, it would be futile, even unreasonable, to put our heads together to think of a different world from the one there is and to flex our muscles to bring it about if we consider it better than the one we are in.
>
> (1999: 1)

Such a foreclosure of possibility, as I have shown, had continued in spite of the financial crisis, and yet this hasn't stopped others from arguing that such limits are beginning to unravel. For Jodi Dean, for instance, while 'aspects of the diagnosis of de-politicization [are] well worth emphasising' the term 'post-politics' is 'inadequate to the task of theorising this conjecture' (2009: 12) as such conceptions 'might have worked a decade or so ago, but not anymore [in the context of] massive uprisings, demonstrations, strikes, occupations, and revolutions' (ibid. 2012: 46). The term 'post-politics', she argues, is 'childishly petulant' (ibid. 2009: 12) and is itself indicative of 'a retreat into cowardice [and] the retroactive determination of victory as defeat because of the left's fundamental inability to accept responsibility for power and to undertake the difficult task of reinventing our modes of dreaming' (ibid.: 10). Or, as Jonathan Dean has pointed out, while such 'narrations of apoliticality are, in principle, underpinned by a desire for a return to politics' it remains that case that 'if one fantasmatically invests in narratives of apoliticality then the emergence of politicisation will very likely be experienced as troublesome, even traumatic, as they potentially disturb the deeply sedimented frames of reference that have come to constitute the symbolic universe of the academic left subject' (2014: 462).

In contrast, then, Jodi Dean sees potential in 'we are the 99%' for the reassertion of collective responsibility and authority on the left, which might underpin a democratic movement for justice and equality. The 'we', on the one hand, fulfils Badiou's (2012) criteria for politics in terms of asserting a collective identity which can then be qualitatively extended to others, while 'the 99%' indicates a common recognition that the injustices and inequalities inherited from history – capitalism, colonialism, racism, patriarchy – can only be addressed by a democratic movement. As Žižek and Butler have also argued, while such a universal identity might (in the process of definition) risk the exclusion of some politics in favour of others, it can also be performative (insofar as it is symbolically efficient) as well as form the basis for democratically negotiating such exclusions.

Non-sensible suggestions

To conclude this volume, I will make a series of non-sensible (naïve, impossible) suggestions. They are 'non-sensible' because in the current distribution of the sensible, they're much easier said than done. While I agree, along with Foucault, that there is no outside to normative power because the authority of voices, appearances, knowledge, and possibility is always socially distributed in relation to a police order of what does or does not count as 'common sense', I nevertheless disagree with Foucault's vague answer to this dilemma which is to simply respond to the decentralisation of power by 'multiplying points of resistance', seeing this as a problematic extension of postmodern and libertarian norms. Instead, I advocate a reflexive return to collective organisation and symbolic efficiency, but this would require the kind of discipline and authority that will not come easily to today's new left, burnt by the authoritarianism of 20th-century socialism and inspired by the subsequent turn towards previously marginalised voices. My suggestion is that 'we' require nothing less than a combination of the two: a collective democratic politics which avoids *pre*cluding the diverse politics of 'the 99%', but also advocates strongly for a collective negotiation of exclusions that would be necessary to create the basis for organisation, solidarity, and symbolic efficiency – something that would require a fundamental shift in the presuppositions and inherited inclinations of left wing activists.

A The art of the impossible

Mounted on a wall in the main quad of Goldsmiths, University of London, in tribute to the late Mark Fisher, there is a quote which reads:

> Emancipatory politics must always destroy the appearance of a 'natural order', must reveal what is presented as necessary and inevitable to be a mere contingency, just as it must make what was previously deemed to be impossible seem attainable.

In 2012, as an unfunded masters student, I remember taking a 12-hour round Megabus trip from York to London just to hear Mark speak at Housmans bookshop, King's Cross. Discussing his book *Capitalist Realism* (2009), he was dismayed at the anti-collective culture on the left. Why, he asked, would the left deny itself in advance the authority of collective organisations? Or the state? Why would it not fight collectively, but in many different arenas – including the state – at the same time?

I have argued above that this problem can be understood as part of the foreclosure of possibility that positions the only legitimate politics as one which is individualised, marginal, and powerless. Movements like Occupy not only incorporate distributions that were attempting to dismiss them as disorganised and structureless 'non-sense' (nothing to see here, move along), but they also saw their own demands as 'impossible' when compared to the entrenched, centralised, cynical power they considered themselves to be up against. Rather than asserting their own authority, in other words, post-crash activists tended to position their authenticity in their non-authority, in the fact that they didn't have power and were therefore uncorrupted by the state or market.

What Occupy stood for, from the perspective of the police order, may have been easily dismissed as 'madness', but it is precisely 'through madness [that] a work that seems to drown in the world, to reveal there its non-sense, and to transfigure itself with the features of pathology alone, actually *engages* within itself the world's time, masters it, and leads it; by the madness which interrupts it, a work of art opens a void, a moment of silence, a question without answer, provokes a breach without reconciliation where the world is forced to question itself' (Foucault 2001: p273–4). Radical intervention, in other words, requires a certain madness, an 'art of the impossible' or 'a call to be equal to the rest of the catastrophe that has befallen us by demanding what, in the framework of our symbolic belief, might appear to be 'impossible' (Žižek 1992: 28). This is an aesthetic *demand* to be heard and seen, claiming for itself the authority to appear, one that cries (as the protestors did in May '68) 'let us be realistic and demand the impossible' (i.e. a just and democratic society). Such a demand will be dismissed as mad, idealistic, and naïve, as evidence for facetiousness and a demonstration that activists 'don't know what they're talking about'; thus, it needs to be countered with collective authority and an assertion that another world is possible. What is needed, in other words, is 'a politics of projects and strategies rather than moral righteousness; a politics of bids for power rather than remonstrances of it' (Brown 2001: 106).

Pointing to the limited successes of the US civil right movement, as well as Ghandi's resistance against British colonialism in India, Brown argues that 'while these movements did not wholly eschew the phenomenon of identity produced by oppression, neither did they build solidarity on the basis of that production; rather, solidarity was rooted in shared beliefs … they eschewed cultivation of identity-bound difference claims' (2001: 26). Despite being designated as 'non-sense' and impossible by the racist/colonial distribution of the sensible, these movements did not fetishise or adopt this marginal position as a signifier of authentic identity, but instead created a collective 'we' on the basis of a universal politics, avoiding any extension of individualism and libertarianism into their movement. What's more, despite adopting a position designated as 'impossible' they were able to turn this into positive solidarity on the basis of those with shared beliefs, rather than fetishising their resistance as 'outside' of such power structures. The art of the impossible begins with a recognition that resistance begins within and in relation to that which it is protesting against, but this cannot mean aesthetic or structural compromise.

The art of the impossible is to make 'non-sense' appear against a context that designates it as such. Such an approach avoids the reduction and foreclosure of possibility and protest by what is normatively considered to be 'possible' – i.e. pragmatic, realistic, rational, sensible – which can only lead to conservative acceptances of the current framework (see Rigby and Schlembach 2013). Instead, the art of the impossible is one 'which seeks to transform the very parameters of what is considered 'possible' in the existing constellation' (Žižek 2008a: 199). It forces the appearance of two worlds in one and an argument for a world in which such 'non-sense' might actually *count* as sensible (Rancière 2001, 2010).

B Genealogical politics

The problem, as demonstrated by the lack of change after the crisis, is how to position the authority of resistance in the context of normative power. One approach is perhaps to start with a more *genealogical* politics, one which seeks to make the familiar unfamiliar and the normative abnormal. As Brown has described it, such an approach would mean developing a politics which, at its heart, is an 'historically conscious critique of the present' (2001: 95) that 'reorients the relationship of history to political possibility' (ibid.: 103). By returning to history and creating an understanding of how we got to the current police order and distribution of 'common sense', it becomes possible to demonstrate the contingency of that order, showing how the world hasn't always been like this, that it's like this for a reason, and therefore it doesn't have to be like this in the future.

By taking such a view of history that recognises how 'we inherit not 'what really happened' to the dead but what lives on from that happening, what is conjured from it, how past generations and events occupy the force field of the present, how they claim you, and how they haunt, plague, and inspirit our imaginations and visions for the future' (Brown 2001: 150), genealogical politics has the potential to open up limits of possibility and challenge claims to objectivity which are made by the nationalist and racist right. Instead of history being something that inevitably controls us and to which we now have to react – something that means that some people are rich and some are poor; that means some people carry legitimate appearance and voice and some people do not; and that's just the way it is – such an approach means that 'history becomes less what we dwell in, are propelled by, or are determined by, than what we fight over, fight for, and aspire to honour in our practice of justice' (ibid.: 155). Recognising that there is nothing objective or inevitable about injustices of the past being allowed to continue to dominate present relations as a natural order, structural legacies of capitalism, colonialism, patriarchy, class, and precarity, suddenly seem optional and therefore open to change.

Therefore, in terms of 'the 99%', such a genealogical politics might help to avoid internal preclusions and marginalisation, by recognising the different sources and histories of democratic deficit and injustice which make up 'the 99%'. In other words, the genealogical approach to politics can help movements 'to entertain the claims to attention of local, discontinuous, disqualified, illegitimate knowledges against the claims of a unitary body of theory which would filter, hierarchise and order them in the name of some true knowledge and some arbitrary idea of what constitutes a science and its objects' (Foucault 1980: 83). Instead of placing resistance as something which needs to be structureless in order to avoid oppression and exclusion, as well as something that needs to be autonomous and morally pure in order to prefigure an alternative future, this approach offers the possibility of a fundamentally reflexive and assertive intervention which 'instead of stigmatising the unacceptable in order to supplant it by the acceptable' calls into 'question the very rationality which grounds the establishment of a regime of acceptability' (Gordon 1980: 157–8).

This can only be achieved, however, if activists avoid the tendency to pursue authenticity and the cunning of impotence, and instead accept the fact that protests need not be perfect or adopt the moral high ground in order to appear, act, and take power. Rather than adopting such self-marginalising positions, movements must go beyond sovereign models of power and 'cut the head off the king' in their self-understanding, recognising that power now tends to operate as a normative distribution. Or, as Foucault put it bluntly, 'nothing in society will be changed if the mechanisms of power that function outside, below, and alongside the state apparatus on a much more minute and everyday level, are also changed' (1980: 60).

C Positing our own presuppositions

Finally, having completed this research on Occupy (in) London, I am convinced that the left needs to rediscover collective politics, which inevitably means creating an exclusive and defined organisation, rather than opting for

open and structureless inclusivity. Formalising a democratic movement not only enables accountability, but also ensures that 'the 99%' don't preclude voices or appearances through a tyranny of structurelessness, while at the same time creating a collective intervention into the police order supported by symbolic efficiency and authority. Assertions of structurelessness, by contrast, not only extend normative presuppositions of neoliberalism and capitalism (individualism, libertarianism, symbolic inefficiency), but also play into accounts of their politics as incoherent, inconsistent, disorganised 'non-sense'. The symbolic efficiency and cohesion provided by a disciplined organisation is therefore the bare minimum for an organisation that can make 'non-sense' appear.

As Blencowe (2013) argued at the beginning of this volume, the ability to speak with authority or from a 'position of knowing better' is premised upon a common idea of objectivity (i.e. what the truth of the matter actually is). So, if the left wants to claim a democratic authority, then it must find a historical premise, while maintaining an emphasis on this being an idea of objectivity (i.e. contingent upon and open to collective negotiation). Unable to form claims about the kind of assertions being made by the populist right (e.g. the racist 'objectivity' of national blood and soil), the 'idea' of objectivity is instead a search for a base which could *support authority without becoming authoritarian*. Such an approach also harks back to notions of genealogical politics (see above), because if history is perceived as contingent and 'past's play in the present is elective, interpreted and imagistic' (Brown 2001: 166); then the possibility emerges for left-wing movements to redeem foreclosed resistances of the past (Benjamin 1999) by retroactively positing *our own presuppositions* (Žižek 2006: 201–8). In other words, the potential arises for movements to find ideas of objectivity through electing their own history and background, which then forms the basis of their authority in the present.

The legacy of post-crash resistance

Ten years after the financial crash, the outlook remains uncertain. On the one hand, attempts to formalise post-crash resistance – such as Syriza in Greece – quickly found themselves up against the limits of the European Union which blackmailed the Greek government by closing banks and denying loans, asserting that there was no alternative and forcing Syriza to break its electoral promises. The democratic movements of the Arab Spring nations have also found themselves policed and limited, facing the reprisals of governments who outlived an incomplete revolution (e.g. Syria) and the rise of right-wing conservatism in the form of religious fundamentalism (e.g. Islamic State). Movements in the global north-west seem to have dispersed into more specific protests, the focus shifting away from socio-economic and democratic justice towards police violence (Black Lives Matter), the refugee crisis in Europe and nationalist isolationism (e.g. Trump, Brexit), as well as environmentalism in the face of ever-increasing occurrences of natural disasters. All this in a post-truth context whereby claims to objectivity have lost all symbolic efficiency, demonstrating how statements can 'remain authoritative despite being untruthful, depending on who declared it and in what circumstances' (Blencowe 2013: 15).

Yet there have been some suggestions that things could be finally changing for the better. Directly against a police order which designated Jeremy Corbyn's democratic socialist agenda as 'impossible' – attempting to use normative dismissals such as 'Comrade Corbyn' or to disparagingly describe grass-roots supporters as 'Corbynistas', insisting that his politics would make the Labour Party unelectable for a generation – the 2017 snap general election in the UK saw a record swing towards the Labour Party which has not been seen since the 1945 post-war election on the welfare state. This could partly be attributed to the perceived arrogance of Prime Minister Theresa May and a disastrous Conservative campaign in which the party refused to take a clear stance on anything, with May appearing robotic and failing to present herself as the rational choice with a 'strong and stable hand'. Yet the swing towards Corbyn's Labour also demonstrates that the post-crash police order, which had automatically designated democratic socialism as an 'impossible' alternative, might be starting to lose its authority. In particular, the young, who have borne much of the brunt of the failed promises of (neo)liberalism, seem to be backing this alternative above right-wing options (as shown by the popularity of Corbyn, which the police order have also attempted to frame as a facetious 'cult of personality' supported by a younger generation who 'don't know what they're doing').

Some have suggested that a direct genealogy can be drawn from the Occupy movement in London and the growing enthusiasm for democratic socialism (e.g. Klug *et al.* 2016), but having conducted this research between 2012–14, before Corbyn had even stood for leadership of the Labour Party, I am not in a position to add to this claim empirically. But in the spirit of positing our own presuppositions and claiming an authority on the basis of an 'idea' of objectivity, the Occupy movement for 'the 99%' undoubtedly led to the return of left-wing party politics. Mainstream journalists of the right and centre will continue to attempt to normatively undermine the alternative that Corbyn represents by pointing to 'common-sense' lessons of history (that movements for democracy and justice through the state always end up with a Stasi-like apparatus, something that demonstrates that 'virtually none of the Bourgeois Corbyn army … know the first thing about the political ideology they are endorsing'[1]; or that Corbyn's unwillingness to condemn outright the Venezuelan government (which was responsible for getting rid of decades of neo-imperialist and neoliberal abuse by the USA, bringing swathes of the population out of poverty) indicates that he is basically the 'same as Donald Trump' when the latter refused to condemn neo-Nazi violence in Charlottesville.[2] That such strange abuses of reason circulate at all is indicative of the post-truth decline of symbolic efficiency, but it also suggests that the police order is running out of normative claims from which to dismiss the politics of 'the 99%'. And if the dismissals are getting desperate, then surely now is as good a time as any for us to organise 'non-sense' with authority. To paraphrase a well-worn saying attributed to George Bernard Shaw, 'people who say it cannot be done should not be permitted to interrupt those who are doing it'.

Notes

1 http://www.telegraph.co.uk/news/politics/Jeremy_Corbyn/12035326/Jeremy-Corbyns-clueless-admirers-have-not-the-faintest-idea-about-his-hard-Left-beliefs.html (accessed: 12th October 2017).

2 http://metro.co.uk/2017/08/17/donald-trumps-comments-on-charlotteville-arent-that-dissimilar-to-jeremy-corbyns-stance-on-the-ira-and-venezuela-6859100/ (accessed: 12th October 2017).

Interviewee demographics

Pseudonym	*Date*	*Interview no.*	*Location*	*Other information*
2012, int. 1	30/4/12	1	Finsbury Square	White, male, 17, long-term activist (Reclaim the Streets/Fields)
'Nick'	30/4/12	2	Finsbury Square	White, male, 45, long-term activist
'Mickey'	30/4/12	None	Finsbury Square	*Observation only, interview refused*
2012, int. 3	30/4/12	3	Finsbury Square	White, male, 30
2012, int. 4	30/4/12	4	Finsbury Square	White, female, 18, former student
2012, int. 5	30/4/12	5	Finsbury Square	White, female, 18
2012, int. 6	30/4/12	6	Finsbury Square	White, male, 28
'Greg'	30/4/12	7	Finsbury Square	*First interview of three*
2012, int. 8	2/5/12	8	Mile End	White, male, 56, long-term activist
2012, int. 9	2/5/12	9	Mile End	White, male, 46, long-term activist
2012, int. 10	2/5/12	10	Mile End	White, male, 27, long-term activist (British National Party)
'Felicity'	2/5/12	11	Friends' House, Euston	White, female, 23, European
2012, int. 12	3/5/12	12	Mile End	Black, male, 48, African
2012, int. 13	3/5/12	13	Mile End	White, male, 37, European

Pseudonym	*Date*	*Interview no.*	*Location*	*Other information*
2012, int. 14	3/5/12	14	Mile End	White, male, 24, European
'Harry'	7/5/12	15	Friends' House, Euston	White, male, 34, new activist, *First interview of two*
2012, int. 16	7/5/12	16	Finsbury Park Café	Bangladeshi-British, female, 28
'Harry'	11/7/13	17	Tower Hill pub	White, male, new activist *Second interview*
2013, int. 2	15/7/13	18	Friends' House, Euston	White, male, older
'Shaun'	16/7/13	19	Parsons Green café	White, male *First interview of two*
'Ollie'	17/7/13	20	Skype	White, male, older
'Sally'	25/7/13	21	At her home	White, female, older
2013, int. 6	26/7/13	22	Bethnal Green café	White, female, younger
2013, int. 7	26/7/13	23	Friends' House, Euston	White, male, older
2013, int. 8	29/7/13	24	Rochester Square Gardens	White, male, younger, European
2013, int. 9	29/7/13	25	Rochester Square Gardens	White, male, older, long-term activist (environmental activism)
'Julia'	29/7/13	26	Rochester Square Gardens	White, female, younger, South American
'James'	30/7/13	27	Bethnal Green café	White, male, younger *First interview of two*
'Brian'	30/7/13	28	Friends' House, Euston	White, male, older
2013, int. 13	5/9/13	29	Victoria Park café	White, male, disabled
'Greg'	5/9/13	30	St Paul's Cathedral	*Second interview of three*

Pseudonym	*Date*	*Interview no.*	*Location*	*Other information*
2014, int. 1	28/5/14	31	At her home	White, female, younger *Second interview*
'Dan'	29/5/14	32	Friends' House, Euston	White, male, South American
2014, int. 3	29/5/14	33	Euston Station	White, male, younger
2014, int. 4	30/5/14	34	Goldsmiths	White, male, younger, Student
'Greg'	5/6/14	35	Cat Hill protest	*Third interview*
2014, int. 6	5/6/14	36	Cat Hill protest	White, male, European
'Shaun'	5/6/14	37	At his home	White, male *Second interview*
'Lucy'	6/6/14	38	Brixton café	White, female, younger, working class
'James'	7/6/14	39	St Paul's Cathedral, café	White, male, younger *Second Interview*
2014, int. 10	8/6/14	40	Muswell Hill café	White, female, older
2014, int. 11	9/6/14	41	Walthamstow café	White, male, older, long-term activist (Socialist Worker Party)
'Jenny'	11/6/14	42	Hammersmith café	White, female, older, long-term activist (Greenham Common)

Bibliography

Adebayo, K. (2016) 'Occupy Nigeria Movement, Organized Labor Unions, and Oil-Subsidy Struggle' in B. Coban (ed.) *Social Media and Social Movements: The Transformation of Communication Patterns.* Lanham, MD: Lexington Books.

Albinsson, P., Wolf, M. and Kopf, D. (2010) 'Anti-consumption in East Germany: Consumer Resistance to Hyperconsumption', *Journal of Consumer Behaviour* 9, 412–425.

Alimi, E. (2012) 'Occupy Israel': A Tale of Startling Success and Hopeful Failure', *Social Movement Studies* 11/3–4, 402–407

Althusser, L. (1971) *Lenin and Philosophy and Other Essays.* London: NLB.

Amoore, L. (2013) *The Politics of Possibility: Risk and Security beyond Probability.* Durham, NC: Duke University Press.

Arenas, I. (2014) 'Assembling the Multitude: Material Geographies of Social Movements from Oaxaca to Occupy', *Environment and Planning D: Society and Space* 32, 433–449.

Armstrong, A. (2008) 'Beyond Resistance: A Response to Žižek's Critique of Foucault's Subject of Freedom', *Parrhesia* 5, 19–31.

Atkinson, R. (2017) 'The (In)visibility of Riches, Urban Life and Exclusion', in R. Atkinson, L. McKenzie, and S. Winlow (eds) *Building Better Societies.* Bristol: Policy Press.

Atkinson, R. and Burrows, R. (2014) 'A City in Thrall to Capital? London, Money-Power and Elites', *Discover Society.* Available at http://discoversociety.org/2014/12/01/a-city-in-thrall-to-capital-london-money-power-and-elites/ (accessed 7 September 2017).

Badiou, A. (2010) *The Communist Hypothesis.* London: Verso.

Badiou, A. (2012) *The Rebirth of History.* London: Verso

Barker, A. (2012) 'Already Occupied: Indigenous Peoples, Settler Colonialism and the Occupy Movements in North America', *Social Movement Studies* 11/3–4, 327–334.

Bassett, K. (2014) 'Rancière, Politics, and the Occupy Movement', *Environment and Planning D: Society and Space* 32/5, 886–901.

Bassett, K. (2016) 'Event, Politics, and Space: Rancière or Badiou?', *Space and Polity* 20/3, 280–293.

Bauman, Z. (1999) *In Search of Politics.* Cambridge: Polity.

Benjamin, W. (1999) 'The Angel of History', *Illuminations.* London: Pimlico.

Bennett, L. and Segerberg, A. (2011) 'Digital Media and the Personalization of Collective Action: Social Technology and the Organisation of Protests against the Global Economic Crisis', *Information, Communication and Society* 14, 770–799.

Benski, T., Langman, L., Perugorria, I. and Tejerina, B. (2013) 'From the Streets and Squares to Social Movement Studies: What Have We Learned?' *Current Sociology* 61/4, 541–561.

Bey, H. (2011) *T.A.Z.: The Temporary Autonomous Zone.* CreateSpace Independent Publishing Platform.

Bhambra, G. (2016) 'Wither Europe? Postcolonial versus Neocolonial Cosmopolitanism', *Interventions: Journal of Postcolonial Studies* 18/2, 187–202.

Birchall, C. (2006) *Knowledge Goes Pop: From Conspiracy Theory to Gossip.* Oxford: Berg.

Birchall, C. (2011) 'Secrecy and Transparency', *Theory, Culture and Society* 28/6–7, 1–15.

Blencowe, C. (2010) 'Foucault's and Arendt's 'Insider View' of Biopolitics: A Critique of Agamben', *History of the Human Sciences* 23/5, 113–130.

Blencowe, C. (2013) 'Biopolitical Authority, Objectivity, and the Groundwork of Modern Citizenship', *Journal of Political Power* 6/1, 9–28.

Boltanski, L. and Chiapello, E. (2007) *The New Spirit of Capitalism.* London: Verso.

Bonnett, A. (1989) 'Situationism, Geography, and Poststructuralism', *Environment and Planning D: Society and Space* 7, 131–146.

Bonnett, A. (2006) 'The Nostalgias of Situationist Subversion', *Theory, Culture & Society* 23/5, 23–48.

Brady, M. and Antoine, D. (2013) 'Decolonize Wall Street: Situating Indigenous Critiques of the Occupy Wall Street Movement', *American Communication Journal* 15/1, 1–10.

Brown, W. (1999) 'Resisting Left Melancholy', *Boundary* 2/26.3, 19–27.

Brown, W. (2001) *Politics Out of History.* Oxford University Press.

Brown, W. (2015) *Undoing the Demos: Neoliberalism's Stealth Revolution.* New York: Zone.

Burgum, S. (2014) 'The Risks of Web Logging', in K. Woodfield (ed.) *Social Media in Social Research: Blogs on Blurring the Boundaries.* NatCen NSMNSS.

Burgum, S. (2015) 'The Branding of the Left: Between Spectacle and Passivity in an Era of Cynicism', *Journal for Cultural Research* 19/3, 306–320.

Burgum, S. (2015b) 'Rancière and Occupy (in) London: An Interview with A.N. Onymous', *Networking Knowledge* 8/3, 1–21.

Burgum, S., Raza, S. and Vasquez, J. (2017) 'Redoing the Demos? An Interview with Wendy Brown', *Theory, Culture & Society.* Available at http://www.theoryculturesociety.org/interview-wendy-brown/.

Butler, J. (1997) *Excitable Speech: A Politics of the Performative.* London: Routledge.

Butler, J. (2000) 'Restaging the Universal', in J. Butler, E. Laclau, and S. Žižek (eds) *Contingency, Hegemony, Universality.* London: Verso.

Butler, J. (2006) *Gender Trouble.* London: Routledge.

CAAT (2017) 'Campaigners 'Occupy the Arms Fair'. Available at www.caat.org.uk/media/press-releases/2013-09-08 (accessed 3 July 2017).

Campbell, E. (2011) 'A Critique of the Occupy Movement from a Black Occupier', *The Black Scholar* 41/4, 42–51.

Castaneda, E. (2012) 'The Indignados of Spain: A Precedent to Occupy Wall Street', *Social Movement Studies* 11/3–4, 309–319.

Catalano, T. and Creswell, J. (2013) 'Understanding the Language of the Occupy Movement: A Cognitive Linguistic Analysis', *Qualitative Inquiry* 19/9, 664–673.

Caygill, H. (2013) *On Resistance: A Philosophy of Defiance.* London: Bloomsbury.

Cissel, M. (2012) 'Media Framing: A Comparative Content Analysis on Mainstream and Alternative News Coverage of Occupy Wall Street', *Elon Journal of Undergraduate Research in Communications* 3/1, 67–77.

Chambers, S. (2013) *The Lessons of Rancière*. Oxford: Oxford University Press.

Chenoweth, E. (2014) 'Civil Resistance: Reflections on an Idea Whose Time Has Come', *Global Governance* 20, 351–358

Chomsky, N. (2016) 'Naom Chomsky on Slavoj Žižek'. Available at www.youtube.com/watch?v=AVBOtxCfan0.

City of London (2017) 'Temple Bar'. Available at www.cityoflondon.gov.uk/about-the-city/about-us/buildings-we-manage/Page/temple-bar.aspx# (accessed 7 September 2017).

Conover, M., Ferrara, E., Menczer, F. and Flammini, A. (2013) 'The Digital Evolution of Occupy Wall Street', *PLoS ONE* 8/5.

Costanza-Chock, S. (2012) 'Mic Check! Media Cultures and the Occupy Movement', *Social Movement Studies* 11/3–4, 375–385.

Cox, L. and Flesher-Fominaya, C. (2013) 'European Social Movements and Social Theory', *Understanding European Movements*. London: Routledge.

The Daily Mail (2011) 'The Thermal Images that Prove 90% of Tents in the Occupy Camp in London Are Left EMPTY Overnight'. Available at www.dailymail.co.uk/news/article-2053463/Occupy-London-90-tents-St-Pauls-protest-camp-left-overnight.html (accessed 18 August 2014).

Davis, M. (1990) *City of Quartz: Excavating the Future in Los Angeles*. London: Verso.

Davis, A. (2011) '(Un)Occupy', in A. Taylor and K. Gessan (eds) *Occupy: Scenes from Occupies America*. London: Verso

Davis, O. (2010) *Jacques Rancière*. Cambridge: Polity Press.

Dean, J. (1998) *Aliens in America: Conspiracy Cultures from Outerspace to Cyberspace*. Ithaca, NY: Cornell University Press.

Dean, J. (2002) *Publicity's Secret: How Technoculture Capitalizes on Democracy*. Ithaca, NY: Cornell University Press.

Dean, J. (2006) *Žižek's Politics*. London: Routledge.

Dean, J. (2009) *Democracy and Other Neoliberal Fantasies: Communicative Capitalism and Left Politics*. Durham, NC: Duke University Press.

Dean, J. (2011) 'Claiming Division, Naming a Wrong', in A. Taylor and K. Gessan (eds) *Occupy: Scenes from Occupied America*. London: Verso.

Dean, J. (2012) *The Communist Horizon*. London: Verso.

Dean, J. (2014) 'Tales of the Apolitical', *Political Studies* 62/2, 452–467.

Debord, G. (1957) *Report on the Construction of Situations and on the International Situations Tendency's Conditions of Organization and Action*. Available at www.cddc.vt.edu/sionline/si/report.html (accessed 2 August 2015).

Dorling, D. (2014) *Inequality and the 1%*. London: Verso.

Douglas, M. (1966) *Purity and Danger: An Analysis of the Concepts of Pollution and Taboo*. London: Ark.

Douzinas, C. (2013) *Philosophy and Resistance in the Crisis: Greece and the Future of Europe*. Cambridge: Polity Press.

Elden, S. (2004) *Understanding Henri Lefebvre: Theory and the Possible*. London: Continuum.

Elden, S. (2017) *Foucault: The Birth of Power*. Cambridge: Polity Press.

Evans, R. and Lewis, P. (2013) *Undercover: The True Story of Britain's Secret Police.* Guardian Books: London.

Feigenbaum, A., McCurdy, P., and Frenzel, F. (2013) 'Towards a Method for Studying Affect in (Micro)politics: The Campfire Chats Project and the Occupy Movement', *Parallax* 19/2, 21–37.

Fischer, K. (2009) 'The Influence of Neoliberals in Chile before, during, and after Pinochet', in P. Mirowski and D. Plehwe (eds) *The Road from Mont Pelèrin: The Making of the Neoliberal Thought Collective.* Cambridge, MA: Harvard University Press.

Fisher, M. (2009) *Capitalist Realism: Is There No Alternative?* London: Zero.

Florida, R. (2002) *The Rise of the Creative Class.* New York: Basic.

Foucault, M. (1980) *Power/Knowledge: Selected Interviews and Other Writings.* Hemel Hempstead: Harvester.

Foucault, M. (1989) *Foucault Live: Interviews 1966–84*. New York: Semiotext(e).

Foucault, M. (1991) *Discipline and Punish: The Birth of the Prison*. London: Penguin.

Foucault, M. (1998) *The History of Sexuality Vol. 1: The Will to Knowledge.* London: Penguin.

Foucault, M. (2001) *Madness and Civilisation*. London: Routledge.

Foucault, M. (2003) *Society Must Be Defended, Lectures at the College de France 1975–1976*. London: Allen Lane.

Frank, T. (1997) *The Conquest of Cool: Business Culture, Counterculture, and the Rise of Hip Consumerism*. Chicago, IL: University of Chicago Press.

Freeman, J. (2013) 'The Tyranny of Structurelessness', *WSQ: Women's Studies Quarterly* 41/3–4, 231–246.

Fukuyama, F. (1992) *The End of History and the Last Man*. London: Penguin.

Gamble, A. (2014) *Crisis Without End? The Unravelling of Western Prosperity.* Basingstoke: Palgrave.

Gander, K. (2014) 'Occupy London Protests: Police to be Allowed to Clear Paternoster Square near St Paul's', *The Independent*. Available at www.independent.co.uk/news/uk/home-news/occupy-london-protests-police-to-be-allowed-to-clear-paternoster-square-near-st-pauls-9657491.html.

Gane, N. (2006) 'Speed Up or Slow Down? Social Theory in the Information Age', *Information, Communication and Society* 9/1, 20–38.

Gane, N. (2014) 'Sociology and Neoliberalism: A Missing History', *Sociology* 48/6, 1092–1106.

Gitlin, T. (2012) *Occupy Nation: The Roots, the Spirit, and the Promise of Occupy Wall Street*. New York: It Books.

Glaser, B. and Strauss, A. (2017) *The Discovery of Grounded Theory.* London: Routledge.

Gleason, B. (2013) '#Occupy Wall Street: Exploring Informal Learning about a Social Movement on Twitter', *American Behavioural Scientist* 57/7, 966–982.

Goodwin, J. and Jasper, J. (2015) *The Social Movements Reader: Cases and Concepts* (3rd edn). Chichester: Wiley Blackwell.

Gordon, C. (1980) 'Afterword', in M. Foucault (ed.) *Power/Knowledge: Selected Interviews and Other Writings.* Hemel Hempstead: Harvester.

Gowan, P. (1999) 'The NATO Powers and the Balkan Tragedy', *New Left Review* 1/124 (March–April).

The Guardian (2016) Available at www.theguardian.com/uk-news/2016/jul/04/squatters-evicted-derelict-london-nursery-camden-town (accessed 17 August 2017).

Guzman-Concha, C. (2012) 'The Students' Rebellion in Chile: Occupy Protest or Classic Social Movement?' *Social Movement Studies* 11/3–4, 408–415.

Habermas, J. (1987) *The Theory of Communicative Action*. Boston, MA: Beacon Press.

Hall, S., Winlow, S. and Ancrum, C. (2008) *Criminal Identities and Consumer Culture: Crime, Exclusion and the New Culture of Narcissism*. London: Willan.

Harvey, D. (2012) *Rebel Cities: From the Right to the City to the Urban Revolution*. London: Verso.

Hayek, F. (1979) *The Road to Serfdom*. London: Routledge.

Heath, J. and Potter, A. (2006) *The Rebel Sell: How the Counterculture Became Consumer Culture*. Chichester: Capstone.

Hickel, J. and Khan, A. (2012) 'The Culture of Capitalism and the Crisis of Critique', *Anthropological Quarterly* 85/1, 203–227.

Hill, J. (1998) *Occupying Architecture: Between the Architect and the User*. London: Routledge.

Ho, M. (2015) 'Occupy Congress in Taiwan: Political Opportunity, Threat, and the Sunflower Movement', *Asian Studies* 15/1, 69–97.

Holloway, J. (2014) 'A Note on Hope and Crisis', *Sociology* 48/5, 1070–1072.

Howard, N. and Pratt-Boyden, K. (2013) 'Occupy London as Pre-figurative Political Action', *Development in Practice* 23/5–6, 729–741.

Jameson, F. (1992) *Postmodernism: Or, the Cultural Logic of Late Capitalism*. London: Verso.

Kaneck, H. (2012) *Occupy Wall Street: A Movement in the Making*, Senior Thesis, Trinity College, Hartford, CT. *Available at* http://digitalrepository.trincoll.edu/theses/245.

Kavada, A. (2015) 'Creating the Collective: Social Media, the Occupy Movement and its Constitution as a Collective Actor', *Information, Communication and Society* 18/8, 872–886.

Kern, T. and Nam, S. (2013) 'From "Corruption" to "Democracy": Cultural Values, Mobilisation, and the Collective Identity of the Occupy Movement', *Journal of Civil Society* 9/2, 196–211.

King, D. (2017) 'Entrenching the New Right: Markets, Financialization and the State' https://www2.warwick.ac.uk/fac/soc/sociology/staff/gurminderkbhambra/research/ (accessed: 2 September 2017)

Klein, N. (2001) *No Logo*. London: Flamingo.

Klein, N. (2008) *The Shock Doctrine: The Rise of Disaster Capitalism*. London: Penguin.

Klein, N. (2011) 'Occupy Wall Street: The Most Important Thing in the World Now', *The Nation*. Available at www.thenation.com/article/occupy-wall-street-most-important-thing-world-now/.

Klug, A., Rees, E. and Schneider, J. (2016) 'Momentum: A New Kind of Politics', *Renewal: A Journal of Labour Politics* 24/2, 36–44.

Kohn, M. (2013) 'Privatization and Protest: Occupy Wall Street, Occupy Toronto, and the Occupation of Public Space in a Democracy', *Perspectives on Politics* 11/1, 99–110.

Koksal, I. (2012) 'Walking in the City of London', *Social Movement Studies* 11/3–4, 446–453.

Kreiss, D. and Tufekci, Z. (2013) 'Occupying the Political: Occupy Wall Street, Collective Action, and the Rediscover of Pragmatic Politics', *Cultural Studies, Critical Methodologies* 13/3, 163–167.

Krippner, G. (2011) *Capitalizing on Crisis*, Cambridge, MA; Harvard University Press.

Lambert, C. (2013) 'Live Art as Urban Praxis: The Political Aesthetics of the City', *Sociological Research Online* 18/3, 12.

Land, C. (2012) 'Occupy Auckland', *Psychotherapy and Politics International* 10/1, 79–82.

Langman, L. (2013) 'Occupy: A New New Social Movement', *Current Sociology* 61/4, 510–524.

Littler, J. (2009) *Radical Consumption: Shopping for Change in Contemporary Culture*, Maidenhead: Open University Press.

Lefebvre, H. (1991) *The Production of Space*, Oxford: Blackwell.

Lefebvre, H. (1996) *Writings on Cities*, Oxford: Blackwell.

Lubin, J. (2012) 'The 'Occupy' Movement: Emerging Protest Forms and Contested Urban Spaces', *Berkeley Planning Journal* 25/1.

Lyotard, J. (1984) *The Postmodern Condition: A Report on Knowledge*, Manchester: Manchester University Press.

Mabrouk, M. (2011) 'A Revolution for Dignity and Freedom: Preliminary Observations on the Social and Cultural Background to the Tunisian Revolution', *Journal of North African Studies* 16/4, 625–635.

Madden, D. and Vradis, A. (2012) 'From Athens to Occupy and Back: Introduction to Cities in Upheaval', *City* 16/1–2, 235–236.

Maharawal, M. (2013) 'Occupy Wall Street and a Radical Politics of Inclusion', *Sociological Quarterly* 54, 159–228.

Marx, K. and Engels, F. (2002) *The Communist Manifesto*, London: Penguin.

Mason, P. (2012) *Why It's Kicking Off Everywhere: The New Global Revolutions*, London: Verso.

Mason, P. (2017) 'BBC Two – Performance Live: Why It's Kicking Off Everywhere'. Available at www.bbc.co.uk/programmes/b08zj2wq (accessed 7 September 2017).

Min, S. (2015) 'Occupy Wall Street and Deliberative Decision-Making: Translating Theory to Practice', *Communication, Culture and Critique* 8/1, 73–89.

Mirowski, P. (2013) *Never Let a Serious Crisis Go to Waste: How Neoliberalism Survived the Financial Meltdown*, London: Verso.

Mottiar, S. (2013) 'From 'Popcorn' to 'Occupy': Protest in Durban, South Africa', *Development and Change* 44, 603–619.

Narayan, J. (2016) 'Fanon's Decolonized Europe', in G. Bhambra and J. Narayan (eds) *European Cosmopolitanism: Colonial Histories and Postcolonial Societies*, London: Routledge.

Nietzsche, F. (2008) *On the Genealogy of Morals*, Oxford University Press.

Occupy Directory (2015) Available at directory.occupy.net (accessed 2 August 2015).

Occupy London (2012) Available at http://occupylondon.org.uk/video-alan-moore-writer-of-v-for-vendetta-the-watchmen-at-occupylsx/ (accessed 17 August 2017).

Occupy London (2015) Available at http://occupylondon.org.uk/about-2/ (accessed 2 August 2015).

Occupy London (2017) Available at http://occupylondon.org.uk/occupy-london-safer-space-policy/ (accessed 17 August 2017).

Oxfam (2017) 'Eight People Own Same Wealth as Half the World'. Available at http://www.oxfam.org.uk/media-centre/press-releases/2017/01/eight-people-own-same-wealth-as-half-the-world (accessed 2 September 2017).

Ozkirimli, U. (2014) *The Making of a Protest Movement in Turkey: #occupygezi*, Basingstoke: Palgrave Macmillan.

Peck, J. (2005) 'Struggling with the Creative Class', *International Journal of Urban and Regional Research* 29/4, 740–770.

Peck, J. (2010) *Constructions of Neoliberal Reason*, Oxford: Oxford University Press.

Pickerill, J. and Krinsky, J. (2012) 'Why Does Occupy Matter?', *Social Movement Studies* 11/3–4, 279–287.

Prentoulis, M. and Thommassen, L. (2013) 'Political Theory in the Square: Protest, Representation and Subjectification', *Contemporary Political Theory* 12/3, 166–718.

Quinn, B. (2014) 'Anti-homeless Spikes Are Part of a Wider Phenomenon of 'Hostile Architecture', *The Guardian*. Available at www.theguardian.com/artanddesign/2014/jun/13/anti-homeless-spikes-hostile-architecture.

Rancière, J. (1991) *The Ignorant Schoolmaster: Five Lessons in Intellectual Emancipation*, Stanford, CA: Stanford University Press.

Rancière, J. (2001) 'Ten Theses on Politics', *Theory and Event* 5/3.

Rancière, J. (2004) *The Politics of Aesthetics*, London: Continuum.

Rancière, J. (2010) 'Ten Theses on Politics', in *Dissensus: On Politics and Aesthetics*, London: Continuum.

Rancière, J. (2011) *Althusser's Lesson*, London: Continuum.

Rashad, M. and Azzazi, I. (2011) 'The Egyptian Revolution: A Participant's Account from Tahrir Square, January and February 2011', *Anthropology Today* 27/2, 22–27.

Richardson, M. (2010) 'Cameron Speech: "We're All in This Together"'. Available at http://news.sky.com/story/811331/cameron-speech-were-all-in-this-together (accessed 2 August 2015).

Rigby, J. and Schlembach, R. (2013) 'Impossible Protest: No Borders in Calais', *Citizenship Studies* 17/2, 157–172.

Roberts, A. (2012) 'Why the Occupy Movement Failed', *Public Administration Review* 72/5, 754–762.

Ross, K. (2002) *May '68 and its Afterlives*, Chicago, IL: University of Chicago Press.

Rushkoff, D. (2011) 'Think Occupy Wall St. Is a Phase? You Don't Get It', *Institute for Ethics and Emerging Technologies*. Available at https://ieet.org/index.php/IEET2/more/4925.

Sadler, S. (1999) *The Situationist City*, London: MIT Press.

Sayer, A. (2015) *Why We Can't Afford the Rich*, Bristol: Policy Press.

Schein, R. (2012) 'Whose Occupation? Homelessness and the Politics of Park Encampments', *Social Movement Studies* 11/3–4, 336–338.

Schlembach, R. (2014) *Against Old Europe: Critical Theory and Alter-Globalization Movements*, Farnham: Ashgate.

Sheets, C. (2013) 'Anonymous Masks' Photo Stirs Controversy on Guy Fawkes Day'. Available at www.ibtimes.com/anonymous-masks-photo-stirs-controversy-guy-fawkes-day-1456790 (accessed 26 October 2015).

Sinha, S. and Back, L. (2014) 'Making Methods Sociable: Dialogue, Ethics and Authorship in Qualitative Research', *Qualitative Research Online* 14/4, 473–487.

Sitrin, M. (2012) 'Horizontalism and the Occupy Movements', *Dissent* 59/2, 74–75.

Skinner, J. (2011) 'Social Media and Revolution: The Arab Spring and the Occupy Movement as Seen through Three Information Studies Paradigms', Working Papers on Information Systems. Available at http://aisel.aisnet.org/sprouts_all/483.

Sky News (2010) 'Cameron Speech: "We're All in This Together"'. Available at http://news.sky.com/story/811331/cameron-speech-were-all-in-this-together (accessed 2 August 2015).

Sloterdijk, P. (1987) *Critique of Cynical Reason*, Minneapolis, MN: University of Minnesota Press.

Stekelenburg, J. (2012) 'The Occupy Movement: Product of this Time', *Development* 55/2, 224–231.

Smith, C., Castaneda, E. and Heyman, J. (2012) 'The Homeless and Occupy El Paso: Creating Community among the 99%', *Social Movement Studies* 11/3–4, 356–366.

Smith, J. and Gidden, B. (2012) 'Occupy Pittsburgh and the Challenges of Participatory Democracy', *Social Movement Studies* 11/3–4, 288–294.

Swyngedouw, E. (2009) 'The Antinomies of the Post-Political City: In Search of a Democratic Politics of Environmental Production', *International Journal of Urban and Regional Research* 33/3, 601–620.

Swyngedouw, E. (2010) 'Impossible Sustainability and the Post-Political Condition', *Making Strategies in Spatial Planning Urban and Landscape Perspectives* 9, 185–205.

Swyngedouw, E. (2011) *Designing the Post-Political City and the Insurgent Polis*, London: Bedford Press.

Taylor, A. and Gessan, K. (eds) (2011) *Occupy! Scenes from Occupied America*, London: Verso.

Taylor, B. (2013) 'From Alterglobalization to Occupy Wall Street: Neoanarchism and the New Spirit of the Left', *City* 17/6, 729–747.

The Telegraph (2009) 'Economists' Letter Spells Out What Went Wrong'. Available at www.telegraph.co.uk/finance/recession/5309591/Economists-letter-spells-out-what-went-wrong.html (accessed 16 August 2017).

The Telegraph (2013) 'Isa Funds: The 10 Biggest Winners during the Crisis Years'. Available at www.telegraph.co.uk/finance/personalfinance/investing/10308150/Isa-funds-the-10-biggest-winners-during-the-crisis-years.html (accessed 16 August 2017).

Thorsen, K., Driscoll, K., Ekdale, B., Edgerly, S., Thompson, L., Schrock, A., Swartz, L., Vraga, E. and Wells, C. (2013) 'YouTube, Twitter, and the Occupy Movement: Connecting Content and Circulation Practices', *Information, Communication and Society* 16/3, 421–451.

Turner, S. (2017) 'Expert Failure and its Consequences: The Case of the IMF'. Available at www2.warwick.ac.uk/fac/soc/sociology/staff/gurminderkbhambra/research/ (accessed 2 September 2017).

Uitermark, J. and Nicholls, W. (2012). 'How Local Networks Shape a Global Movement: Comparing Occupy in Amsterdam and Los Angeles', *Social Movement Studies* 11/3–4, 295–301.

Vaneigem, R. (1983) *The Revolution of Everyday Life*, London: Aldgate.

Van Gelder, S. (2011) *This Changes Everything: Occupy Wall Street and the 99% Movement*, San Francisco, CA: Berrett-Koehler.

Venn, C. (2007) 'Cultural Theory, Biopolitics, and the Question of Power', *Theory, Culture and Society* 24/3, 111–124.

Wasserstrom, J. (2014) 'What Hong Kong's Occupy Movement Can Learn from History', *The Nation* (12 September 2014).

Weber, M. (2003) 'The Three Pure Types of Legitimate Rule', in S. Whimster (ed.) *The Essential Weber: A Reader*, Routledge: London.

Winlow, S. (2012) 'Is It OK to Talk about Capitalism Again? Or, Why Criminology Must Take a Leap of Faith', in S. Winlow and R. Atkinson (eds) *New Directions in Crime and Deviance*, London: Routledge.

Winlow, S. and Hall, S. (2012) 'A Predictably Obedient Riot: Post-Politics, Consumer Culture and the English Riots of 2011', *Cultural Politics* 8/3, 465–488.

Winlow, S., Hall, S., Treadwell, J. and Briggs, D. (2015) *Riots and Political Protest: Notes from the Post-Political Present*, London: Routledge.

Winner, L. (1980) 'Do Artefacts Have Politics?', *Daedalus* 109/1, 121–136.

Worth, O. (2013) *Resistance in the Age of Austerity*, London: Zed.

Wright, E. (2010) *Envisioning Real Utopias*, London: Verso.

Wright Mills, C. (1981) *The Sociological Imagination*, Oxford: Oxford University Press.

YouTube (2015) Available at www.youtube.com/watch?v=3252FSW7OC4 (accessed 2 August 2015).

Zamora, D. (2014) 'Can We Criticize Foucault? An Interview with Daniel Zamora', *Jacobin*. Available at www.jacobinmag.com/2014/12/foucault-interview/.

Žižek, S. (1992) *Looking Awry: An Introduction to Jacques Lacan through Popular Culture*, London: MIT Press.

Žižek, S. (2000) 'Class Struggle or Postmodernism?' in J. Butler, E. Laclau, and S. Žižek (eds) *Contingency, Hegemony, Universality*, London: Verso.

Žižek, S. (2006) *The Parallax View*, MIT Press.

Žižek, S. (2008a) *The Ticklish Subject: The Absent Centre of Political Ontology*, London: Verso.

Žižek, S. (2008b) *Violence*, London: Profile.

Žižek, S. (2008c) *Did Somebody Say Totalitarianism?* London: Verso.

Žižek, S. (2008d) *The Sublime Object of Ideology*, London: Verso

Žižek, S. (2009a) *First as Tragedy, Then as Farce*, London: Verso.

Žižek, S. (2009b) *In Defence of Lost Causes*, London: Verso.

Žižek, S. (2010) *Living in the End Times*, London: Verso.

Žižek, S. (2011) 'Don't Fall in Love with Yourselves', in A. Taylor and K. Gessan (eds) *Occupy: Scenes from Occupied America*. London: Verso.

Žižek, S. (2011b) *Revolution at the Gates: Selected Writing of Lenin from 1917*, London: Verso.

Index

abstract empiricism (Wright-Mills) 13–15
Adbusters 9, 94
aesthetics 20–21, 33; as strategy 37–38, 39, 55; *see also* distribution of the sensible (Rancière)
Althusser, Louis 33–35
anarchism 81, 93, 108; neoanarchism 85
Anonymous (movement): in the USA 10, 104, 116; in London 64, 94–96, 105–106, 122
Arab Spring 1–2, 4, 9–11, 32, 135–136, 149
art of the impossible (Žižek) 145–147
authenticity: and autonomy 24, 39, 44, 57, 60, 111, 129; and the new spirit of capitalism (Boltanski & Chiapello) 88–90, 106–110; and activist identity 90–95; hierarchy of authenticity 95–101; as moral high ground 101–106; with powerlessness 119–120, 137–139, 146–147; *see also* co-optation
authority: from 'above' 8–9, 22, 131–132; from 'below' 20–21, 28–30, 32–39, 48–49, 53, 66, 143–146; lacking authority 136–139; authoritarianism 30–31, 45, 65; as an idea of objectivity (Blencowe) 25–26, 149–150; internal hierarchies of expertise 68–70, 73–74, 97–101, 119; collective authority 80–81, 84–86
autonomy 15, 24, 38–39: in the creative city 57; and prefiguration 58–60, 148; outside social structures 66; as authenticity 24, 39, 44, 57, 60, 111, 129; *see also* tyranny of structurelessness (Freeman)

Badiou, Alain 3, 101, 145: on political organisation 30–32, 46, 64
Balcolme (Anti-Fracking Protest) 63
Bank of Ideas 11
Bilderberg 41, 134–136
Black Lives Matter 71, 149
boycotting 93, 97, 102–103, 107–110: *buy*cotting 93–94, 101–103, 105–107, 109–110
Brexit 4, 149
British National Party (BNP) 75–76
Brown, Wendy: on normativity 7; on melancholia 16–17; critique of Foucault 20, 27–28; on siege mentality 116, 139; neoliberal Frankenstein 141; on solidarity 146–147; on genealogical politics 147–149
Butler, Judith 38: on power and resistance 25–26, 131; on universality 83–84, 145; on reverse discourses 25, 36, 60, 131

Cameron, David 1, 140
capitalism: capitalist realism (Fisher) 1–9, 17, 90, 97, 145–146; colonialism 1, 6, 141, 145, 148; Wall Street 10; City of London 45, 143; anti-capitalism 12, 42–43, 50, 65–66, 82–83, 111; post-modern capitalism 20–21, 28–30, 56–57; modernity 22, 27–28; new spirit of capitalism (Boltanski & Chiapello) 88–90, 106–110, 142; *see also* consumerism
Cat Hill (Protest Camp) 79–80
class 2, 31, 59, 70, 72, 83, 148: middle class 16, 57, 68–69, 71; working class 30, 66–68, 89, 141; creative class (Florida) 56–57; ruling class 126–127; *see also* Marxism
conspiracy theory 24, 114–116, 138–139, 142: as strategy 116–121; undercover

agents 121–125; corporate-state collusion (the 1%) 126–132; international pan-historical networks 132–138
consumerism 20, 29, 110, 142: as unproductive enjoyment 56, 109; as flexibility 82–83, 94; as artificiality 93, 95, 107–108; ethical consumption 102, 106; rebel consumers 89–92, 100, 105–106, 109; *see also* co-optation
co-optation 89, 107–109, 111, 128: precorporation (Fisher) 107–108
Corbyn, Jeremy 150
cynicism 4–5, 29, 51, 108: in academic research 16–17; of collective organisations 118–119; of elites and the state 127–128, 130–132; enlightened false consciousness (Sloterdijk) 132–133; in activism 138–139

Dean, Jodi: on strategy 9, 29–30, 32, 37, 111, 131; on 'we are the 99%' 65–66, 118; on conspiracy theory 118, 136; on post-politics 7, 85, 144–145
democracy: liberalism 2, 10, 37, 140; direct 3, 71; in practice 4, 11–12, 47, 86; as inclusivity 8, 70, 76; as politics itself (Rancière) 21, 33, 36, 38; and neoliberalism 27–28, 130, 150; disenfranchised 127
détournement 25, 36, 39, 57, 60: examples in London movement 44, 49, 114, 143–144
distribution of the sensible (Rancière) 8, 20–21, 26, 33–39, 111–112: external distributions of the movement 44, 48–50, 55–57, 81, 85, 101, 104, 106, 131; internal distributions 64–65, 69–72, 90, 96–97, 99, 101; *see also* police order
diversity: between different movements 2, 10; as a democratic value 11–12, 46, 59–60, 67, 79, 142, 145; within London movement 63, 65, 70–71, 75; in consumerism 89, 95, 107
DSEI Anti-Arms Rally (Campaign Against Arms Trade) 113–114

European Summer 2, 9–11, 92,
European Union (EU) 4, 7, 75, 149
exclusion 12, 20, 53, 60–61, 145: within London movement 68, 70, 72, 74–75, 83, 95–96, 125, 139; as disciplinary power 22–23, 25, 38; negotiated as part of organisation 32–33, 39–40, 44, 65, 80, 82, 84–86, 148; preclusion 64–65, 71, 81, 84–86, 90, 95–97, 99–101, 116, 123, 125, 142, 145, 148–149

financial crisis 1–7, 9–11, 16–17, 45, 61, 66, 81, 103, 114, 126–127, 138, 140–141, 143–144, 147
Fisher, Mark 1, 97, 107, 145–146
Foucault, Michel: as a neoliberal 19; on power 19–24, 33, 60, 145, 148; on resistance 24–26, 32, 36, 57, 111, 146; on neoliberalism 26–28; on truth 133
French Communist Party (PCF) 33–35

G8 and G20 10, 43
gender 2, 59: feminist values with London movement 66–67; patriarchy within London movement 66–67, 69–72, 85
genealogical politics (Brown) 21, 147–149
General Assembly (GA) 11–12
Greenham Common 100–101, 124–125

hierarchy 12–13, 33, 39: in disciplinary power 19, 22–23, 34–35, 148, 60; anti-hierarchical values 48, 64, 66, 131; internal hierarchies 25–26, 40, 44, 71–74, 77, 90, 142; hierarchies of authenticity 95, 97, 99–101; hierarchies of trust 123, 125; *see also* tyranny of structurelessness (Freeman)
homelessness xii, 12, 44: the homeless question 50–52, 61, 67; defensive architectures 55
horizontality: in technology 3; leaderlessness as a value 4, 11–13, 33, 39–40, 59–60, 64, 67, 79; as problematic 70, 73–74, 81–82, 101, 131, 141–142; *see also* hierarchy

inclusivity: openness as a value 4, 12, 25, 33, 37–38, 46, 59–60, 126; as problematic 30, 39–40, 74, 76, 81–82, 141–142; inclusivity for the sake of it 40, 64–72, 85–86 *see also* tyranny of structurelessness (Freeman)
Indignados (15M) *see* European Summer
individualism 3, 8, 20, 28–31, 39–40, 60–61, 65–66, 72, 75, 83, 109, 146; in consumerism 89–92, 94, 107, 109–110; *see also* libertarianism
International Monetary Fund (IMF) 5, 7

Johnson, Boris 50

Klein, Naomi: on the Iraq war 7; on alter-globalization movements 9, 109; on Occupy 15–16

Le Pen 30
Lefebvre, Henri 40, 44: on power 45, 55–57
Lehman Brothers 1
libertarianism 3, 8, 37, 77–82, 85–86, 124, 140, 142, 147, 149 *see also* symbolic efficiency

Marxism 19, 22, 27–28, 65, 68, 69,
May '68 21, 33–35, 68, 89, 146
May, Theresa 150
melancholia 16–17
Mirowski, Philip 6–8, 16, 77
Mont Pelerin Society 6

neoliberalism 1–2, 5–9, 12, 17, 20, 27–28, 30, 35, 37, 39, 59, 119, 138, 143, 150; neoliberal normativity 130, 140–142, 149; neoliberal city 43–45, 47, 54, 56–57, 61; crossovers with left-libertarianism 65, 81, 85, 109–110; austerity 68; social media 77; state-corporate collusion 126–127
new social movements (NSMs) 14, 81, 89
new spirit of capitalism (Boltanski & Chiapello) *see* capitalism
Nietzsche, Friedrich: on the cunning of impotence 116; on powerlessness 137, 139
non-sense *see* distribution of the sensible
normativity 1, 3, 6–8, 15, 17, 140–141, 145; normative power 19–26, 31, 33–36, 39–41, 60, 138, 143, 148; normative foreclosures 27–30, 57, 64–65, 70, 81, 85, 90, 101, 104, 106–111, 142, 147, 149–150; spatial norms 44–45, 50, 54–55, 61; challenging normativity 115–116, 119–121, 132, 136, 139; authority 127, 131

occupation (tactic) 4, 31, 38–39, 44–49, 53–55, 61, 143–144; challenges 49–53
Occupation Finsbury Square xii-xv, 11–12, 42–43, 45, 47, 51–52, 75, 92, 102, 105–106, 143
Occupy Leyton Marsh 11
Occupy LSX 10–12, 44–62, 66–69, 73, 99, 117
Occupy (global movement) 10–11, 32, 92
Occupy Nomads 11, 75–76
Occupy St Paul's *see* Occupy LSX
Occupy Wall Street: the American Fall 9–11; the homeless question 51; organisation 58, 67; race 71
Occupy Working Groups 11, 74, 77–78

police order (Rancière) 20, 33–39, 44, 49–50, 53, 57, 60–62, 65, 68, 79, 90, 101, 106, 111, 116, 118–119, 130, 132–133, 136, 138–139, 141, 143, 145–147, 149–150
postmodernity 20–21, 28–30, 39, 56–57, 65, 81–82, 88, 109, 116, 120, 132–133, 138, 142, 144–145 *see also symbolic efficiency*
post-politics 7, 144–145
post-truth 135, 149–150
prefiguration 40, 58–61, 64, 66, 74, 84–86, 88, 142, 148

racism 2, 31, 59, 65–67, 70–72, 75, 84–85, 141
Rancière, Jacques 8, 20–21, 26, 33–38, 43–44, 50, 54–55, 98, 147
Reclaim the Streets 98
riots 30–32, 35, 71, 143
Rochester Square Gardens (squat) 87–89
Romanticism: in academic research 15–17, 142; within London movement 59, 137–138

Seattle 1999 98
social media 3, 11–12, 14, 48, 63, 73, 77
Starbucks 29, 43, 90, 101–104, 106, 111
Storerdijk, Peter 132
symbolic efficiency: declining under postmodern capitalism 3, 20, 29, 82, 120, 144, 150; necessary for aesthetic organisation 37, 39, 65, 78–79, 81, 86, 118, 145, 149

The 1% 5, 41, 79, 115–116, 118–119, 126–132, 138, 142
Trafalgar Square (Protest) 63–64, 117
Trump, Donald 3, 4, 30, 149, 150
tyranny of structurelessness (Freeman) 40, 64, 72–86, 88, 90, 95–99, 149

UK Independence Party (UKIP) xii, 30, 129
undercover police 40, 53, 91, 114–118, 121–125, 132, 138; *see also* conspiracy theory

V for Vendetta (Guy Fawkes Masks) 64, 90, 104–106, 133

We are the 99% 5, 10, 15, 24, 65–68, 70–73, 75, 79, 82–85, 124, 126, 129, 141, 144–145, 148–151

World Bank 7

Žižek, Slavoj: on pseudo-events 4; on financial crisis 7; on social theory 16; on melancholia 17; as a charlatan 19; on postmodern capitalism 20, 28–30, 82, 106; on the symbolic order 23, 34; criticism of Foucault 24–25; on the universal 84; on conspiracy 131–133; on cynicism 139; on the art of the impossible 145–147; on positing pre-suppositions 148–149

For Product Safety Concerns and Information please contact our EU
representative GPSR@taylorandfrancis.com
Taylor & Francis Verlag GmbH, Kaufingerstraße 24, 80331 München, Germany

www.ingramcontent.com/pod-product-compliance
Ingram Content Group UK Ltd.
Pitfield, Milton Keynes, MK11 3LW, UK
UKHW011016180926
475701UK00004B/768
9780367438968